Me and My Hair

Me and My Hair

A Social History

PATRICIA MALCOLMSON

CHAPLIN BOOKS

www.chaplinbooks.co.uk

ISBN 978-0-9571128-9-6

A CIP catalogue record for this book is available from The British Library.

Design by Michael Walsh at The Better Book Company

Cover design by Helen Taylor

Printed in the UK by Ashford Colour Press

Chaplin Books
1 Eliza Place
Gosport PO12 4UN
Tel: 023 9252 9020
www.chaplinbooks.co.uk

DEDICATION

To my family
Bob, Stuart, Kim, Charlotte, and Sasha

CONTENTS

A hair advertisement from 1940
© *The British Library Board,* Hairdresser and Beauty Trade, *8 March 1940/535*

PREFACE

This is a book that takes hair seriously – though I hope not too seriously. It shows how women have felt about their hair since the late nineteenth century, how the hairdressing industry grew from almost nothing to its current spectacular prominence, how changes in hairstyles have been linked to larger social changes since 1900, and how hair care has been closely tied to commerce, social psychology, and feminist attitudes (or their absence). Women often hold firm views about their own and other women's hair. For generations hair has been linked to strong feelings – envy, pride, admiration, anxiety, even self-loathing. Hair is an important signifier of a woman's 'worth', whether she is young or old or middle-aged. How a woman does her hair is not just a matter of style or a minor expression of taste, it is also testimony to her judgment and sense of self. Hair can speak volumes about the character and taste of its wearer.

There is a lot more to hair than meets the eye, and this book is intended to explore below the surface of ephemeral fashion. Hair always – whether consciously or not – makes a statement. I am concerned mainly with hair in Britain and how British women over the past 150 years have managed their hair. *Me and My Hair* explores the changes in hairstyles and the ways of treating hair – for hair cannot be ignored; it has always had to be treated in *some* way – and it links these changes to larger issues of Britain's social history since the late nineteenth century. The sources for this history are, for the most part, magazines and newspapers, short stories and novels, diaries and memoirs, trade and commercial directories, interviews and oral history, and ephemera from different parts of Britain. The voices of women in the past are often heard in these pages, as are the voices of those trying to influence them – journalists, advertisers and professional hairdressers. Much of my research has been done in London, mainly at the British Library and its newspaper library in Colindale, and this research has been supplemented by visits to libraries and archives in other parts of Britain, of which the Mass Observation Archive at the University of Sussex is the most important. I have also benefitted from the resources of some excellent libraries in Canada, notably those at the University of Toronto and Queen's University in Kingston, Ontario, and also from the admirable Interlibrary Loans service both at the latter and through the Nelson Municipal Library in British Columbia, where I now live.

While British experiences predominate in this book, I have felt justified in ranging beyond Britain and citing evidence from other areas of the (mainly English-speaking) world. This is because the history of hair in modern times has often not been particularly defined by nationality. Styles and aspirations have tended to cut across national borders. What was done in, say, New York or Paris in one year was probably adopted in Brighton and Norwich and Bristol not long after. In the 1920s bobbed hair was prominent almost everywhere in the transatlantic world. A little later, machines for the permanent waving of women's hair were pretty much the same in South London as in Spokane, Washington. Ideas about good looks and good hair in the 1950s and 1960s were not much different in Britain, Canada, and the United States. Given these realities, I have felt at liberty often to draw evidence from outside Britain, usually when I am virtually certain that experiences documented in North American sources would have been replicated in many parts of the United Kingdom. So, this is a book on British social history that is linked fairly often to social changes elsewhere in the modern world, because modernity – in art, architecture, graphic design, fashion, and much more – was inherently international, and new ideas and technologies spread easily and quickly from one country to another.

✄ ✄ ✄ ✄

In the making of this book I have become indebted to so many people. My largest debt is to a man I met when I was 19 and to whom I have been married for 45 years (in the present age, no doubt a source of amazement). Bob is also a historian – a very encouraging one – and has provided much sound advice and practical assistance (with a touch of uxorious cajoling). He even volunteered to slog through a decade's worth of the weekly magazine *Hairdresser and Beauty Trade*. Given his penchant for understatement, I'll say no more. But I am grateful.

I also wish to thank my editor and the publisher of Chaplin Books, Amanda Field, for her interest in my work, and her enthusiastic response to my book proposal. Since our first meeting in September 2011, she has been reliably and constructively supportive. Her innovative ideas and insightful suggestions have made the production of this book a true collaboration.

Many individuals have given me the benefit of their reflections and insights, or pointed me to an interesting source, or perhaps kick-started a train of thought that otherwise might not have occurred. Among those who helped and whom I am pleased to thank are Janet Bailey; Jenna Bailey, whose thoughtful comments have helped to shape this book more than she probably knows; Katherine Baird of the London School of Fashion; Robert Bell of the Wisbech and Fenland Museum; Denise Brackett; Jamie Brooks of Brooks and Brooks, London; Trisha Buller and her colleagues at Cienté, Berkhamsted, Hertfordshire; Sam Carroll; Fiona Courage and the excellent staff at the Mass Observation Archive at the University of Sussex; Rose Krause at the Ferris Research Library and Archives, Northwest Museum of Arts and Culture, Spokane, Washington; Caroline Dyer and her colleagues and students at the College of West Anglia, King's Lynn, Norfolk; Laura Fortier, Archivist, Touchstones Museum of Art and History, Nelson, British Columbia; the late eminent hairdresser and hairdressing educator, Joshua Galvin; Rita Galvin; Sindi Gordon; Kim Hartzell; Sandra Holtby, former Head, London School of Fashion; Camilla Hornby, formerly of Curtis Brown; Margaretta Jolly; Stuart Malcolmson; Debra McDermott and her colleagues and students at the Academy for Hairdressing in Bournemouth; Mary Ann McPhail; Mass Observers B2760 and

H260; Bob Mitton; Jeff Moon of Queen's University in Kingston, Ontario; Felicity Pope; Pat Reid; Bill Robbins; Chavez Roddick of Bellacabello, Nelson, British Columbia; Krissy Sampy of Toni and Guy, London; Jessica Scantlebury; Peter Searby; Lydia Sharman; Kath Shawcross, Local Studies and Archives Centre, London Borough of Sutton; Sue Sharman; Dorothy Sheridan, former Head of Special Collections, University of Sussex; the late Pino Spadafora of Rapunzel, Toronto; Andrea Stark; Amanda Stewart of House of Attitudes, Cobourg, Ontario; Debbie Stirton; Nancy Sutherland; Kathleen and Joyce Tipper; Gail Wells; Sebastian Wormell, Archivist, Harrods; Gordon Wise of Curtis Brown; the staff members of the Music Department of the British Library, the Colindale Newspaper Library, and the National Art Library; and those British women who, in the spring of this year, supplied Chaplin Books with a lovely collection of photographs of various twentieth-century hairstyles. This book could not have been written without these many people's diverse contributions.

Patricia Malcolmson
Nelson, British Columbia
July 2012

The author and her hair over the decades

1965

1970s

1980s

1985

1990

Patricia today

CARNIVAL
HANDBOOK 6ᵈ

EASTLEIGH
12-19ᵗʰ
AUGUST
1967
CARNIVAL

HAVE
FUN!

Marlene Barns in 1967,
Carnival Queen of Eastleigh in Hampshire

1

HAIR STORIES

'She sits at her dressing-table and vigorously brushes her hair, a mop of copper-coloured curls, natural curls, as tight and springy as coiled steel. Some would say her hair is her finest feature, though Robyn herself secretly hankers after something more muted and malleable, hair that could be groomed and styled according to mood – drawn back in a severe bun like Simone de Beauvoir's, or allowed to fall to the shoulders in a Pre-Raphaelite cloud. As it is, there is not much she can do with her curls except, every now and again, crop them brutally short just to demonstrate how inadequately they represent her character.'

(David Lodge, Nice Work, 1988, Part One, Chapter Two)

'Her hair was a joy. It lay folded round her little well shaped head in waves and little curls formed in the damp air. It was black and burnished, as a bird's wing.'

(Nella Last, in her Mass Observation diary, 4 April 1940, said of a young gypsy, 'the loveliest girl I'd seen for a long time')

'If my hair's alright, then I'm alright.' Many women have felt – and still feel – this way. Hair is a vital aspect of a woman's identity. It conveys so much about who she is or would like to be. Hair has been a source of pride and a source of agony. 'My hair caused me misery and shame', says British writer Jenny Diski, talking about how she felt as a young woman in the 1960s.[1] She undoubtedly had lots of company.

What is hair that is 'alright'? What is alright in one decade is decidedly not alright a few years later. As the changes in hairstyles, colour, and cut over the past century have repeatedly revealed, our sense of self is pliable. There is a widely used advertising slogan that declares 'Your hair defines who you are', a claim that, putting aside the patent hyperbole, most women would not completely deny.

Numerous celebrities have been defined, in part, by their hair. Country singer Dolly Parton is perhaps as well known for her wigs as she is for her voice and breasts. Cher virtually is her hair, just as actress Veronica Lake was in the early 1940s. The late British singer Amy Winehouse's heavily backcombed and sprayed hairdo was nearly as outrageous as, though less sad than, her offstage behaviour. The late Princess Diana spent almost £4,000 a year on having her hair bleached, while that other prominent British blonde of the later twentieth century, Margaret Thatcher, was well known for her ever-blonder helmet of hair, whose immoveable rigidity was a very visible symbol of her authority, inflexible convictions, and self-assurance.[2]

'It was a tenfold return on my investment', said Pam Hague-Wilton, a 44-year-old businesswoman of the £1,600 she had spent on hair extensions some two months earlier. 'It makes me feel more confident, more feminine, more relaxed. I see myself differently. My husband loves it – he was thrilled. I'm a bit of an instant gratification person – I want long hair so I go and get long hair!'[3] Hair this extravagant is costly in time, money, and professional maintenance (and is frequently uncomfortable as well). For many women today all this is worth it. But the experience is not for everyone. 'I bought the hairpiece six months ago to make me feel better about my post-baby paunch. I figured that if people saw great hair, they'd overlook the gut.' Canadian comedian and actress, Jessica Holmes, made this confession in Canada's major newspaper at the end of 2009. She thought the extra hair would not only distract attention from her figure but would also make her look glamorous when she hosted an upcoming prestigious event, which she had been invited to do. With long, lush hair she imagined she would feel worthy of her prominent role. The hairpiece didn't do its job. Instead, with every toss of her head it slipped a bit more from its mooring. It was an embarrassing disaster, but one that she had already put in perspective. She still had the hairpiece – 'cause you don't throw away something that cost $150, even if it is a hunk o' junk.' It also served as a cautious reminder, for when she clips it to her children's heads as a joke, she knows that 'a big gut is small price to pay for having great kids'.[4]

Hair, for women – at least for most of them in the past century – has not been a given. It is a bounty of nature that has needed to be managed, arranged, and frequently enhanced. Hair-extensions were and still are one major means of improving on nature, and this 'artifice' has been viewed in different ways. One 21-year old woman, identifying herself only as Sylvia, recounted her adventure with clip-in hair extensions. She was on the prowl for a new boyfriend and had prepared herself with special care for a party. Her new look attracted the man she had her eyes on, but when he kissed her he also tousled her hair, and the extensions came away in his hand. Looking with horror at the false hair, he dropped it, ran to the bathroom, and avoided eye contact with Sylvia for the rest of the evening. Understandably, she concluded that she would avoid that particular beauty tool on future first dates.[5] On his wedding night in late Victorian England, Jude Fawley in Thomas Hardy's *Jude the Obscure* (1894) had an unsettling experience that highlighted his and his new wife's incompatibility. 'A little chill over-spread him at her first unrobing. A long tail of hair, which Arabella wore twisted up in an enormous knob at the back of her head, was deliberately unfastened, stroked out, and hung upon the looking glass which he had bought her. "What – it wasn't your own?" he said, with a sudden distaste for her. "O no – it never is nowadays with the better class."'

Helping nature along, even if it was sometimes effective, has rarely been cost-free. In New York Meredith Bryan invested $1200 for 'five wavy blonde horsetails' to attach to her head with tiny barrettes which, her stylist assured her, 'total hair idiots' could snap in and out with ease. Nearing 30, as she put it, she wanted to achieve something of the high-volume 'Farrah Fawcett look' that once took 45 minutes with her blow dryer. With her new extensions in place she felt she looked '10 years younger and semi-famous' and noticed a 'striking and immediate difference' as she attracted stares from men in suits, construction workers, and from other women. Her boyfriend told her she looked like she was in a hair commercial and other friends didn't recognise her immediately but thought she looked fabulous. After a while, though, she found clipping and unclipping the extensions and carefully backcombing her own hair to hide the barrettes rather tedious and the washing and styling of the extensions 'about as sexy as rinsing dentures'. Returning to her everyday frumpiness, she packed the extensions away, lovingly, to await some special occasion or the next time she might need to remind herself 'that I can turn heads when I *want* to'.[6]

Sitting, blearily, waiting for an early morning flight, I have sometimes wondered who would buy clip-on hair extensions in an airport before breakfast. Now I know. They are people (almost all of us some days) who need a pick-me-up and confidence booster – what a smart new hat may have achieved for our mothers or grandmothers. A glance at the TV monitors in the departure lounge will reveal them to be advertising grooming products promoted by models with heads of hair so long, lush, and full that very few women could look this way in real life (especially those above, say, their early thirties) unless they employed artifice. These idealised images may be selling shampoo, but they undoubtedly stimulate the market for hair extensions as well. I have to admit that I might be tempted to purchase them myself if I really thought they could restore my youth. Just as television advertising manifestly assumes that men are obsessed with cars, so it also assumes that millions – no, tens of millions – of women obsess about their hair (and both assumptions are surely correct). Beauty salons that play on the idea of hair as a vital expression of personal identity are now found everywhere in the Western world and are usually more common on the High Streets of British towns than grocery shops.

These salons are virtually everywhere because so many women see their hair as a vital sign of self. This obsessing has taken many different forms. In 2007 an American journalist, Anne Kreamer, wrote a whole book about letting her hair go grey. In chapter after chapter she recounted her personal anguish with her decision – noting at one point that in Los Angeles she saw no woman of any age with grey hair. Tough decision made, she described the repeated hairdressers' appointments needed to allow her hair gradually to regain its natural colour without leaving her striped, badger-like, in the process. This saga, from final decision to weeks of execution, was, she suggested, almost as difficult as her struggle with a major personal crisis decades earlier. The dust-jacket of the book shows classic 'before' and 'after' shots: the silver haired after-view is of a slim, fit, confident-looking woman who is undoubtedly more attractive than her former dark-headed self.[7] The mere fact that someone could write, and expect people would want to read, a whole book on going grey is testimony to just how important hair is to the self-image of many women of a certain age.

The meaning of hair is often more in the head than on it. Anne Kreamer's friend and prominent New York writer, the late Nora Ephron (think *Sleepless in Seattle*), revealed in her humorous age-obsessed book *I Feel Bad About My Neck* that she never willingly managed her own hair but went instead several times a week to have someone else blow-dry it. 'It's cheaper by far than psychoanalysis', she observed, 'and much more uplifting.'[8] Wash and blow-dry services are increasingly available for those who want to appear their best without personal effort. Ephron was a rich, pencil-thin, fashionable, black-clad celebrity then in her sixties with lots of chutzpah, but apparently hadn't the confidence to manage her own fashionably coloured hair. Indeed, the effort of achieving the right hair seemed to her so overwhelming that she observed 'sometimes I think not to have to worry about your hair anymore is the upside of death.'[9] A wash and blow-dry is a luxury widely available in large cities. Blow-dry lounges or salons in many cities offer to blow-dry a woman's hair to a flawless, confidence-boosting coif for around £15 or £20 in Britain, $28 and $35 a session in North America, and this is one way of looking good that is rapidly becoming a necessity for many moneyed women two or three times a week – over and above their usual cuts, tints or styling.[10] British novelist Barbara Taylor Bradford shared these thoughts with her readers: 'I can be wearing the worst dress or the oldest piece of clothing, but if my hair is the way I like it, I'm satisfied. I go to the hairdresser's twice a week. My hair is blondish, a little streaky. I don't like it to be too blonde, and if it's not right – not only the colour, but the style – I get very unhappy.'[11]

Many women who live their lives far from celebrity circles or the paparazzi also define themselves, to some degree at least, by their hair. A former teacher, mother and new grandmother from Edmonton, Alberta with whom I discussed hair acknowledged that 'Hair is always a concern. If I think my hair looks bad, I feel bad. I can be put into a bad mood by a comment about my hair. I am a slave to feelings about my hair.' She would like to have naturally curly hair and is jealous of those who do. 'However, at least I do not have thin hair!'[12] One accomplished Englishwoman who shared with me her lifetime of hair anxieties reported that when she had her hair coloured she was often less than confident of the result: 'I was never quite sure and sometimes felt that I combined the worst features of two awful looking famous blondes, Myra Hindley, the Moors murderer, and Andy Warhol.'[13] The importance that these women attach to the presentation of their hair is, I am certain, shared by many, many other women. And this concern for one's hair has a colourful history. Here, in the pages to follow in this chapter, are some of the voices of the 158 women who responded in 2001 to a questionnaire about their hair from the

British social survey organisation, Mass Observation. (Fifty-four men replied as well but they mostly they talked about their wives' or partners' hair and little about their own.) These women's answers, many detailed and self-disclosing, others succinct and more matter-of-fact, make for a rich repository of sources for anyone interested in women and their hair.[14]

'My hair is light brown, slightly red, fine, about two feet long, with a centre parting and a medium fringe [known as 'bangs' in North America]', wrote a 44-year-old author from Watford. 'I do not dye it, curl it or use any substances on it other than shampoo. I suppose it accurately expresses who I am as a person. I consider myself to be quite an honest, straightforward and sincere person, rather sensitive, romantic, cautious, spiritually inclined and unconventional.' 'My hair is tremendously important to me', said a retired Londoner, 'and, in a quite powerful way, I think it embodies the good, bad, and indecisive elements in my character … It has always been a problem – at least since my teens – and still is, although I now know exactly how I want it to look. The trouble is, most of the time it refuses to oblige.' Sadly, one woman observed, 'I have never had hair I could be proud of. It is too fine and thin.' 'My present severe style fits the sort of person I am', reflected a retired headmistress. 'When I was young, I gave the impression with my fluffy waves or curls of being far less serious than I am or was.' Her severe style, however, was softened by a golden blonde tint, which she thought made mature women look younger in contrast to 'that permed all white hair known locally as cauliflower style.'[15]

A mature student of 36, living in Herstmonceaux, East Sussex, didn't think her hair reflected accurately who she was: 'I feel a lot more outgoing than my hair shows. I feel tempted to throw blue or green streaks into my hair, but think I may be getting too old for that … My favourite hairstyle was still one where my perm was growing out, the top was cut short, the rest down to my shoulders and it was coloured a subdued red.' A 66-year-old Justice of the Peace from Bedfordshire counted herself fortunate because, as she said, 'I actually like my hair which, I think, is quite unusual'. Her light brown hair suited her well and she was pleased it hadn't faded much with age. Much as she liked her look, she also recalled the fun of wearing appearance-altering wigs which, earlier in her career, she had used as disguises while working as a store detective. A different sort of disguise appealed to a 30-year old London Museum curator: 'My hair is probably my best physical feature ... long and thick and curly and a kind of brown with a ginger tinge... I consider it an integral part of who I am and how I perceive myself. It does also play a sort of camouflaging role, or at least I think of it doing so. I think, perhaps hope, that it draws attention from the rest of me.' A similar view was expressed by a 52-year old retired social historian who said: 'I like my hair... My hair is right for my face... I've always liked a bit of camouflage – my face is fatter now and I need hair to balance it.' She dyed her hair chestnut to go with her relatively unwrinkled face, adding 'I'm not ready to be old yet... I feel better as a person when my hair looks nice.' She summed it all up this way: 'I'm an artist at heart, my body is my canvas – decorate it nicely'. Another woman in her fifties spoke of 'the torture of not being able to have your hair as you would like it'. 'If my hair isn't quite right', she added, 'then I'm not quite complete.' [16]

'Oh great. Something I can write reams about', enthused a woman from Tunbridge Wells when Mass Observation gave her the opportunity to write about hair. For her, hair was a very high priority. 'I wouldn't dream of leaving the house without styling my hair', she said, and recalled that, as a young woman and competitive ballroom dancer, she had taken two part-time jobs to maintain her bleached platinum-blonde hair: 'Spent every penny I had on my hair ... I went without clothes, shoes, sweets, everything...to pay for my retouches.' In 1978, she estimated that she spent about £760 a year on her hair out of a take-home salary of £4,500. A former inspector of engine parts, who herself favoured the 'neat, no nonsense style' of her childhood, recalled the views of a younger sister who had died the previous year: 'She would not open the curtains in her home until her hair was beautifully styled, and her makeup complete. She always looked the picture of elegance.' A retired librarian had a very different perspective. 'I am in despair about my hair', she said. 'It doesn't let me down. I let it down. It used to be very thick … It is now very thin'. Yet she added: 'I don't think it is important to have my hair cared for regularly to look well groomed. That wouldn't suit my personality, which is that of a wild Irish intellectual that won two scholarships to public school and two to Oxbridge when I was barely 17. Got a First Class Honours Degree … As for sex appeal, my husband and lovers preferred the natural look.' 'DULL, DULL, DULL', complained a 29-year-old communications consultant in an information technology company of her straight, mousy brown hair. She added that her hair was 'not one of my priorities in life'. Nonetheless, she saw the social importance of hair care and confessed to going to 'posh saloons' and spending between £20 and £30 for a good low maintenance cut. 'I just look scruffy', concluded a Manchester technician of her hair which was straight, an insipid mouse colour, now graying, and plagued by a crown 'in a bad position so I can never get any fullness on top.' She tried to compensate with colouring but got 'sick of the effort of being blonde' following the birth of her daughter; she abandoned the dye bottle and, she reported, frightened her toddler who at first didn't at recognise the woman with short, dark hair as her mother.[17]

Managing one's hair is commonly a critical component of a woman's well-being in times of stress: dishevelled hair was sometimes used to represent women in distress in nineteenth-century literature. A former civil servant commented that she 'would rather go naked than go with dishevelled hair… If my hair says anything about me it is that I am a control freak, and my hair is the first thing to control. Once that's done I can face anything. For example, before going into hospital last December, I had my hair done, and before starting radiation therapy in February I did the same.' Other women recalled that making an appointment with the hairdresser was the first thing they did on returning home after a hospital stay. 'I begin to feel better quickly if my hair looks good', said a woman who had had several hospital stays over the previous six years. In late 2009 a television journalist, reporting on the release of a female hostage after a long incarceration by terrorists, noted, as evidence she was recovering well, that she had asked to have a hairdresser visit her in hospital. A woman in her late fifties lamented the erosion of confidence that had come with the thinning of her once thick, gingery red hair of which people used to say 'what lovely hair you've got'. Her sympathetic GP arranged for her to have an open appointment to consult a National Health facility about hairpieces, even though she had no medical problem. This kindly gesture of comfort – it spoke to a certain consensus on the importance of hair – she greatly appreciated. It is clear from the replies of older women to Mass Observation's questionnaire that for many of them thinning hair was a source of anguish and humiliation, and that retaining 'a good head of hair' into middle and old age was a source of pride and self-respect. Several women described their efforts as they aged to conceal the sparseness of their hair. One wore hers up in a clip, 'typical old woman's style', she remarked, though many of the hair slides or clips she had collected over the years were now too heavy for her thin hair.[18]

A few women were less preoccupied with their hair. A 23-year-old Brighton student of Afro-Caribbean background said she thought little about whether her hair reflected her personality, adding that she had more important things to worry about. On a whim, she traded her thick dreadlocks for a short style without much consideration beyond alarm at what the barber charged for the haircut. 'I am happy with my own hair, it takes little time to wash or dry', another apparently relaxed woman reported. 'I hate "fiddling" with hair – or having it fiddled with – hence my lack of "style"... I have never needed to wear a wig or hairpiece. I have never permanently dyed or bleached my hair.' This sounds like someone at peace with her tresses. But I noted that she took 6½ pages of print to record her lifetime's experiences with and thoughts about hair.[19]

For many women a question put to them about their hair evoked powerful and sometimes anguished responses. 'How can such a small part of your body assume such terrifying proportions?' lamented a Derbyshire administrator. 'Your hair can have a terrible effect on your confidence … I always say that when you have anything different done to your hair it feels like you are walking round with a Belisha beacon [a traffic pole topped with an orange lamp] on your head!' 'My hair has ALWAYS been a problem', moaned a receptionist from Preston. 'I feel as though my hair is the greatest thing about my appearance that lets me down. I wear smart clothes and put make-up on and I try to keep my figure trim but all of this is no use because my hair nearly always looks a mess.' 'My hair and its appearance is of paramount importance to me!' commented a woman of 71 who admitted spending £1,000 a year on her hair. 'Never being gifted with a beautiful face,' she continued, 'I was fortunate enough to have good thick hair, so I have made the most of it. I could never imagine not caring about my style of hair, and am always having it coloured and trimmed to shape. It gives me great confidence to know it looks good, and I constantly get remarks about how "lucky" I am to have such good hair.' One 60-year-old woman was thankful that she had aged her way into hair that she now saw as one of her best features, 'pure white and quite distinctive' in contrast to the mousy, non-descript colour of her earlier years. An unemployed, single, 35-year old in York was less self-satisfied. 'My hair is a disaster area, drives me mad, and often makes me miserable. I'm currently a bit obsessed about it, to be honest! … I notice other people's hair and am constantly on the lookout for a style I might copy.' She added that in childhood 'I was infamous for bad hair. It was very fine and you couldn't do much with it … As those around me became trendy and cool, I remained incredibly uncool with hair that was dull and greasy-looking and kept in some sort of order only by gallons of hairspray.'[20]

Other women's words were ironic, or at least more muted and analytical. One writer described her hair thus: 'It was a dark and stormy night, when I looked in the mirror, and I thought IT was coming to get me! The Creature from the Black Lagoon!

With writhing, matted locks, made from snakes. Then I realised: no, it was just my old perm. It had dropped shortly after I had it done (December 2000) and I couldn't do anything with it.' A Cheshire civil servant concluded, in a spirit of realism, that her short hair style was an asset. 'I feel it has improved my looks and is fashionable, it also says something about me as an independent woman ... It goes with the image I have of myself as being able to be smart as well as sexy.'[21] Some women paid their hair little heed, simply scraping it back into a knot or ponytail and just letting it hang loose, but such a casual outlook was rare in this – admittedly self-selecting – sample of women who were prepared, even keen, to talk about their hair.

A few respondents cared deeply about hair in general. 'Ever since I was a young girl I just loved hair', wrote one woman. She always wanted to be a hairdresser 'to fulfill my passion', but her father wouldn't permit it, saying it was a dirty, smelly profession that didn't pay well. She became a civil servant instead. Her daughter, gifted with a similar love of hair care, wanted (in 2001) to be a hairdresser on leaving school, a career choice her mother enthusiastically endorsed. 'I should have been a hairdresser, it would have been a proper career, instead of the various jobs I've done', lamented a widow from Leeds. She had always cut her mother's hair, and later that of both her husbands and her son until the latter was a teenager. She also cut and set the hair of workmates, which included, at one site, doing the secretary's hair as her first job of the day. Using a three-way mirror and good scissors, this woman reported that she had cut her own hair until very recently. Since then, finding the task more difficult, she found a good hairdresser – and still gets a lot of 'nice compliments' on her hair, so, as she concluded, 'all is not lost'.[22]

In September 2009 I interviewed students and faculty at the hairdressing school at Bournemouth and Poole College. Virtually all of them expressed a real vocation for hairdressing, telling me that they had always loved playing with hair and occasionally bribed friends or siblings to let them experiment on them. I couldn't help but notice that few of them could go for long without touching a client's hair, or their own, or fiddling with their practice-models' heads of hair while they talked to me. Three of the four instructors with whom I had coffee that day still own the hairpieces they had made as students. Several came from families of hairdressers. They also liked their chosen occupation because of its role as a helping profession. Lorraine Hawkins, an instructor at the College, observed that people sometimes seek out hairdressers instead of therapists. A big part of her role, she thought, was to have people leave her salon feeling better as well as looking good – a lesson she took pains to pass on to her students.[23] Exposure to hairdressing at home did not, naturally, convert everyone. An acquaintance in Ontario told me that, as a child, she actively disliked being made to help out in her mother's hairdressing shop. Her reaction was certainly not a consequence of any lack of enthusiasm on her mother's part, for when Marian McPhail talked me it was clear that her passion for hair care was undiminished, even after several decades in the trade. She recounted many hair stories, including dressing the hair on corpses; her eagerness to take courses to keep up with the latest trends and techniques; her enjoyment in being on friendly terms with her clients; and her lifelong joy in the work. As she signed off, this hairdresser in her mid 70s was on

Meg Thompson of North Shields at age 16 in 1946 and with a 'Jane Wyman' look at age 22 in 1951, when she became engaged to Bill Stephenson

her way to dress a neighbour's hair.[24]

✂ ✂ ✂ ✂

A woman's intense relationship with hair often began in childhood. Memories abound of hair washed infrequently, often attended to in the bath to save precious hot water, and dried in front of the fire; and painful tugs as hair was combed, plaited, or wound in curling rags. Washing and doing up one's hair was something of an event, as were, for a few young girls, scary visits to barbers. Personally, I recall having my hair washed in the bath which I shared with my three younger siblings. Our mother used a sort of plastic, crownless hat, that we called the halo, to shampoo our hair without getting soap in our eyes. (Only decades later did I learn that ancient Roman women wore somewhat similar headgear when sitting in the sun and hoping that their hair would bleach.) Instead of drying our hair in front of an open fire, my siblings and I put the hose at the opposite end of the vacuum cleaner to produce an ad hoc hairdryer. After babyhood, our mother sent us all to the barber to be shorn. I loathed the results, particularly when my fringe was eliminated and I was forced to present myself with a really short haircut – 'like a boy and shaved at the nape of the neck', as one Mass Observer put it; she hated it and so did I.[25] This was no way to be feminine in the 1950s. At least I was spared visits to hairdressers that some children found excruciating. One woman remembered loathing the small cramped cubicles at her mother's hairdresser, along with the noise from hood hairdryers and the overpowering fumes from perming solutions, and by age 11 she refused to return ever again. At 44 she still had not visited any other hairdresser.[26] Other people remembered family haircuts performed in the garden in summer by a parent or family friend; drying hair before a gas fire in strict rota at boarding school; fathers who cut the family's hair, and some who 'hated fringes with an irrational vengeance'. Fathers and grandfathers of traditional tastes sometimes wanted the girls in their families to leave their hair uncut until late adolescence, which meant, of course, that it might hang down to their waists, and thus require regular brushing and troublesome washing and drying.[27]

The nit comb was the bane of some childhoods. Wielded by the school nurse or by mother, it was usually followed by unpleasant dosing with coal tar or other anti-lice shampoos, repeated painful combings, nauseating crushing of the creatures between fingernails and, perhaps worst for a sensitive child, an irritated parent who was forced to launder every hat, towel, or sheet that might have touched the infected head. And, particularly among middle-class parents in the 1950s, head lice were regarded as an excruciatingly embarrassing failure of hygiene, even though outbreaks of lice were near universal in some schools. Along with these everyday experiences, some children absorbed family hair prejudices. There was, for example, the common superstition that it was ill-advised on health grounds to wash hair while menstruating; the notion that washing hair on Friday was bad luck was a bit more unusual.[28]

Early hair experiences sometimes coloured a child's relationships with parents, siblings or peers, and, all too often, negatively influenced her view of herself. 'What a disappointment I was to my mother!' recalled one woman (aged 69) of her childhood. 'She longed for a "curly-knob" like Shirley Temple. She struggled with special shampoos in the hope of achieving a miracle.' Efforts to conform to the fashions of the day were routinely frustrated. 'Sunday school was a special occasion, with straw hats atop dangling ringlets favoured by an elite minority. To silence my pleading my mother wrestled with "curl-rags" some Saturday nights to enable me to ape the elite. But my hair was so fine and slippery the pitiful clusters of six or eight ringlets had collapsed before we were led out before the sermon.' This little girl internalised her mother's disappointment, longing by eight or nine to be beautiful, envying her closest friend's thick wavy hair, and continuing to hope for that miracle. Then there were the struggles between mother and daughter. 'Hair was a constant battle in our house', wrote another woman (aged 54). 'My mother believed that all little girls should have curly hair. Unfortunately

I was born with dead straight, very fine and wispy hair. She liked short hair, I wanted it long.' 'I did not like my hairstyle when I was a child', reported a 44-year old married woman. 'It was rather short, and my mother used to curl it with plastic curlers or metal ones with a little brush inside so that the bristles of the brush protruded through the outer metal mesh. I would sit near the fire until my hair was dry. I also wore an Alice band for many years. I found that hairstyle unattractive, unfeminine, old-fashioned and embarrassing, and it set me apart from other little girls of my age in a way that made me feel awkward and self-conscious. I was a very shy, nervous, anxious child. I did not make friends easily, was unadventurous and did not really fit in in many ways, so having an embarrassing hairstyle was an impediment for me.'[29]

Other women also remembered well the indignities they had suffered at the hands of mothers or other family members. 'I hate my hair', was the stark opinion of a 48-year old woman with three grown-up children, and she attributed this feeling to experiences in childhood. 'You see, my Mother allowed me to grow my hair long on one condition, that I had it tied back. I had to wear it in plaited braids. Now my sister, who is six years older than me, was given the task of plaiting it. She didn't like me and she didn't like to have to tend my hair so when she plaited it she pulled so hard it made my eyes smart and water. When I complained she just told me to shut up. As this was a daily task I quickly learned to hate my hair.' Her sister likened her hair to 'rats' tails', and some four decades later, in middle age, 'I cannot look at my hair without thinking it looks a mess. It doesn't help to know now that she only said that because she was jealous of my long hair and she really thought it looked lovely.' Even a child with blonde, curly Shirley Temple-like hair, which a doting mother adorned with blue ribbons, could be troubled by her mother's predilections. 'By the time I was 13 I was likened to another film star, Harpo Marx' – not a flattering association. A 45-year-old Londoner recalled her hair in childhood as 'unruly', despite her mother's efforts to keep it looking decent. 'By the time I reached 10, I was convinced that I was so ugly that I would never marry. My hair – frizzy, mousy and uncontrollable – played a major part in this self-loathing.'[30]

Hair, clearly, was often a source of frustration and dissatisfaction, both for young girls and their elders (who were sometimes quick to be censorious). In a 1960 BBC radio broadcast, Shivaun Cunningham (her real name was Julie Lanchester) described the loss of her ringlets as 'the main tragedy of my childhood'. Without her ringlets her hair was straight, and her distress was such that every night she added a fervent postscript to her prayers: 'please, God, give me back my curls'. God, it appears, eventually listened, though only after she had served several years as a nun. When Cunningham re-grew her shorn hair upon leaving her convent, she reported with satisfaction that it grew back in curls – and was still curly two years later.[31] She was perhaps more fortunate than the girl who was teased about the shoulder length ringlets she still had – at her own request – when she started secondary school. She asked to have her hair short again, but the short cut executed by her stepmother in the 1950s was incompatible with the reigning fashions, and she was made the butt of derision at Girl Guides for wearing a haircut which, the author admits, would later be regarded as quite stylish. Perhaps the most frequently cited hair woe was straight hair, the second an unappealing mousey colour. As one woman put it, 'My hair has always been a problem – it is very, very fine and mousey in colour, also DEAD STRAIGHT. As a small child my mother constantly bemoaned my unattractive hair.' Other women also remembered mothers and grandmothers deriding hair that they saw as 'straight as a yard of tap water'. In order to counteract the unpleasantness of straight hair, children might be subjected to curling tongs, which were probably heated over an open fire – 'regarded by me as instruments of torture, but worth enduring in the cause of vanity.' Whatever measures were taken to tame their hair, some girls continued to be subjected to taunts, such as the 50-year old social researcher who remembered being chastised by a junior-school teacher for not combing her hair – "'You look as if you've been pulled through a hedge backwards!"'[32]

A prominent feature of the hair experiences of women several decades ago was the permanent wave. The perm was expensive and time-consuming – it normally demanded at least three hours of a woman's time, maybe as many as five or six hours – and it involved equipment that was cumbersome and smelly, perhaps even dangerous. Central to the perming process was an assemblage of electrified rollers, hanging above a client's head, which cooked the hair. It could lead to some alarming incidents. A veteran hairdresser told me about one of his (later famous) colleagues' experiences of giving a woman a perm in London's East End in wartime. When the air raid siren sounded, the hairdresser had no choice but to leave his client, hair tied up in spiral rollers attached to an overhead electrically powered 'halo'. When he returned from the shelter his client was alive and unhurt but when he unrolled the 'overcooked' waves, much of her hair came away in his hand.[33] One woman remembered the prospect of having a perm in 1937, when she was around 17, as a 'great event'. But she found the actual process a trial – stinky and painful – and when the rollers were taken off 'there were chemical burns right along my neck that formed horrible scabs'.[34] Such disasters were not the norm, but many women did risk discomfort or danger in order to rid themselves, temporarily, of the humiliation of straight, unfashionable hair, and a few mothers in the 1930s put their daughters through the rigors of a perm (this was before home perms existed). Hairdressers, unsurprisingly, were keen to market – and they had convinced themselves and their clients of this – the perm's many and remarkable merits.

Much social significance came to be associated for some women with getting a perm. A perm could be an assertion of independence bought by a young woman from her first earnings; a gift from an elder that might signal the end of childhood or emerging adulthood; or a preparation for a life outside the family home. In the late 1950s and early 1960s, according to one woman, 'a sign of growing up was to have your first perm, then your hair set every week'. 'By working in the holidays I earned enough money to visit a hairdressing salon', wrote a woman in her seventies. 'I felt very grown up when I had my first permanent wave.' She also recalled it as 'quite a frightening experience. I was wired to an overhead contraption, and left there for what seemed liked hours. The smell of the lotion brought tears to one's eyes, and the resultant frizz must have looked awful.' Many memories of these perms were often less then serene. 'I had my first perm at thirteen [around 1945], in time for boarding school', wrote another woman; 'it was a somewhat threatening experience. The victim was attached by wires to an electric device which energised each individual curler. Fuzz and split ends sometimes resulted. I had a perm every school holiday.' One woman remembered that when she was about to start work around 1950, her mother 'treated me to a perm at the hairdressers', even though her hair was naturally curly. 'I recall being put under a load of wires and enduring the most awful stink of ammonia or some such. I never liked the resultant frizz ... I have never ever had a perm since.'[35] Many girls made a perm an early priority once they had full-time wages of their own. Sisters Kathleen and Joyce Tipper, who lived in south-east London, recalled getting perms when they began their first jobs as late adolescents in the 1930s. Hair care continued to be of central importance to them: they had perms and visited their local hairdresser regularly all through the Second World War, despite being bombed out of their house, earning slender wages, and spending long hours (on top of their full-time jobs) as volunteers, helping the troops from various nations that were stationed in London.[36] And a visit to a decent hairdresser never came cheap.

Adolescence and young adulthood has always been a time to experiment – a time for a woman to try out who she wanted to be, or to be seen to be. Hair has been very much a part of this search for identify, in respect of the public presentation of self. Women reported to Mass Observation a wide variety of hair experiments, from backcombed bubble-cuts and fun wigs in the 1960s, to 'Afro' perms in the 1970s, to allowing hair grow very long, to playing around with wild hair colours and even spiking the hair. 'When I was 17', around 1943, recalled one woman, 'I went to Ray in Oxford Street for a perm to make me look like Ingrid Bergman in For Whom the Bell Tolls ... It was the best perm and the best hairstyle I've ever had. A feather cut? That was my favourite. It was a great success with American soldiers.' Some hair experiments, of course, were flops. One woman with an extensive and sometimes difficult hair history appreciated that 'one of life's blessings is that mistaken hair does at last grow out'.[37]

Women think a great deal about hair, but what have men thought about it? In 2008, a Toronto fashion magazine convened a meeting of 'a few of the city's coolest men' to discuss what they found truly alluring in a woman. When asked the first feature they noticed in a beautiful woman they saw across the room, they gave answers like: ass, face, legs, skin, teeth. Not one mentioned hair. When the conversation did eventually turn to hair, the men held two principal views. First, they thought that a very short hairstyle showed confidence or could be fashion-forward but generally needed a special (or especially beautiful) woman to carry it off. Secondly, they displayed irritation at women who frequently changed their hair colour, with one man saying that it was usually a 'sign of insecurity – a red flag'.[38] On the whole they would have agreed with the woman who said her husband didn't notice hair: 'he's more a legs and tits man'. After childbirth in the 1950s one woman's hair lost some of its thickness and bounce, and she 'did buy a blonde wig which quite turned my husband on' (but it was hot to wear and flattened her natural hair so didn't get a lot of use). A woman whose husband didn't much notice her hair took solace in the fact that he probably wasn't aware when it was a mess.[39] The men's responses to Mass Observation's 2001 Directive (three times more women than men responded to it) confirm that hair, their own or their wives', does not and (I think) still does not deeply engage most men's emotions. I have found that my own fretting about my thinning hair is not shared by my husband, who claims to think about it infrequently (and offers me the typically simplistic advice, 'Wear hats'). For most men women's hair is and has been no big deal.

Men have been known, however, to give their partners practical hair assistance. A Watford man washed his arthritic wife's long hair and trimmed its ends about twice a year. In return she combed his hair, 'otherwise he often wouldn't bother', and for some years she helped him to dye it with henna which 'made it very nice, silky and an attractive colour, but was

Joan Shepherd from Cardiff in 1943, aged 20. Joan's upswept crown and rolled long pageboy showed Britain's young women at their best

messy and difficult to apply'. Another woman decided early in her marriage to be a blonde 'and for the next eight years my husband was stuck with touching up the roots with a toothbrush every few weeks. He is an engineer', she added, 'and so found it quite easy to part my hair in sections and methodically apply the solution'. The same husband also trimmed his partner's shoulder-length hair, a fairly common form of spousal assistance when a woman's hair was worn long in the 1970s. Other husbands simply offered occasional opinions: 'My husband now does notice and when it is different will always say whether he likes it or not.' At one end of the spectrum, a woman reported that her husband not only took an active part in the management of her hair, occasionally persuading her to go to a hairdresser, accompanying her there, and even 'instructing the hairdresser as to how she should deal with me'. One woman's husband 'was the person who suggested that I should start to go to the hairdressers' on a weekly basis, after I had difficulty keeping up to it at home', according to a 63-year old from Cottingley, West Yorkshire. A consequence of this suggestion, she calculated, was that she spent £586 on hair in a year, and wondered if she should spend less.[40]

Most respondents for Mass Observation admitted to noticing other women's hair and often making assessments of it, some rather guiltily, others not. One hair-sensitive and perhaps insecure 35-year-old regretted this attitude: 'It's a shame judgements are made so readily about a person according to hairstyle – judgements about attractiveness, personality, self-awareness, confidence, capability etc.' Another woman – older, in her sixties – was more self-accepting, and worldly wise. 'I notice other people's hair styles and always tell people if their hair looks exceptionally nice', she said. A less self-confident woman of about the same age admitted to being envious of women with 'thick, beautiful or easily managed hair. I am impressed by the skill acquired by friends and acquaintances utilising heated rollers, heated brushes, blow dryers, back-combing, flicking, tumble dryers, you-name-it. Our local Light Opera Society put on a show after Christmas. In the jam-packed dressing room, where the swinging of a cat would present serious difficulties, I watched with envy and amazement as eighteen women, from sixteen to sixty-five, flicked, combed, snatched, swatched and blew their hairs into shape, performed miracles on one another with the tongs, drooped forward their lovely heads to get the desired level of lift. I had to be content with extra visits to the hairdresser!'[41] Interestingly, few women who wrote about hair for Mass Observation revealed any of the commonly held stereotypes from around the mid twentieth century about blondes, that is, dyed or 'bleached' blondes – who were once seen as rather trashy, fast, attention-seekers (natural blondes, of course, have traditionally been associated with youth and innocence).

Diaries, in which women often confided their candid views, have occasionally recorded harsh – or bemused – judgments on other women's hair choices. On 7 May 1942 Nella Last, of Barrow-in-Furness, Lancashire, aged 52, wrote of her working day at the Women's Voluntary Services Centre and of how 'Mrs. Wilkins turned up after a new perm yesterday with her hair in flapperish curls and rolls and rolls – and jet black! Try as we would our eyes would stray to her glistening black locks although no one mentioned it, of course. Later she came into the kitchen and patting her hair she said "Have you never thought of having a rinse when you had a shampoo? You could make a lot more of your appearance if you liked." I made a non-committal reply but could have told her candidly that her bright glittering black curls made her 54 year-old face look older!' (Such censorious thoughts have surely passed through millions of women's minds.) Some months later, on 22 February 1943, Mrs Last encountered another woman who must also have attached a lot of importance to the presentation of her hair – and this was after three and a half years of war, when personal grooming was becoming more and more a challenge. The woman, whom Nella Last likened to a Dresden doll, had 'a tiny face with huge blue eyes, nearly lost in a tangle of platinum curls as big as black puddings heaped on top of her head and tumbling down on to slender light-blue clad shoulders. A beret hung – by willpower alone, evidently – at the back of her head and made up a picture of musical comedy cum revue.'[42] A striking hairstyle was one way to stand out, though clearly it took care to avoid ridicule.

The self-described sweeps and bangs of one Mass Observer, 1948

Picture courtesy Mass Observer H260 and the Mass Observation archive, University of Sussex

Going grey has been notably contentious and open to a range of attitudes. Some women have gone grey contentedly (or at least so they say), others have resisted greyness with zeal. 'A lot of judgements are made when a woman has grey hair, which is why I have my hair tinted a lighter colour so people can't see the grey roots', confessed a 52-year-old receptionist. 'I know myself if a female customer comes in and she has grey wispy hair I immediately think she is "old" even though she may only be my age! All sorts of pre-conceived ideas come into play.' Looking old and grey, some felt, was equivalent to being invisible – and who wanted that? One woman recalled that her last discussion with a recently deceased neighbour (she was 79) had been about hair. Her dyed 'lovely head of auburn hair' had been criticised at the over-60s club both for its colour and the fact that she still coloured it at her age. 'In fact I heard remarks about her smartness and coloured hair (which was actually a quite natural looking colour) being referred to as her "London ways"'. By contrast, a 45-year-old objected to the 'unnatural' colouring of hair, but 'I think that "natural" looking dying of hair looks good if hair is grey. A cousin who is younger than me is completely grey and, although I've not spoken to her about it, I often wonder why she does not dye it to her natural colour as it was.'[43]

A lovely 1959 pageboy
Picture courtesy Nelson Museum of Art and History, Renwick Collection, TN-Renwick 3324001

Particular hairstyles or colours were regularly evaluated, and these views were certainly varied. 'Straightening hair is pathetic and absurd', declared a 75-year-old. 'It never looks as good as naturally curly or Afro hair. Often true of permed hair too.' A woman of 60 whose hair 'is now pure white and quite distinctive' was alert to bad dye jobs. 'I do hate to see older women with such obviously dyed hair, which as been done in too dark a shade for their older complexions. It really does look artificial. I often feel they should go to a hairdresser and get some professional advice upon the shade of colour that would be better for them.' A 49-year-old London civil servant had several reflections on hair: 'After a certain age people look older if the hair hangs around the face as it seems to emphasise the wrinkled skin texture,' she said. 'A hair dye also looks odd with an old skin tone and emphasises the age. On the other hand, early grey hair with a fresh complexion can look younger. I prefer to accept the ageing process and find it a pity when others do not.' And perhaps men were not entirely blind to women's hair, for when she wore her own hair longer, 'I sense a little more personal and less professional response from older male colleagues'.[44]

The 158 women who responded to Mass Observation's 2001 Spring Directive ranged in age from their twenties to late seventies. Almost all were aware that hair – how it was presented, how it changed both by design and from aging – carried powerful messages, messages that signal health and well-being, confidence, social standing, and perhaps even political inclination. Most important, their hair played a critical role in most of these women's self-esteem. Hair also often marked significant changes in women's lives. Altered style or colour could celebrate a success, mourn a death or failed relationship, or highlight a changed direction in life. 'It made me feel like a different woman'; 'it was a bit of a statement about me getting a life and doing my own thing'; 'made me feel bubbly'; 'a real step forward in self confidence' – these were some of the feelings reported about changing one's hair. The act of thinking and writing about their hair induced many women in 2001 to write at length, probably more than they had expected to write, and perhaps more personally than they had planned. 'I'm amazed writing this', concluded one respondent, 'to see how inextricably my psyche and my hair are linked!'[45]

A change of hairstyles has, for decades, been seen – or imagined – as linked to a change in personal identity. In a short story from 1941, Dorothy Whipple had one of her two main characters, a middle-aged spinster, ponder her recently permed and curled hair: 'It made a great difference to her appearance, and Miss Morley spent much more time admiring her back hair with the aid of a hand-mirror than anyone in the village would have believed. In fact, if Miss Morley had had her hair waved years ago, she might have been a different woman altogether.'[46]

Almost every woman has a hair story. And so did many of their mothers and grandmothers and great-grandmothers. The following chapters are intended to show what these previous generations thought about hair and changing fashions, how the commercial dressing of hair became ubiquitous – it had not been for women before the twentieth century – and how the management of women's hair was closely linked to larger changes in culture and society, including good times and bad, war and peace, and times of freedom and of constraint. Hair has a history, and this history is much deeper than the mere vagaries of fashion. Hair, as I hope to show, is an important – and an interesting – aspect of Britain's social history.

Patience Watson Turnbull from Gateshead, pictured in 1966 aged 25, with her cats' eyes spectacles accenting her bouffant hairstyle

References

1   Jenny Diski, *The Sixties* (London: Profile Books, 2009), p. 17.

2   Joanna Pitman, *On Blondes* (London: Bloomsbury, 2003), captions to photographs between pp. 134 and 135.

3   As quoted in Katie Glass, 'Hair Today Gone Tomorrow', *The Sunday Times Magazine*, 12 February 2012, 42.

4   Holmes, Jessica, 'My Last Stupid Purchase', as told to Deidre Kelly, *Globe and Mail*, 22 December 2009, L, 2.

5   *Cosmopolitan*, December 2009, 66.

6   Meredith Bryan, 'I want more hair', *Marie Claire*, January 2009, 113-4.

7   Anne Kreamer, *Going Gray: What I Learned About Beauty, Sex, Work, Motherhood, Authenticity, and Everything Else that Really Matters* (New York: Little, Brown and Company, 2007).

8   Nora Ephron, *I Feel Bad About My Neck: and other thoughts on being a woman* (New York: Alfred A Knopf, 2006), p. 34.

9   Ibid, 32.

10 Deirdre Kelly, 'Say you want a (beauty) revolution', *Globe and Mail*, Saturday, 21 February 2009, L, 2.

11 Barbara Taylor Bradford, 'What I See in the Mirror', *Guardian Weekend*, 26 September 2009, 67.

12 Janet Bailey, personal communications, November 2009-January 2010.

13 Dorothy Sheridan, personal communication, 2 March 2010.

14 This material, collected in response to MO's Spring Directive in 2001, is part of the Mass Observation Archive (MOA), which is housed in Special Collections in the Library of the University of Sussex in Brighton. Each respondent, as a writer for MO, had been assigned an identifying number (MO's volunteers were promised anonymity), and this number is used below to refer to the quotations and individual evidence cited in the text. All these documents are in MOA, SD (2001), and all the references below are from this file unless otherwise indicated.

15 A 2212, married, author, Watford; D 996, 74, divorced Londoner, retired from Citizens Advice Bureau; G 224, 75, widow; E 174, 77, retired Headmistress, Manchester.

16 H 2911, 36, married, mature student; B 2760, 66, JP; D 2899, 30, single; R 2247, 52, Walthamstow, London; A 1706, 55, artist/gardener, Shoreham-by-Sea.

17   B 1898, 69, married, ex-claims assessor; R 1469, 77, widow, Derby; G 1041, married, Purley; G 2776, 29, communications consultant; J 931, 55, married, part-time technician, Manchester.

18   R 1760, 70, widow, former civil servant; H 2639, 60, married, retired library assistant, Ipswich; D 2585, late 50s, secretary, near Bristol; E 174.

19   B 2917, 23, student; N 2912, 45, married, part-time student and former pharmacy technician.

20   H 1703, 55, married, Derbyshire; C 1713, married, receptionist; H 260, 71, ex-shop manageress, Brentwood; H 2639, 60, retired library assistant, Ipswich; A 2801, 35, single, unemployed, York.

21   J 2830; T 1843, 51, married, civil servant.

22   N 2890, 40, Local Government officer, Shoreham, West Sussex; Z 53, 74, widow, Leeds.

23   Lorraine Hawkins, personal communication, 23 September 2009.

24   Telephone conversation with Mary Ann McPhail of Cannington, Ontario, 15 May 2008.

25   N 2912.

26   A 2212.

27   A 2212; N 1592; T 1843; C 2053; H 266.

28   C 2929; C 2053; H 1703; W 2588; M 1979.

29   N 1592; P 1796; A 2212.

30   D 156; B 1180; B 2728.

31   Shivaun Cunningham (pseudo), 'My Hair and Me', 16 November 1960, BBC file # FX 16/11/1960. The author's son, John Lanchester, discusses this episode in his mother's life in *Family Romance: A Love Story* (Toronto: McClelland and Stewart, 2007), pp. 291-92.

32   P 1326; P 1637; H 1371; P 2138; H 1145.

33   The late Joshua Galvin, personal communication, November 2009.

34   N 2148.

35   A 1706; D 1685; N 1592; B 1771.

36   Kathleen and Joyce Tipper, personal communications, 2008 and 2009.

37   G 1041; M 1979.

38   *Fashion*, Summer 2008, 108.

39   G 1041; K 130; J 931.

40   A 2212; J 931; B 2760; B 2197; W 571.

41   A 2801; B 2760; N 1592.

42   MOA, Diarist no. 5353.

43   C 1713; G 1241; N 2912.

44   G 1041; H 2639; G 2089.

45   R 2247.

46   Dorothy Whipple, 'Youth', in *After Tea* (1941), pp. 208-09.

"Mamma, shall I have beautiful long hair like you when I grow up ?"—"Certainly, my dear, if you use Edwards' ' Harlene.' "

"HARLENE"

THE GREAT HAIR PRODUCER AND RESTORER. The finest dressing, specially prepared and perfumed, fragrant and refreshing. Is a Luxury and a Nece to every Modern Toilet. "HARLENE" PRODUCES LUXURIANT HAIR. Prevents its Falling Off and Turning Grey. Unequalled for Promoting the Growth of the Beard and Moustache. World-Renowned Remedy for Baldness. For Preserving, Strengthening, and Rendering the Hair Beautifully Soft ; for Removing Scurf, Dandruff, &c. ; also for Restoring Grey Hair to its Natural Col

Why neglect your Children's Hair ?   Edward's "Harlene" Preserves, Strengthens, and Invigorates it !   Prevents and Cures all Species of Scurf. Keeps the Scalp Clean and allays all Irritation.

*Victorian and Edwardian enthusiasm for long hair created markets
to restore and grow abundant hair*

Advertisement in The Sketch, *April 1896, from author's own collection*

2

'SHALL I HAVE IT BOBBED OR SHINGLED?'

Monday she goes to be shingled and shaved,
Tuesday she goes to be hennaed and waved,
Wednesday she's massaged because she's so stout,
Thursday she has all her wrinkles ironed out,
Friday she goes to have a nice mud bath,
Saturday she goes out in the rain;
And all day Sunday she's longing for Monday
To be beautified all over again. (1925)[1]

Before the Great War – and indeed for centuries before that – women wore their hair long. While it may occasionally have been trimmed or the ends singed, usually it was allowed to grow, and grow, and grow some more. Mothers boasted when their daughters had hair long enough to sit on; the popular press featured pictures of women with astonishingly long and abundant tresses. A famous set of American sisters made their fortunes travelling to display their extraordinarily long hair and promote their Seven Sutherland Sisters Hair Grower; and one enterprising woman, Madame Walker, reputedly became the first Afro-American female millionaire, largely on the strength of her patented hair growth products.[2] Since hair was, according to longstanding conventional wisdom, a woman's 'crowning glory', the more of it the better. Hair cut short in the Victorian and Edwardian periods was mostly restricted to the inmates of prisons, workhouses, and hospitals for the insane and incurable.

Of course, long hair could be presented in different ways. In the early decades of Victoria's reign, hairstyles were fairly simple, often parted in the middle and drawn back into a simple bun or twist, a mode of hairdressing necessitated by the virtually universally worn poke-bonnet that concealed most of a woman's hair. Sometimes decorative curls or ringlets might be seen at the sides. Young girls wore their hair loose, sometimes restrained by a ribbon, braided or plaited, or (this was more labour-intensive) curled in rags or wound as ringlets, probably for special occasions. As these girls became women, they began to wear their hair up. Margaret Cunningham, born in 1900, described her hairdressing evolution when she was at boarding school in her mid teens:

> *I was growing up; my pigtail was turned up and fixed at the nape of the neck with a large bow. We called this style a doorknocker. In the evening for high tea Miss Boyce liked us older girls to practice doing up our hair. Mine was very fine and unmanageable. In the oratory, the elder girls sat at the back and behind them the maids. One evening the row of servants almost strangled themselves with laughter, even the stern black-browed Kilby, the parlour maid. I had rolled a pair of gloves in my bun to give it bulk and one of the fingers was pointing straight out at them.[3]*

Annabel Huth Jackson aged 20, about 1890

Picture from A Victorian Childhood *by Annabel Huth Jackson (née Grant Duff) published by Methuen 1932*

Ample hair, as the young Margaret Cunningham and most women acknowledged, was a sign of health and vitality. To help achieve it mothers admonished their daughters to brush their hair one hundred strokes daily from the scalp to the ends – and most mothers followed this advice themselves. This practice was meant to encourage hair growth and keep the rarely washed tresses free of dust. Young girls probably tried to follow their elders' example, perhaps in the hope of looking like the beautiful, long-haired princesses in fairy tales; maybe they could grow their hair long enough and strong enough – Rapunzel-like – to support the courting of a prince ('Rapunzel, Rapunzel, let down your hair'). Around 1950 my own grandmother warmly commended the virtues of hair-brushing. As a girl with a boyish bob and a disposition to

A glamorous photo from Viola Bawtree's unpublished childhood newsletter 'Skylark', Autumn 1914
Picture courtesy of Local Studies and Archives Centre, London Borough of Sutton

read books rather than dress like a prospective princess, I gave that bit of grandmotherly advice a pass. She always wore her own long hair in a tidy, severe bun. How often she brushed it was, to me, never disclosed. (I was only six when she died and never had the nerve to ask this formidable lady such an impertinent question.)

An abundance, if not a super-abundance, of hair was highly valued in later Victorian and Edwardian times. On most women's dressing tables sat a hair receiver, a small glass, silver, or ceramic vessel into which her daily hair brushings would be put, or an embroidered 'hair tidy', a small bag for the same

Hair receiver
From author's own collection

Long-haired mother and daughter, early 1880s

Picture from A Victorian Childhood *by Annabel Huth Jackson, published by Methuen 1932*

purpose. This saved hair was sometimes kept for years until it could be made into a switch or other hairpiece. Formal and evening hairdressing was elaborate, and even simple daytime dressing often required large coils for plaits, buns, or chignons. During the Edwardian period hats almost as big as cartwheels necessitated a considerable bulk of hair beneath them just to keep their wearers from being completely engulfed by their headgear. Since what nature supplied was often inadequate, artifice was called into play. Responding to the demands of fashion, Parton and Sons' 1912 catalogue, *Guide to the Requirements of the Hairdressing Trade*, devoted more than a dozen pages to women's false hair products alone.[4] An early twentieth-century fashion commentator summed it up this way:

> *Hairdressing is an art which is all important at the present. The early Victorian woman could perhaps dress her head with her own locks and be in the mode. Not so the Edwardian fashionable person. For her it is better to give up the struggle to be natural and fall back on the hairdressers' art... The innumerable little curls that are now the fashion can hardly be achieved satisfactorily with locks... If you abhor false hair you must do the best you can, but you will hardly be able to appear quite fashionable save in the rare case of possessing the combination of an exceptional quantity of natural locks and the services of a very clever maid.[5]*

Children, when allowed into mother's boudoir, were sometimes astute observers. The visually perceptive society photographer Cecil Beaton recounted his mother's struggles with the elaborate Edwardian hairstyle: 'Since she had no personal maid, my mother was usually obliged to dress her own hair. It was worn wide at the sides, stuffed out with pads and garnished with amber, tortoise-shell, or imitation diamond combs. On black Mondays, after a long solitary session with her arms upraised, pulling the waves and curls into place, the effect might still not please her. Then

THE PRACTICAL STYLE.

A fairly simple style from 1912 that would have benefited from professional styling and (usually) hairpieces

© *The British Library Board,* Hairdressing, *December 1912/751*

she would take out the rats [pads, usually made from human or horse hair, intended to add volume to the hairdressing], glancing with alarm into the looking glass as the whole business started again. The face became flushed, her arms would be aching, and by the time she was finished she was more than late for dinner.'[6] Violet Hardy, who was a child when adult women's enormous hats were 'perched on a pyramid of hair', observed what happened when the edifice was undone. 'My sister and I were amazed to see how much false hair and pads were shed at "brushing time". Mama adopted a mass of curled fringe, which was called a "front", made fashionable by Queen Alexandria. In most cases it was disfiguring and very unhygienic, and as make-up was scarcely worn, it created a hardness to the face and a top-heaviness which was most unbecoming.'[7] Even if the result of so much effort was, for some viewers, lovely to behold, it was certainly not appealing to touch. In 1877 the writer Octave Uzanne complained of long, curled, upswept hairdressings which were backcombed (a technique that predated the 1960s

25/855.—Pearl Quakeress Cap.

The "DAINTIE"
- Series -

IS A GUARANTEE OF STYLE
AND EXCLUSIVE DESIGNS.

For Prices, see page 646 of Journal.

Manufactured in England by . .
PARKER & SMITH,
4/5, Bridgewater Square, London, E.C.

25/854.—Pearl Boudoir or
Matinee Cap.

25/332.—A Pretty Bandeau, in Gold and
Silver, with Hand-made Rose
Cluster Side Ornament.

25/1105.—Boudoir Cap, Gold or Silver
Tinsel, with Beaded Band.

Pretty caps to cover elaborate hairstyles at home
© *The British Library Board,* Hairdressers' Journal, *December 1911/370*

by generations), blended with false hair, supported by various frames and rolls, and rarely washed. 'Mixed with shams of every sort, burnt by acid, dried up by ammonia; this dead hair, which fell in curls or frisettes under the cap, was not indeed the most agreeable thing.'[8]

Elaborate hairstyles, huge hats, and hobble skirts sharply limited a woman's physical autonomy in the early twentieth century. Laws and conventions hemmed in the political and social freedom of women, yet many of these women were better educated than their mothers and grandmothers. Many were also attracted to the active lifestyle being offered or soon to be offered by bicycles, cars, aeroplanes, dance halls, and new employment opportunities. The stage was set for change.

Cascades of hair fell to salon floors in the 1920s and early 1930s – and in some places even earlier – as women adopted short, simple haircuts. It was a dramatic change. The 'bob', in which the hair fell straight to the neck and then curled under at the ends, and the even shorter shingle, in styles with androgynous names such as the Garcon, the Eton crop, and even the Gigolo and the Coconut, swept not only through Britain but across other Western countries, particularly the United States and France. Many women of all ages and social classes abandoned long, fussily styled hair. For some of them it would be the first time their hair had ever been cut. It was a social and sartorial revolution – a revolution that, like so many, was led by the young. Short hairstyles first appeared on both sides of the Atlantic during the Great War and within a decade became the norm for fashionable young women. Short hair was easier for active women to manage, whether working in a military hospital, behind the wheel of an ambulance, doing farm work, playing tennis, driving in open cars, or dancing new fast-paced dances. The trainer of a girls' football team in the early 1920s reported that practically all those who took up football at all seriously eventually bobbed their hair. Hairpins, it had quickly been discovered, were an impediment – and hazardous – to heading the ball.[9]

Ada Fishlock of Hampshire in the 1920s. Right through to her 90s, Ada never missed her weekly appointment with her hairdresser

For many younger women, short hair was a gain in comfort and freedom. In 1925 the American actress, Julia Hoyt, commented that 'it certainly looks as if "woman's crowning glory" is soon going to be a relic of the past…Well, speaking for myself, I had an enormous amount of "woman's crowning glory", and, as far as I can now tell, I'll spend the rest of my life with the small amount of my crown that is with me now.' She went on to recall the day four years earlier when she had her first short haircut: 'It was a very hot day,' she said. 'My hat, as usual, was cutting my forehead in two, owing to the large knot at the back of my head, and my head was dripping from the heat. I walked into a hairdresser's establishment and said: "Cut off my hair". I must say the first snip of the scissors gave me a shock [but]… as my head began to feel cooler and lighter, I derived an enormous amount of pleasure from seeing the long pieces of hair fall to the floor.'[10] The freedom, ease, coolness and comfort of the bob was endorsed in *Good Housekeeping* the next year by Nora Mullane, who added that 'hats are easy to buy, headaches from hairpins and heavy coils disappear, and hairdressing takes less time'.[11] The bob was soon wildly popular on both sides of the Atlantic. 'All the young women at the office were having their hair shorn', one young flapper recalled. 'My mother and I went to the hairdressers on Wardour Street, where we sat at the end of a long queue of women who, like us, were patiently waiting to let down their beautiful long hair. An hour later with hats too big for our diminished heads, feeling very self-conscious and anxious to be home where we could make a minute, pitiless examination of our changed appearance, we emerged as new women.'[12]

✄ ✄ ✄ ✄

Where did the bob come from? In the early twentieth century short haircuts for children of both sexes, with thick straight fringes and one length cut straight round at about ear level, often called the Buster Brown or Dutch Cut, were appearing in Britain and America. Later the bob for adult women was a practical response to the conditions of wartime factory work and is sometimes thought to derive from the easy-to-care-for styles adopted by wartime nurses. It was also an imitative response to Parisian high fashion; a flouting of the conventions of a society that had created the horrors of the Western front; an endorsement of the styles of the Jazz Age; and a testimony to the influence of the silver screen. The notoriety attached to the bob led many to claim authorship. The name 'bob' itself likely goes back to the eighteenth century when wigs were widely worn and merchants and other men of relatively modest means often wore a shorter and

Two stylish inter-war bobs
Picture courtesy Pat Reid

relatively cheaper bobbed wig with the ends curled under. (The epithet 'bigwig' derives from the wealthy man who could afford the more elaborate full-bottomed wig.) 'Bobbing' was also the word used to describe a short dressing of a horse's tail.

Olivia Cockett, aged 19 sports a fashionable short bob in 1931

Picture courtesy Hilary Munday

Josephine Baker, the sensual American exotic performer, was almost as well known for her greased-down bob as she was for her 1925 Paris debut performance wearing little other than a strategically placed bunch of bananas. Antoine, the celebrity hairdresser, was reputedly responsible for her sleek, brilliantined head. And according to one envious hairdresser interviewed in the 1970s, so big was the bob phenomenon that Antoine sold his business for '$17,000,000, and he just lies around the Waldorf in a big suite of rooms'.[15]

(By that time he had added celebrities from Coco Chanel and Claudette Colbert to Simone Signoret and even the 'sex kitten' Brigitte Bardot to his client list.) The dancers Irene Castle in New York and Isadora Duncan in Paris adopted short hairstyles to go with their shortened skirts. In artistic and theatrical circles cropped hair was labelled the 'Castle Bob' after Irene, and when the dancer wore a seed pearl necklace around her forehead, another iconic 1920s style was born and nicknamed either the 'Castle Band' or the headache band. Of Iris Storm and her shingled hair, the novelist Michael Arlen wrote in *The Green Hat* (1924): 'Her hair was thick and tawny ... It was like a boy's hair, swept back from her forehead ... Above her neck her hair died a very manly death, a more manly death than "bobbed" hair was ever to die.'[16]

The bob was widely taken as a sign of the independence that women had won through their vital work on the home front during the Great War, and as testimony to the cynicism about the bankrupt values that had taken so many young men to the killing fields of Europe. Bobbed hair was also associated in Britain with gaining the vote (though voting restrictions continued until 1928 and prominent suffragettes were better known for their hunger strikes than their haircuts) and the growing economic clout of young women. At its most basic the bob was a blunt cut, level with the bottom of the ears, and worn either with a fringe or with the hair brushed off the face. It was straightforward and readily cared for, and could liberate affluent women from the costly, time-consuming ministrations of hairdressers and ladies' maids. 'Bobbing was exhilarating and rejuvenating; it made the face more alive and alert, well in keeping with the modern spirit in woman', declared a male artist in 1925. He thought the bob 'a masterful stroke, complete and final, in the march of woman's emancipation'.[17] Amelia Earhart, the pioneering aviator, wore her blonde hair in a short, fuss-free bob. The bob fitted in smoothly with the active, healthy-body culture of avant garde modernism. The modernist youth of the 1920s were self-consciously different from previous generations. They flaunted an athletic style with slimmer, fitter and tanned bodies. Sleek, short haircuts and, at times, body-revealing clothing became the outward signs of modernity.

The bob also reflected the growing impact of films and the new film magazines that spread news of fashion across the globe. When famous film stars such as Mary Pickford, after much personal angst, bobbed their hair, legions of young women took note. During one frenzied week in 1924, it was reported that no less than 3,500 women had their hair bobbed in one New York salon, where stylists kept smelling salts close to hand to revive clients who grew faint as they saw their tresses fall.[18] After the war an expanded consumer society created new jobs for office workers and shop girls; more flexible views about employment for single women drew many thousands into the workforce; and, most significantly, a dramatic decline in the number of possible husbands kept them

Bobbed, permed and waved – a 1930s classic

kept them there. Legions of single women, most with slender means, dreary lives, and scant prospects for a brighter future were drawn to the distractions of the new cinemas which sprang up across Britain in the 1920s and 1930s. Beyond simple amusement, motion pictures spread new styles, of which the bob was one of the most accessible, to a mass audience on both sides of the Atlantic, and well down the English social scale. Joyce Storey, writing of her working-class childhood near Bristol in the later 1920s and early 1930s, recalled that 'everyone who could afford it went to the pictures every week ... As schoolgirls, we copied hairstyles and tried to emulate them. The false became the real.'[19] Meanwhile women in the labour force found the bob to be very practical as well as fashionable: many lived in cold-water flats or rooming houses and lacked the time and facilities for elaborate hairdressing, and the bob, especially when nicely waved, could project a sleek image of professionalism and efficiency.

Bobbed hair became very, very popular. By 1925 it was estimated that fifty-three percent of the female students at Mount Holyoke College in the United States had bobbed hair.[20] On the other side the Atlantic, short hair became similarly popular. The bob suited most women; it could be adapted for wear by children, the middle-aged, and even the elderly (some of whom may have welcomed it particularly warmly after a lifetime of the wearisome brushing, tugging, untangling, plaiting, and pinning that long hair involved); and it lent the wearer an air of modernity. One prominent hairdresser thought that English women 'took more quickly to the short bob (shingle) than those of any other nation'.[21]

In the first two decades of the twentieth century short hair was worn only by a tiny minority of fashion leaders, eccentrics, and theatrical women; after the war it spread rapidly across social classes and geography. And it has proven extraordinarily durable in the usually fickle world of fashion – as demonstrated by the numerous heads on which it is still worn in the second decade of the twenty-first century. James Stewart, both a hairdresser and a Member of Parliament from Glasgow in the 1920s, told the *Evening News* of London that in 1927 in Britain 'women spend approximately £20,000,000 a year on bobbing, shingling, Eton crops and other methods of hair treatment. This works out at about 30s. a year for every adult woman in the country!' While prices could run to several guineas in Mayfair, he noted that in his own part of the country shingling was 'as low as 1s 6d' and he had 'heard of cases in mining districts where it is as cheap as 1s'.[22] The fact that short hair had reached mining villages and become a priority in tight budgets was a measure of its appeal. A Cheltenham hairdresser, when speaking at his Rotary club in 1928, offered the extreme claim that short hair had been more important than the Great War.

By the 1920s American polls found that girls were going to cinemas almost weekly and others revealed that, in contrast to the early years of the century, young people more often named movie stars as their role models than contemporary political, business, or artistic leaders.[23] In England, too, film actresses inspired young women to cut their hair, but in a society in which the elite presented themselves as fashion leaders there might be a price to be paid by a plebeian girl who enthusiastically endorsed the modern look. One young girl with stylishly bobbed locks who applied for work as a domestic servant in Lord Litchfield's home in Shugborough was curtly informed that she must grow it again. One member of the family had just had her hair similarly cut and as a servant she should have known better (as she later reflected) than to imitate her superiors.[24]

In Paducah, Kentucky, five nurses in training were suspended for cutting their hair and elsewhere conservative employers in business offices fulminated against the carefully waved, bobbed head that would, a decade later, become virtually synonymous with the efficient, well-groomed professional secretary.[25] Another young woman, Kathleen Hale, author of the *Orlando* children's books, recalled that she narrowly missed being expelled from Reading University when she cut her hair short.[26] Her offence seems to have been less that she emulated her betters than that her action was unladylike since she planned to sell her hair to defray some of her student expenses. In an earlier century, the heroine of Louisa May Alcott's *Little Women* (1886) cut her hair to sell it to benefit her family.[27] The famous Christmastime short story by O Henry, 'The Gift of the Magi', recounts the sale by a newly wed woman of her glorious hair so she could buy a watch-fob for her husband. As readers of this story will recall, her husband had sold his watch to buy combs for the long hair he had so admired.

✂ ✂ ✂ ✂

Early adopters of the new short cut, especially in conservative circles, often found that acquiring a hairstyle that was associated with rebelliousness (or at least nonconformity) could be stressful. A short story by F Scott Fitzgerald, originally published in *Saturday Evening Post* on 1 May 1920, was devoted to this theme. In 'Bernice Bobs Her Hair', a pretty but socially insecure young woman is browbeaten into bobbing her hair at the local barbershop before a gaping and mocking audience of her peers. Her declaration that she intended to bob her hair gained the naïve girl some social cachet, but the consequences of carrying out her brave intention is more than she bargained for: 'Twenty minutes later the barber swung her round to face the mirror, and she flinched at the full extent of the damage that had been wrought. Her hair was not curly, and now it lay in lank lifeless blocks on both sides of her suddenly pale face. It was ugly as sin – she had known it would

Wisbech competitors in a beauty competition
wearing iconic 1920s cloche hats

The same group photographed without hats to highlight their bobbed and
permed hair
Both pictures courtesy Lilian Ream Exhibition Gallery Trust, Wisbech

be ugly as sin. Her face's chief charm had been a Madonna-like simplicity. Now that was gone and she was – well, frightfully mediocre – not stagy, only ridiculous.'[28] Bernice finally enjoys an ambiguous triumph when she takes revenge on the cousin who started it all – by cutting off her rival's blonde braids as she sleeps, and then tossing them onto the porch of a faithless boyfriend.

Opinion was divided on the merits of short hair for women. Monica Dickens' heroine in *Mariana* says to her mother, 'But, Mummy, I *must*, I simply *must* cut my hair. I've tried putting it up, but it simply won't stay.' She then decides to take the plunge and finds that 'as the great chunks fell to the floor from the skilful scissors of Mr Pee-aire, whose accent was more Cockney than continental, the pale face that stared back at Mary from the mirror became more and more scared. She looked naked, she looked almost bald. "Haven't you cut it rather short?" she asked timidly, fingering the bare, bristly nape of her neck with horror. "Oh no, it's a lovely bob," said Mr Pee-aire.'[29] In the 1920s a literary reference to bobbed hair was one way of signifying a woman's character. In her 1923 novel *None-Go-By*, Cecily Sidgwick has one of her characters describe a bohemian friend of his niece as 'squat in figure, and obstinately set on wearing what the plain and squat should not wear; screaming colours and jazz cubes and stripes. Her hair was bobbed, she was neither clean nor godly.'[30] Sidgwick portrayed a fashionable young woman in another novel: 'It was Sylvia who smoked, bobbed her hair and wore an orange-coloured jumper over a skirt that almost showed her knees.' Then followed the comment, 'There was no reticence in girls now in appearance or behaviour. No wonder they did not marry.'[31] Perhaps the reader is meant to assume that she swilled gin and danced the Charleston as well.

While the bob was essentially a classless style for everywoman, it became in Britain very much a marker of high society, favoured by the sophisticates of the kind of world portrayed by Noel Coward. It was a hairstyle synonymous with the flapper, a glamorous young woman freed from corsets, convention, long skirts and elaborate hairdos who danced the night away with a carefree toss of her newly freed locks. In the 1920s the pages of *Queen*, a weekly paper catering to Society, were full of advertisements from hairdressers highlighting their skills at bobbing and shingling as well their aptitude for using hairpieces and jewellery to embellish these simple hairstyles for evening events, to suit the 'bright young things' of Mayfair. Wigmakers also quickly adopted bobbed styles – and raised their prices. Their products could provide the wealthy woman with the latest modern look along with an attractive accent of waves, and without much effort. They could effect a transformation in a woman's appearance. In fact, wigs were usually called 'transformations' in the trade. Maison Nicol of New Bond Street, Posticheurs d'Art and Hair Specialists, carried a large advertisement in *Queen* in January 1923 advising readers that 'when your own hair is thin and straight, and difficult to dress, a Transformation of natural wavy hair would prove and a great boon and "friend" to you'.[32] These transformations could cost fifteen guineas for a full wig and seven for a smaller version that covered part of the head and blended with a woman's natural hair (though wholesale merchants of human hair offered shingled and bobbed wigs to the trade at prices from 45 shillings).[33] The well-coiffed woman was expected to own at least two transformations; she had no need to depend entirely on her own growth of hair. Artificial hair products, however, were well beyond the means of many ordinary working women; in the 1930s a young secretary might earn 30 shillings a week and a senior school teacher up to £5 weekly.

Hairdressers to the elite saw their business thrive. The need for frequent hair trims, the sale of curled postiches for more formal wear, the already very profitable Marcel waving process, using specially designed curved curling irons, and the recently invented permanent wave, all made hairdressers smile. Skilled barbers, many soon to re-label themselves hairdressers, also benefitted from the haircutting boom. Monsieur Eugene, inventor of a permanent wave system, observed in 1925 – not without a little self-interest – that 'the short-haired vogue is assured for at least one generation, for all school girls have their hair cut now, and it is scarcely likely when they reach eighteen or so, that they will burden themselves with long hair... Most likely "milady" of former days now plays a vigorous game of golf all afternoon, arrives home at 6, and has to be ready for dinner at 7.' For his sophisticated clientele he added that a permanent wave was what made a shingled hairdo successful. 'In unskilled hands there is something horribly masculine about the shingled head, but when the correct line is obtained, and the natural contours of the head are emphasized by a soft wave, the effect is adorably feminine.'[34]

✄ ✄ ✄ ✄

Hairstyles were widely discussed in the 1920s, and not just in publications targeted at women. The London *Evening Standard*, with a keen appreciation of a topical and somewhat controversial issue, conducted a survey on women's hair fashions in the spring of 1928 and even sought the views of the nation's political leaders. 'The result of the poll has been that the House of Lords gave a three to one majority in favour of long hair, and there was a similar majority, though much smaller, in the House of Commons', the trade journal *Hairdressing* reported. The Earl of Lonsdale responded to the survey forthrightly: 'Personally, I think bobbed hair is awful. Some of the longer and curled types I quite understand and they are very pretty. But the "Eton crop" is disgusting.' Lord Riddell, more thoughtfully, declared long hair to be 'a relic of barbarism, when, metaphorically, men used to drag their wives about by their hair'. 'Short hair must be a boon to those girls and women who are bound to lead a working life', thought Viscount Dunedin. 'But to those who are not so compelled, the sacrifice of luxuriant hair is the sacrifice of a great asset.' A weary Earl of Birkenhead observed that he knew nothing about women's hair – 'I am much too old'. An apparently practical Earl of Essex applauded short hair since it was 'a great aid to punctuality at breakfast'.[35]

Women themselves, when interviewed, more often than not endorsed the bob, the shingle, or the Eton crop. 'For comfort I prefer the shingle', said Lady Bland-Sutton, while a sportswoman declared that shingling had saved the sporting woman's appearance, and a third woman said of her short hair that she could not 'ever imagine myself changing it'. Miss Ursula Jeans vowed that sensible women would never return to long hair and a 75-year-old grandmother announced she was going to have her hair shingled the following week.[36]

That women had strong views about their hair is, perhaps, not surprising. What is remarkable is that the debate over short haircuts occupied no less that seven features and several letters to the editor over a three-week period in a major London newspaper.[37] Of course, some women must have realised that, fashion or no fashion, short hair did not suit them. Margaret Powell, a free-spirited and feisty young woman from Hove who was working as a domestic servant in London in the 1920s, later recalled her own reservations. 'I couldn't help thinking how pretty and sophisticated the London girls looked in comparison to those from my home town. Some of them had got Eton crops which were coming into fashion at that time. My sister used to have an Eton crop but you've got to have the right face for it. With my kind of features if I'd had an Eton crop I'd have just looked like a hard-boiled egg with a top knot.'[38] The short story writer, Alice Munro (born 1932), examining family photographs, has written that 'bobbed hair did not suit my mother's full, soft face'.[39]

Skittish aristocratic Englishwomen could rejoice in the fact that the King, in public at least, had little to say about bobbed or shingled hair, while his wife, the elegant, statuesque Queen Mary, who retained her abundant Edwardian hairstyle all her days, merely asked that ladies with short hair conceal this fact when at court or official functions. Hairdressers were only too keen to oblige, creating a range of small curled hairpieces that could be added to bobs to create an elegant look. In fact, touches like these were the bob's saving grace. They helped hairdressers to show their aristocratic clients that a simple barber's shears were not enough. It was not difficult to move from selling little hairpieces to selling expensive hair jewellery. And somewhere along the way most of them learned to cut hair well, not just comb and dress it. They invented more sophisticated cuts and tried their best to popularise hair embellishments. Still, some parents complained that from the back it was hard to tell their sons from their daughters: 'Since the advent of this shingle bob, I have to look twice at my own offspring to tell which is which.'[40] (When long hair was worn by both sexes in the late 1960s, the same complaint was sometimes heard.)

Shorn hair was frequently decried (usually by men) as immoral, too masculine, and an encouragement to vices such as smoking and cocktail drinking. Some educational institutions passed twentieth-century sumptuary rules forbidding bobbed hair, makeup, and cigarettes. In Chicago the famous Marshall Field Department Store announced in 1921 that 'girl employees who bobbed their hair would have to seek other employment' and followed this edict with further proscriptions of 'extremely short skirts' and 'stockings rolled below the knees'.[41] Some religious leaders argued that the Bible said that a woman should not cut her hair: 'if a woman have long hair, it is a glory to her: for her hair is given her for a covering' (*First Corinthians,* ch.11, v.15). In the 1920s a tract circulated in England entitled *Bobbed Hair: Is it well-pleasing to the Lord?* In it the author conceded that many people 'cater for the world's amusements and fashions ... in order to provide something fresh', but wondered 'why should Christian women fall victim to all this?' He claimed that 'a "bobbed" woman is a disgraced woman! Surely a very serious consideration for all who fear God!' If the verses of *Corinthians* were not enough to restrain women from cutting their hair, he reminded them of the woman who dried the feet of Jesus with her hair. 'Where would our present-day defaced sisters have been in such a scene? What services could they have rendered the Lord in their unnatural condition? ... The refusal to utter the word "obey" in the Marriage Service, the wearing of men's apparel when cycling, the smoking of cigarettes, and the "bobbing" of the hair, are all indicative of one thing! God's order is everywhere flouted ... but the hour of Divine intervention in judgment approaches fast.'[42]

It was important, some said, not to blur boundaries. John R Rice, in his *Bobbed Hair, Bossy Wives and Women Preachers*, reinforced the view that 'the Bible expressly teaches that a women should have long hair',[43] noting that even if truly devout Christian women declined to use lipstick, rouge, and paint on their fingernails, the Bible did not specifically prohibit them. But, he said, it was clearly 'a sin for a woman to appear like a man' by cutting her hair; worse still, a bobbed woman might tempt the holy angels. 'How are angels concerned about a woman's hair?' he asked rhetorically. 'I think that not only would angels be grieved by this mark of rebellion against husband or father and against God, but angels would be tempted, likewise to rebel.' For, he argued, 'the sin of angels is the sin of rebellion'.[44] Such patriarchal rigidity was common.

Others spoke of the physical hazards of short hair. Karl Nestler, later Charles Nestlé, coiffeur and inventor of the permanent wave machine, warned women that if they kept cutting their hair they would weaken their scalp muscles and eventually begin to go bald like men. Some people argued that short hair caused headaches – even 'shingle headaches' – allegedly the result of too short hair.[45] This is a somewhat strange view, and others (more plausibly) blamed heavy Edwardian hairstyles and the huge accompanying hats for similar uncomfortable results. 'Some medical men argued in print that bobbing would result "in the ultimate baldness of the species," while others held that it would increase the growth of hair.'[46] The real concern may have been that bobbing hair in barbershops was seen as an insult to a remaining bastion of male supremacy as well as a commercial threat to traditional hairdressers.

Rants against short hair did no good. Fashion triumphed – as it usually does. In fact, the cutting of one's hair into a stylish bob or shingle soon became a rite of passage from childhood to adulthood with much the same meaning as when a girl of an earlier generation first put her hair up or her brother donned long pants. Hairstyles were now part of an enlarging consumer culture, fuelled by advertising and mass media, and funded by expanding discretionary income. A bold, flashy hairstyle was a perfect fit in a culture that increasingly valued youthfulness over maturity. Soon hairdressing manuals were describing how best to bob the hair of older women to permit them to look as fashionable as their daughters. Wigs in bobbed styles were also available for those who did not want to commit themselves.

The hairdressing profession, largely serving a wealthy clientele, initially regarded the bob with alarm. Straight, short hair was seen at first with displeasure, for these professionals had made their livelihood by creating and arranging complex styles that no woman could care for at home and by selling the costly hairpieces and jewelled baubles that went with them. Any simple or straight cut was seen as a threat to business, as were hair-concealing hats such as the 'disastrous' turban look that suppressed the Marcel wave that had kept hairdressers happy and solvent for thirty years up to the 1920s. The wildly fashionable cloche, which covered almost all of the hair, was similarly feared. There was, as well, the alarming expectation that bobbed hair would not soon disappear, whatever new fashions might in time emerge.

Hairdressers, however, were not stupid – and they adapted. They learned or relearned how to cut hair. Regular haircuts, happily, became a necessity for their customers. Hairdressers upgraded their establishments with electricity and hot and cold running water. And they made technology work for them – adopting electric curling irons and permanent wave machines, and employing new, safer vegetable-based hair dyes such as henna. A permanent wave was favoured by both short-haired and long-haired women, and permanent waves were profitable for the profession and much easier to perform on relatively short hair. It would be decades before products were available that allowed women to do their 'perms' at home. A hairdresser had to cut 'nearly thirty shingles to get the same revenue' as he could on one permanent wave, even when price cutting was taking place, according to an industry expert in 1928.[47]

Hairdressers also innovated by creating postiches that could be used to embellish a short hairdo with curls and what *Vogue* in 1924 called a 'dignité de circonstance' for the evening.[48] A 1927 editorial in *Hairdressing* commented that 'short hair is good but must not be too short for fear the electric hair-clipper (barber) may take the place of the artiste-coiffeur', but it concluded that 'short hair has brought prosperity to the great mass of ladies' hairdressers and observed that the graduates of the hairdressing section of the London County Council Trade School had no difficulty finding work.[49] Without doubt, haircutting was seen as profitable.

> *If you like we can cut a crop*
> *Just take a big hair-dresser's shop*
> *You'll find a fortune can be got*
> *By – shingling, shingling, shingling!*[50]

In fact, the craze for short hair, combined with an increasingly robust consumer culture, and given more widely available hot water and electricity, greatly expanded the industry by creating a market for reasonably priced haircuts among women who had never before visited a hairdresser.

Short hair figured prominently during the 1920s in popular culture. The Music Department in the British Library holds some 25 song sheets dating from between 1921 and 1928 whose lyrics feature women with bobbed hair. Several of these songs originated in America and crossed the Atlantic in some form; others were composed in Britain and performed there, often in the still-vibrant music halls. The titles include *Bobbed Haired Betty*, *Shingled Susie*, *My Wife has had her Hair Cut*, *The Bobbed Haired Family*, *Bobbed and Shingled or Nicely Bingled*, *Bobbie "Bobs" and "Shingles"*, *Oh Clare Why did you Bob your Hair?*, *I Don't Want a Girl with a Shingle*, and *Monday She Goes to be Shingled*.[51] 'Baby get your hair cut, hair cut' was the refrain of a popular song from 1921 that connected short hair with fast living – jazz, frenetic dancing, short skirts.[52] The songs of this decade conveyed the wide range of sentiments associated with a woman cutting her hair. One girl's boyfriend 'gave me the dump ... the trouble all came of me bobbing my hair'. 'Nobody loves me now', she lamented, though hardly seriously: 'But don't forget/ I'll get his goat yet/ I'll wear it in a net'.[53] The refrain of another song was alert to a young woman's struggle to find a husband (and after the Great War there were many more young single women than young single men):

So, single or even bingle,

Be sure to get a crop,

Then no longer you'll be single,

If this fashion you adopt.[54]

Young women with cropped hair were sometimes viewed with patronising affection:

Now I want to introduce you

My dear l'il bobbed hair girl

Well, she's a cute, a saucy l'il puss,

Sends your head in a whirl.[55]

In other songs short-haired girls were portrayed as decidedly attractive to the opposite sex. 'The boys are all crazy today, to flirt with the girls with bobbed hair', according to one song, while another celebrated 'the shingled pet that I've recently met'.[56]

Other songwriters were not so gushy. There was, for one, the raw fact of social pressure on the insecure:

Sweet Susie Simpson had such lovely hair,

It reach'd down to her waist;

Till friends sweetly told her that around Mayfair

Having hair was thought bad taste.

'Bobb'd or shingl'd it must be, dear',

Said they, 'if you wish to be wed'...

The third and final verse of this song recalled one of the most famous growths of hair in English folk lore:

Lady Godiva on a snow-white mare
Once rode thro' Coventry,
And all she was wearing was her lovely hair
Oh, it reach'd down to her knee.
Peeping Tom at his window pane
Exclaimed when he saw the sight,
'Oh, your hair's all wrong, 'cause it's much too long!'
And Godiva replied, 'You're right!'[57]

Short hair gave rise to all sorts of social commentary and ridicule. A bob that might be considered acceptable for young women was thought much less suitable for the middle-aged, and several songs mocked the bob when worn on aging heads. *Sister Hasn't Got a Chance Since Mother Bobbed Her Hair* (1924) ridiculed trend-seeking middle-aged women.[58] 'Grandmas now', declared another song,

With their shingled crown
Are striving and craving
Their old age to drown.[59]

Since Mother Bobbed Her Hair had mother not just wearing her hair short, but colouring it, riding a motorbike, fast dancing, taking up golf, attracting the romantic affections of the curate – and 'She's altered all her views on dress/ Each night she's wearing less and less'.[60] If racy behaviour was sometimes linked to short hair, for others the cut hair itself was important. 'Save me the curls of the bobbed haired girls/ For I love what they toss away', pleaded the lyrics of a song composed on behalf of those with thin and faded locks.[61]

For half a dozen years short hair was the butt of many jokes in the hands of singers and entertainers. The word 'bobbed' readily conveyed a sense of flippancy and lack of seriousness. *Bobbed Hair* is the title given to a particularly frivolous piece of 1925 American fiction by 20 authors, each of whom took a turn in unveiling, chapter by chapter, the saga of the heroine's newly bobbed hair. Some social observers tried both to treat hair seriously and maintain a tone of levity. 'Does Shingling Destroy Beauty?' is the title of a 1925 essay in *Pearson's Magazine*, a monthly geared to women readers, and in it various illustrators offered their opinions on bobbed and shingled hair. The bob tended to be better regarded than the more radical shingle, which tapered hair mannishly to the neck in the back – one artist spoke of 'this wretched vogue of shingling' and another thought that it 'robs the average woman of her beauty'. Albert Bailey, who wrote a preface to this article, tried to present a balanced assessment – though still with tongue in cheek. 'If the hair is neatly bobbed and carefully waved, the present-day girl looks very slick and pretty; but looking around one gets the impression that a big majority of girls let their "bobs" go to seed, which is disastrous both for the girl and the hairdresser. A girl can remedy this by spending half her life and all her money at her hairdresser's salon.' As so often when a man talked about women's hair, he adopted a comedic pose. 'The most absurd mode of hairdressing is the Eton crop, which transforms a girl into a decadent, weak-looking youth masquerading in female attire. The girl who has just jilted me has, of course, an Eton crop.'[62]

Whatever were the reservations about ultra-short hair, the bob was becoming respectable and a part of mainstream fashion. Advertisers used fairly closely cropped models to symbolise modernity at its most desirable.[63] Some short stories, such as those by Dorothy L Sayers, were accompanied by illustrations of women with bobbed hair. In 1924 visitors to a Women's Institute's handicraft exhibition at Drapers' Hall could view a 'Noah's Ark, with a magnificent zoo, and Mr. Noah with a long white beard and Mrs. Noah with bobbed hair'.[64]

Hair styles, then, were widely observed and evaluated in the years after the Great War. They were another expression of the

The bob and perm were widespread by the early 1930s
Picture courtesy The Wisbech and Fenland Museum

rise of mass culture, and of an enlarging consumer economy in which more and more people found roles to play. The emerging beauty salons of the first forty years of the twentieth century offered a cost-effective way for women of modest means to be stylish, and they provided work for many small proprietors while leaving established high-end businesses to enjoy 'more trade than they had before the war'.[65] Beauty salons spread in cities and towns. Their numbers greatly increased in the 1920s and 1930s. Close to 1,500 ladies' hairdressers were listed in London's *Post Office Directory* for 1937 – and this number was almost certainly much smaller than the actual number of practising hairdressers. At this date there were around 160 ladies' hairdressers in Hertfordshire and some 360 in the three counties of Cambridgeshire, Norfolk and Suffolk; Hampshire had about 240 in 1935; and at the start of the Second World War slightly more than 1,000 ladies' hairdressers were doing business in Derbyshire, Leicestershire and Nottinghamshire.[66] All these numbers were undoubtedly underestimates since they would not have included the many hairdressers who worked only part-time or episodically.

At the end of Victoria's reign, commercial ladies' hairdressers had hardly existed; by the 1930s they were ubiquitous. Hairdressers served both a youth culture – something that would grow enormously in the twentieth century – and older women who wanted a perm (big business from the 1920s and 1930s) and could afford a modest 'pick-me-up' when they could not afford an entire new costume. Whether hair was short or long, styling it became an important new service industry in the early twentieth century. People were living longer, and hairdressers were, as they still are, eager to market to women age-denying products and services – age-enhancing for the young. How they went about this is the subject of the following chapter.

References

1   'Monday She Goes to be Shingled', Foxtrot song, words by R P Weston and Bert Lee, music by Harris Weston, 1925. See below, note no. 51.

2   The Sutherland hair tonic business reputedly earned $3 million over its 38-year history (Victoria Sherrow, ed., *Encyclopedia of Hair: A Cultural History* [Westport, Connecticut: Greenwood Press, 2006], p. 374).

3   Brunel University Library, Collection of Autobiographies, Margaret Cunningham, 'End of Exploring: An Autobiography', typescript (deposited 1979), pp. 179-80.

4   *Guide to the Requirements of the Hairdressing Trade* (London and Birmingham, 1912), 352ff.; held in the National Art Library, London.

5   Quoted in 'One Hundred Years of Hairdressing', *Hair and Beauty*, January 1966, 9-10.

6   Cecil Beaton, 'Take One Hundred Larks', in Mary Elizabeth Edes and Dudley Frazier, eds, *The Age of Extravagance: An Edwardian Reader* (New York, Rhinehart, 1954), p. 122.

7   Lady Violet Hardy, *As It Was* (London: Christopher Johnson, 1958),

p. 79, as quoted in Caroline Cox, *Good Hair days: A History of British Hairstyling* (London: Quartet Books, 1999), p. 20.

8 Quoted in Mary Trasko, *Daring Dos: A History of Extraordinary Hair* (Paris: Flamarion, 1994) p. 102.

9 'The Football Girl Arrives', *Pearson's Magazine*, February 1922, 121.

10 Quoted in Richard Corson, *Fashions in Hair: The First Five Thousand Years* (London: Peter Owen, 3rd edition, 1971), pp. 611-12.

11 Quoted in Corson, *Fashions in Hair*, p. 613.

12 Quoted in Trasko, *Daring Dos*, p. 112.

13 Antoine [Antek Cierplikowski], *Antoine by Antoine* (New York: Prentice Hall, 1945), pp. 47-8.

14. Ibid, pp. 92-3.

15 David Schroder, *Engagement in the Mirror: Hairdressers and their Work* (San Francisco, California: R&E Research Associates, 1978), p. 59.

16 Michael Arlen, *The Green Hat* (New York: G H Doran, 1924), p. 53, quoted in Modris Eksteins, *Rites of Spring: The Great War and the Birth of the Modern Age* (Toronto: Lester & Orpen Dennys, 1989), p. 259.

17 W H Barribal, *Pearson's Magazine*, December 1925, 522.

18 Diane Simon, *Hair: Public, Political, Extremely Personal* (New York: St Martin's Press, 2000), p. 27.

19 Joyce Storey, *The House in South Road: An Autobiography*, ed. Pat Thorne (London: Virago, 2004), p. 72.

20 Simon, *Hair*, p. 27.

21 *Antoine,* p. 93.

22 *Evening News*, 1 June 1927, 7.

23 Rose Weitz, *Rapunzel's Daughters* (New York: Farrer, Strauss & Giroux, 2004), p. 13.

24 Robin Bryer, *The History of Hair* (London: Philip Wilson Publishers, 2003), p. 117.

25 Antoine, *Antoine*, p. 95.

26 Bryer, p. 116.

27 Louisa May Alcott, *Little Women* (London: Children's Press, 1963; originally published 1886), p. 129.

28 F Scott Fitzgerald, *Novels and Stories 1920-1922* (New York: Library of America, 2000), p. 377.

29   Monica Dickens, *Mariana* (London: Penguin Books, 1940), pp. 116-17.

30   Cecily Sidgwick, *None-Go-By* (London: Collins, 1923), p. 88.

31   Cecily Sidgwick, *London Mixture* (London: Collins, 1924), p. 16.

32   *Queen*, January 18, 1923, following 92.

33   *Hairdressing*, November 1927, 16.

34   *Hairdressing*, December 1925, 210.

35   Quoted in *Hairdressing*, June 1928, 44.

36   *Evening Standard*, 8 May 1928, 3.

37   *Evening Standard*, 8 May, 13; 9 May, 18; 11 May, 18; 21 May, 16; 22 May, 16: 23 May 3; 31 May, 18, all 1928.

38   Margaret Powell, *Climbing the Stairs* (London: Peter Davies, 1969), p. 20.

39   Alice Munro, 'Personal History', *New Yorker*, 19 September 2011, 45.

40   www.hairarchives.com/private/1920s/ht

41   *The Times*, 15 August 1921, 8.

42   Corson, *Fashions in Hair*, p. 615.

43   John R Rice, *Bobbed Hair, Bossy Wives and Women Preachers* (Wheaton, Illinois: Sword of the Lord Publishers, 1941), p. 67.

44   Rice, *Bobbed Hair*, pp. 72-3.

45   Simon, *Hair*, p. 29.

46   Bill Severn, *The Long and the Short of it: Five thousand Years of Fun and Fury over Hair* (New York: David McKay, 1971), p. 122.

47   *Hairdressing*, July 1928, 61.

48   *Vogue,* July-December 1924, p. 52, as quoted in Steven Zdatny, ed., *Hairstyles and Fashion: A Hairdresser's History of Paris 1910-1920* (Oxford: Berg, 1999), p. 15.

49   *Hairdressing*, January 1927, 565.

50   'Shingling', by E M Robinson, c.1927.

51   All these songs in the British Library are catalogued under 'VOC', followed by the year of composition and the surname of the composer.

52   'Bobbed-Haired Babies Ball' (USA, 1921), words by John W Bratton, music by Percy Wenrich.

53   'The Girl with the Bobbed Hair' (USA, 1924), music by E S S

Huntington, words by Lauretta S Ross.

54 'Shingle' (1926), words by Bryn Jenkins, music by Keith Hampton.

55 'My Dear L'il Bobbed Hair Girl' (London, 1926), by H C Stewart.

56 'Mary's Bobbed Hair' (London, 1926), by Ernest Holdom; 'My shingled baby' (London, 1925), music by Noel Gay, words by Clifford Harris.

57 'Shall I have it Bobbed or Shingled?' (1924), written and composed by R P Weston and Bert Lee.

58 Lyrics by Nat Vincent and Blanche Franklyn, music by Harry Von Tilzer.

59 'Shingle' (1926), by Jenkins and Hampton.

60 'Since Mother Bobbed Her Hair' (c.1924), composed by Billie Hayes, written and sung by Charles Hayes.

61 'Save Me the Curls of the Bobbed Haired Girls' (USA, 1924), words by John Storm, music by Harry Jay.

62 'Does Shingling destroy Beauty?' *Pearson's Magazine*, December 1925, 521-27 and 489.

63 *Punch*, 23 April 1930, following xiv.

64 *The Times*, 23 October 1924, 12.

65 *Hairdressing,* June 1927, 33.

66 Various issues of the *Post Office Directory* and *Kelly's Directory*.

3

BEAUTY SALONS

'She tried her best to doll me up
as all hairdressers do.'[1]

I dry hair, I dye hair, I try hair that's new to 'em,
I stick it with glue to 'em, it fits 'em like a mop;
They may not come round again once I've done my stuff
But at the prices I charge 'em once is quite enough.[2]

In his 1933 essay 'From Lather Boy to Chain Shop Proprietor', Albert Langley talked about his successful career in hairdressing for the trade journal, *Hairdresser and Beauty Trade,* in its series 'Story of my Business'. Despite economic and political storm-clouds scudding across Britain, Langley had established several prosperous hairdressing establishments in Wales. One, in Bridgend, halfway between Swansea and Cardiff, 'in addition to having rather a fine and well-equipped ladies' hairdressing department', also had a separate department for such items as gowns and silk underwear, while his flagship store in Swansea featured a new arcade front with expansive window space and an interior renovated 'on ultra-modern lines' with handsome showcases housing high-class jewellery, powders, perfumes and lotions. In another location, Neath, he installed a special massage room, 'decorated in green and silver grey, with elaborate fittings of black opaline glass. Here all sorts of beauty treatments have their home – eyebrow arching, mud and yeast packs, and the latest bleaching masks.'[3]

Langley emphasised cleanliness as the dominant theme, claiming that his businesses resembled the modern American surgery. Hairdressers routinely stressed hygiene, partly to separate themselves from insanitary establishments that sometimes gave rise to lawsuits, partly to associate themselves with the medical profession. As early as 1913, a major trade journal, after noting a report from Colorado of hygienic problems alleged in 'rats' (that is, pads used to heighten a hairstyle) made of 'low grade Asian hair', quickly turned to consider the ways hairdressers could benefit economically from highlighting the issue. 'If you can't bully the fair sex,' it advised, 'scare them until they see smallpox lurking in every cheap piece of hairwork. And then reap your harvest in a larger demand for your goods, and a maximum of profit.'[4]

Since hairdressers provided an intimate service that involved touching their clients and having their trust, they were tempted to link themselves with other health-care professionals: large hairdressing establishments advertised their high standards of cleanliness as a means of attracting and retaining clients. One core business strategy was to encourage frequent washing of the hair (though not very often by today's standards) – something done rarely even by the elite before the early twentieth century – and, crucially, to suggest that only a professional could do this right. Since the best hairdressers had running water, electricity, and hair dryers well before most of their clients, it could be said that this advertising actually had the merit of being based on fact. As late as the 1930s many country houses lacked these amenities, sometimes quite explicitly valuing ponies over plumbing, as Diana Athill recounts in her memoir, *Yesterday Morning: A Very English Childhood.*[5]

In the days before detergent shampoos, whose development was stimulated by the lack of fat to make soap during the Second World War, rinsing hair clean of soap scum was no easy business. 'No hairdresser who wants to earn a living would advise women to wash their own hair at home', wrote a trade journalist in 1938 to an audience of his peers. Happily, he thought, it was a battle already won. 'I should think that the percentage of women who wash their hair at home is decidedly small.'[6] The growing numbers of women employed in offices and retail shops in urban areas were encouraged to view salon care of their hair as an indispensable part of their professional image. And many did. Of 48 female respondents to a 1939 Mass Observation Directive on personal appearance, 32 reported regular visits to their hairdresser. 'When I went into an office job', said one woman, 'I found it paid me to dress. This led me to increase my expenditure on clothes and hairdressing.' [7]

In order to expand their businesses, many hairdressers added quasi-medical functions to their offerings. These included facial massages, often aided by electrical wands, along with the usual range of face and hand creams, hair dyes, shampoos (many of these made in-house to the hairdressers' formulae), manicures, pedicures, hot towels, comb cleaning, and even rather arcane devices such as electric combs. 'Beauty Care Now Will Yield Dividends of Loveliness in Later Life', advised the 'Beauty Editress' of *Queen,* to encourage her readers to adopt the vibratory massages and lotions offered by a new very up-to-date salon in Mayfair.[8] Another new business in the early twentieth- century beauty salon was chiropody, and hairdressing journals at this time are full of advertisements for vicious-looking chiropody knives. Occasionally they include a rather incongruous photograph of a client in a hat and fur-collared coat, bare feet stretched towards the woman with the knives. Stove-heated and then electric curling irons had long been a routine part of the business, particularly since the growth of the Marcel waving system, which was enormously successful by the 1880s and had been then popularised by the celebrities of the day.

Many women had their hair 'Marcelled', that is, set in a series of undulating waves made possible by the specialized curling irons developed by Marcel Grateau (1852-1936). His technique produced a regularly waved hairdo that could last for up to two months or until the hair was again washed. Marcelled waves – and this was a drawback – required a woman to cover her head with a net or sleep-cap at night to preserve their beauty. Hairdressing trade periodicals

Crest designed to honour Marcel Grateau, incorporating his famous curling tongs and undulating waves

Picture courtesy
London School of Fashion

and women's magazines featured a wide variety of coiffure-preserving night-caps. The technique Marcel invented and the tools that made the graceful waves possible spread round the world and made its eponymous inventor, a former horse currier, hugely wealthy and an international celebrity. The Marcel laid the foundations of the twentieth-century hairdressing industry and turned thousands of struggling hairdressers into well-heeled professionals. When properly executed, Marcel waves produced graceful styles suited to most heads. The curling irons were affordable enough for virtually all full-time hairdressers to acquire them; waves could be created fairly quickly, particularly on short hair; and, critically, the Marcel was a method virtually impossible for a woman to execute for herself at home.[9] Good Marcel waving required skill in handling hair and for this reason the technique continued to be taught in hairdressing schools, to give students a feel for hair, long after it had been superseded by more modern methods.

Women used curling irons at home in the late nineteenth century and earlier, but graceful, undulating waves of hair curved fully around the head were a challenge that was usually beyond them. For more modest results at home, most department store catalogues offered women a range of crimping and curling irons; several versions were featured in Harrods 1895 catalogue and two years later the store advertised that 'a very neat little present would be a traveling curling lamp, fitted with tongs and mirror, for 2s 6½d; the 4s size including a box for matches'.[10] Well into the 1930s and 1940s non-electric curling irons were in fairly widespread use. The simplest could be heated on any open fire, their heat tested on a piece of paper, and then applied to a woman's own hair or that of a sister or child.

In the fickle world of fashion, the more reliable Marcel waves remained stylish for about fifty years, partly aided by evolving hairdressing methods (including electricity and setting lotions) that made the style longer-lasting and easier to implement. It proved especially popular during the 1920s and 1930s, when many women wore their hair bobbed and waved closely around their heads. Her hair when cut might look a lot like the straight, fuss-free bob or Buster Brown style popular on children's heads, but it was the rare woman who was content with such simplicity. Even women who usually wore their short hair uncurled sometimes adopted curls or a waved hairpiece for dressier occasions.[11] All this was a blessing to the trade. The *Hairdressers' Weekly Journal* enthused in 1908 that 'we cannot recall any fashion or device in hair which as ever produced so much revenue and continuous revenue to hairdressers as the Marcel wave ... Now there is not even a modest work-girl or shop assistant who does not resort to its infinite possibilities.'[12]

To return to Albert Langley – he was an ambitious man, and a fine example of a small entrepreneur who chose to try his hand at a newly growing business. By the age of 28 he had achieved a lot. How did he do this? Was he exceptional? In fact, his career tells us much about the growth of the profession.

Langley's business, like that of other successful hairdressers, was rooted in tradition and alert to innovation. He learned his trade young. He started at the age of eleven, in 1916, when he cleaned and brushed out a two-chair barber's shop for an hour before school, half an hour at lunch time, and again in the evening. At fourteen his mother apprenticed him to the only ladies' hairdresser in Swansea. Here he learned the rudiments of hair care as well as wig-making, a craft that was included in the syllabus of the new trade schools including the pioneering Barrett Street Trade School in London. While the shorter hair of the 1920s meant that hairdressers had to learn fine haircutting, wigs and postiches were still an important and very profitable part of the business. Hairpieces were used to embellish new modern hairstyles, and they remained a prominent component of the longer, more traditional hairdressing that was still favoured by many mature and often affluent clients. (Solid business thinking underlay why Langley maintained a wig-making room in the 1930s.) Langley was fairly typical in learning his trade by apprenticeship – a training system that had become standard by the 1930s and was still in place as late as the 1970s. Over a period of years the average apprentice graduated from floor sweeping to learning the correct way to shampoo, lather, rinse, comb and dry the hair; to assisting the hairdresser; to preparing rinses and bleaches; and eventually to cutting and curling the hair of a client.

Before a young person could dress hair on his or her own, much practice took place using boards and wig-forms in order to learn such skills as cutting, waving, and singeing. (Today students in the hairdressing programme at The Bournemouth and Poole College are still issued with model heads fitted with human hair on which to practise. The heads influence the curriculum since only at the end of training can these heads be given a very short haircut!) Women since at least the nineteenth century had saved their own hair-combings from which to make hairpieces and often stored their hair in specially designed jars, known as hair receivers, on their dressing tables or in custom-made decorative bags (cleaning and sorting this hair was a frequent and often despised task for new apprentice hairdressers). Long tresses, harvested when a woman first had her hair bobbed or shingled, were made into switches that could be used in many ways to enhance later hairstyles. But purchased hair was the mainstay of hairpieces; Langley's wig-making room probably served as a training ground for his staff as well as a workshop for sales to customers.

It was not primarily the Marcel wave, however successful, that made Albert Langley's career. Rather it was the technology that replaced it – the permanent wave. The breakthrough was the invention of a process that essentially baked a curl into a head of hair. Boiling or baking had been used for centuries to fix curls into hairpieces but it was only in the first decade of the twentieth century that electricity was harnessed in a way that made durable waves possible on the head of a living person. After several years of experimentation, Karl Ludwig Nessler, who changed his name to Charles Nestlé, developed a curling process suitable for use with electricity and advertised it widely to the trade in 1909.[13] While Nestlé is usually credited with the invention of the permanent wave, others had been working along the same lines, sometimes borrowing methods first used by the textile industry to process wool fibres before they were woven.[14] But he was the first to make it a process for which equipment could be readily mass produced. Soon Nestlé's advertising was cautioning against 'imitations, which are growing up like mushrooms'.[15]

The first permanent wave machines were cumbersome affairs with electrical cables suspended from the ceiling or from a circular ring above the client's head. They looked like medieval torture devices and must have seemed very close to that for the women prepared to try them. The whole process could take up to ten hours; it involved heavy heaters, borax rods, and chemicals; and too often it could result in burns, ulcers, or even bald spots. Advertisers of the new machines naturally tried to allay the public's concerns, but as hair historian Caroline Cox has concluded, 'injuries during the perming process were fairly common as the chemical solutions involved had to be heated to above two hundred degrees and burning the scalp was a distinct possibility'.[16] Despite attempts to reduce risk by putting felt pads between curlers and a woman's head, electric shocks were common; sometimes, too, bakelite (an early form of plastic) curlers melted on unfortunate women's heads.

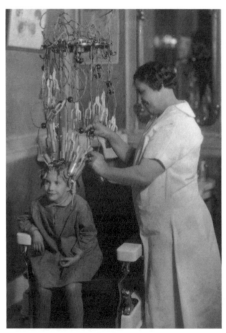

Children were sometimes used in 1920s advertising to make consumers comfortable about the safety of perming machines

Picture courtesy Northwest Mueseum of Arts and Culture/ Eastern Washington State Historical Society, Spokane, Washington L871.31155-26A

Inventors and advocates of the perming process actively promoted their products at trade demonstrations, sometimes emphasising their product's safety by displaying toddlers with appealing permed curls. Hairdressers themselves were quick to show that they were up-to-the-minute in the services they had to offer. In Ipswich in November 1913, at an exhibition of women's work, a special feature was made of Nestlé's permanent waving, with a young lady seated having half of her hair permanently waved while leaving the other half straight.[17] Half-permed heads were in fact a common feature of the early advertising for perming machines.

Early perms were time-consuming, expensive, and available at first only in a limited number of shops. Electrical currents could be unpredictable; several processes were involved, each of which had to be carefully timed; and sometimes the result was uncontrollably frizzy waves, or brittle, damaged and broken hair. So common was the latter that in the profession some hairdos were nicknamed 'pocket perms' after the hairdressers' trick of surreptitiously slipping broken hairs into a pocket and hoping to avoid detection by their patrons.[18] Perms could always go wrong, as the Barrow-in-Furness housewife, Nella Last, discovered once in 1940. On 20 March she returned to her usual salon to have her permanent wave 're-set' – it had fallen out – and remarked that 'I'll never let anyone persuade me to make a change of sachet again, even if made by same firm. When I've had perfect Eugene [*system of perming*] for eight years it's a good test and not for anything will I change from their original sachet.'[19]

All these drawbacks did not, however, deter women. Across the social spectrum women were attracted to the new – and widely advertised – hair procedure. They wanted the modern miracle of curls that only grew out gradually instead of vanishing with one wash, and (for the most part) they accepted the risks.

✂ ✂ ✂ ✂

When Albert Langley, not yet 18, opened his first business in February 1923 in one small room above a shop in Oxford

Street, Swansea with £10 of his own capital and £50 borrowed from his mother, he was on the leading edge of a growing service industry. In the late nineteenth century, hairdressing as a profession had barely existed outside the elite; by the 1930s hairdressing shops were everywhere, especially in cities and towns. One expert, in 1926, was trumpeting hairdressing's future. 'Bobbing, Bingling, Shingling and the Eton crop has [sic] given a fill-up to hairdressing, in that now, it is safe to assume that the majority of women visit the hairdresser's. Our profession is now accepted as a necessary custom of modern life, instead of, as before, just a luxury for those who could afford it. Hairdressing has become popularised and democratised.'[20]

Certainly the fashion for short hair encouraged many more women to have their hair professionally cut, and, once cut, it needed to be cut again and again, and often. In particular, the very shortest cuts needed frequent attention to maintain their stylish smartness. No wonder that many of those initially called 'barbers' transformed themselves into hairdressers. One C W Brown, for example, who was apprenticed at 12 to the men's barbering and tobacco trade, soon moved on to ladies' hairdressing establishments in Bournemouth, London, and Manchester before rising to manage salons in Mayfair and Bond Street and then to supervise 'the many hairdressing departments owned by the Royal Arsenal Co-operative Society'. [21] His last position – with a Co-operative Society – in itself reflected the growth and democratisation of hairdressing services. More young women were in the labour force by the 1920s and 1930s; they had money to spend on themselves, and they wanted to look professional. At the same time many of their mothers also wanted to be stylish – and they could afford to be once services were available that did not assume a ladies' maid or an elite stylist.

New businesses were springing up across the country. These were small businesses that could grow, as Langley's certainly did. After serving his three-year apprenticeship, he 'decided to take a great plunge – emulate Dick Whittington and turn my footsteps in the direction of London', where he went to Eugène Ltd, the headquarters of a hairdressing enterprise established by

Eugene Suter, the inventor of a permanent wave system which was thought to have improved on Nestlé's version. Langley was told kindly to get more experience. But he returned from London brimming with entrepreneurial ideas. These included 'the advantages lying in store for whoever got in first with the new fashion – shingling – which was then taking the West End by storm'. He applied the lessons he had learned. He was successful enough that he was able to repay his mother's £50 loan in eight months plus £21 interest. (Most mothers would be charmed by that kind of interest rate!) But the real trick, he thought, was that lynchpin of the emerging consumer society – advertising. It was advertising, 'one of the cornerstones of commercial success', that soon enabled Langley to win over conservative Welshwomen to the 'new-fangled notion' of permanent-waving of which they were 'frankly scared'.[22]

✂ ✂ ✂ ✂

Langley and his peers did an extraordinary job of convincing women that proper hairdressing would help them to feel better about themselves, and they were helped by lavishly illustrated women's magazines that emphasised that to be fashionable a woman needed to change her hairstyle frequently. Ann Seymour, a prominent hairdressing columnist for *Woman and Beauty*, urged women to try new styles each season – long, short, and all spots in between, or embellished with added hairpieces, or coloured in a new way. In May 1936 she announced that 'Hair can be dressed in a thousand or more winning ways this Spring'. The following year she cheered on another new era with 'hair higher and higher off our faces, waves are going out, but curls are still riotously with us'.[23]

Most magazines in the 1930s devoted a lot of attention to Hollywood and the hairstyles of its celebrities, while *Queen*, like other publications targeted to the social elite, featured the newest styles on the heads of the season's debutantes and female royals. Then, as now, advertising pages in women's magazines were amply laced with enticements to buy the services of hair-care professionals who could help a woman achieve the look she craved – or, more accurately, could be persuaded to crave. One entrepreneur observed that a key principle of his salon was that 'the client rarely knows what is best for the enhancement of her own style or personality', a strategy that encouraged the sale of costly services.[24] Writing of *Woman's Crowning Glory* in 1933, one hairdresser suggested (not entirely without truth) that 'where hair is fine and on the thin side … waving has the effect of making it appear to be twice as much as it really is'.[25] For many women, having a friend or sister or other relative with abundant, curly locks was advertisement enough. It also helped that perms were more readily and conveniently applied to relatively short hair and, from the 1930s, setting lotions made them less likely to dry and damage hair.

A perm came to be seen as a necessity, and the demand for hairdressing services dramatically increased across the country. The Great War had destroyed potential boyfriends and husbands, thus making the pursuit of the men who remained more competitive, while also creating female job opportunities – these were women of the generation of the men killed in the trenches. Somewhat younger women, born during the dozen or so years after 1905, grew up wearing short hair, practical for cleanliness, ease of care, and vigorous outdoor activities. Women who earned their own incomes could justify a little self-indulgence. They had a perm when a fur-trimmed coat would have stretched their meagre resources. If they could afford it or were prepared to spend a little more, many hairdressers were pleased to offer the spa-like services of manicure, chiropody, and facials; and perfume, silk knickers, or hair adornments were temptingly displayed for during the long process of perming.

For the many spinsters in cold, dreary flats and hostels (as well as for some of their more affluent sisters), a hairdresser offered ambience – visual and material. He listened to his clients and learned that they 'appreciated the luxury of warmth' and, when he provided it, they were eager to linger; and, in the cozy salon, they might become open to suggestions for further treatments.[26] One entrepreneur remodelled his ladies' department into a self-styled 'miniature fairyland' with birdsong, a central goldfish pond, and cubicles, each with its own British-born assistant (they did not hire foreigners) with at least a four-year apprenticeship.[27] These extras did much to inflate the hairdresser's profits. Today they are labelled the 'lipstick effect', the small personal indulgences that can generate lots of money for the service providers.

Hairdressers in the 1920s and 1930s were skilled at the art of persuasion. The best of them exploited the thirst for modernity and the taste for efficiency among women who saw themselves as household scientists rather than mere housewives. Hairdressers decorated their premises to appeal to the values of modernism. Ladies' hair salons, whether in Harrods or on the High Street, were among the first businesses to adopt the sleek modern or 'streamlined' style. It was a style with clean, curved lines that employed new materials; evoked the glamour of the ocean liner; mimicked the hygiene and efficiency of scientific domestic management; and employed the soft colours, indirect tubular lighting, and frosted glass of the most fashionable interior design. The redesigned hairdressing shop in the Harrods was described as 'modern but unobtrusive'. The walls were 'of flesh toned panels, with half pillars to break them, in a light walnut veneer with metal inlays' and its fittings picked out in pale shades of blue and yellow.[28] Fresh flowers in modern vases added to the appeal – and distanced the salon from its origins in the darkly masculine world of the barber/tobacconists' shop.

These were buoyant times for hairdressing. From Glasgow in March 1925 came the good tidings that 'it can be said without any fear of contradiction that the big boom in business – as far as ladies' hairdressing is concerned – continues. All the salons are being kept working at high pressure, and all the members of the different staffs have a full daily diary of engagements Glasgow can pride herself on'.[29] Seven years later the *Daily Herald* estimated that women were spending £30,000,000 a year on permanent waves alone. The article further noted that 'in many small shops permanent waving is done at a cost of 25s. Except in the best London shops where rents are high, or in establishments equipped with the most elaborate appliances, more than 50 per cent of this charge is sheer profit'. The perming apparatus only cost £15; assistants were only paid small commissions, and had to rely on tips.[30] In the United States, according to one estimate, women spent $150,000,000 on permanent waves in 1925; another report said that beauty operators, as they were commonly called, gave more than 35 million permanents in 1936 alone.[31]

To this reality were added three more profitable facts. First, women were almost always charged more for haircuts than men – still, in the twenty-first century, a common complaint. Second, a permanent wave was not considered complete without also setting and combing out the hair into a final style. 'The essential culminating feature of the permanent wave is the setting', noted one industry analyst in 1938, adding that 'a permanent wave without a set is like a bark without a dog.'[32] Third, women were encouraged to return to have their hair set between perms and cuts, thereby enhancing an increasingly profitable business. Regular visits to the hairdresser, which had been rare at the beginning of the twentieth century, were commonplace by 1940.

✂ ✂ ✂ ✂

By the 1930s slightly longer cuts and more elaborately curled styles further enriched hairdressers. Ann Seymour of *Woman and Beauty* repeatedly urged her readers to give up the shingle in favour of longer hair because 'it can be dressed almost anyway, finger-rolled and pinned into one soft curl, or allowed to escape in delightful childish curls in the nape of the neck'.[33] But she could be mercurial and inconsistent, sometimes encouraging readers to set their hair at home, touting the return of the shingle or, shortly before the Second World War, the page boy.[34] Analysing women's changing views, one columnist observed that 'once convinced bobbing was the thing to do, we "bobbed" in spite of age, opposition, personal disabilities and terrible hairdressers'. But in 1930 she argued that women were more flexible and progressive and, significantly, that they had the confidence to grow their hair if popular short styles proved unbecoming. 'Everywhere you see the young things with their hair tucked at the back of their ears and curling in their necks behind. It's quaint, becoming and a delightful change.'[35] And a highly profitable one.

Another editorial writer urged that 'if every hairdresser were to din into his, or her, customers that longer haired dressings were an absolute necessity for evening there would be a swelling of the demand for postiche that would reinforce the hairdressers' banking account and cause a feeling of joy among makers of hairpieces.'[36] Fake pin curls were also popular, as were chignon hairpieces and, of course, full wigs. Gilbert Foan, a leading hairdressing specialist, designated the *Ten-inch bob* as the most popular of the longer bobs in Britain in the 1930s, no doubt because it could be styled so many ways. An innovative approach for the indecisive or those caught in the awkward stage of growing out part of their hair was offered in January 1931 by the M André Hugo salon on Sloane Street. 'What struck me most', reported the editor of *Queen's* beauty page, 'was his ingenious new device for dressing growing hair. This is a small oblong-shaped appliance with a hole at each end. The hair is divided down the centre and one portion pulled through each hole, then these ends are crossed over to form a figure of eight, and the ends are tucked in, so that the result is a very fashionable and distinctly neat looking little bun on the nape of the neck. The price for this is the very moderate sum of half-a-guinea.'[37] In such ways new demands were routinely created.

Hair colouring was another major source of profit. Once hair was bleached or dyed, the path back to natural tresses was long and costly, if done gradually, and potentially embarrassing if not accompanied by graduated rinses as the hair grew out. Appointments for dye jobs were still often booked in secluded private cubicles, sometimes even with an entrance apart from the main salon to provide clients with the consolation – or the illusion – of secrecy. To disclose one's secret was unthinkable for many women. 'Your hair makes all the difference', enthused one journalist, echoing the sentiment, in all likelihood, of the majority of her readers.[38] To allow 'ugly grey roots' to show 'as they grow out' was unthinkable; tinting had to be continued.[39] To look smart required the investment of both time and money.

By the 1930s the business of hairdressing had become mainstream, as a glance through any local trade directory will attest. Before that decade there were lots of hairdressers but they were not usually identified as being exclusively for ladies. Figures from the London County Council, apparently based on the 1931 census, estimated 3,500 hairdressing establishments in the metropolis and 8,000 professional hairdressers.[40] In the 1930s they became a significant presence in large and small towns across the country. Around Lancaster and Morecambe in 1934, some 65 ladies' hairdressers were practising; a few years later there were 40 in Burnley and 53 in Blackpool; while in 1939 *Kelly's Directory* records 393 ladies' hairdressers in Hampshire, 108 in Wiltshire (as compared with 23 in 1931), and 85 in Dorset (there had been only 14 in 1931). In the Bournemouth region in 1935 a total of 63 hairdressers restricted their services to women. Some 113 ladies' hairdressers were in business in Brighton and Hove in 1936, serving a population of over 200,000, and over 400 practised in the county of Sussex as whole, which had a population of about 800,000.[41]

Businesses were conducted in different ways. Some served the aristocracy, often listing themselves as court hairdressers, and were found mainly in or near London and a few fashionable county or resort towns. A salon in Bournemouth, *Zara*, styled itself in *Kelly's Directory* (1940) as a Court Hairdresser, Beauty Specialist and Health Spa. Others appealed to women of affluent but untitled families and went out of their way to imply that their services were high-end. Many gave French names to their establishments – 'Chez', 'Maison', or 'Monsieur' – to suggest connections with high fashion and exclusiveness (a marked contrast to such names as Scissors, Taps, Hairport, Pigtails, Tangles, Smile, Tressez, Rapunzel, and the like that are favoured by the current generation). These pretensions were commonly accompanied by modern stylish décor, obsequious service, and staff who styled themselves Miss, Mr, or Madame and Monsieur, and usually worked hard to rid themselves of accents that betrayed their true, unremarkable origins. Trade listings sometimes advertised a shop's credentials and prize-winning at competitions, such as the annual hairdressing exhibition at Olympia or Earl's Court in London, the hairdressers' version of the Chelsea Flower Show.

Major department stores almost always included beauty salons. In fact, the very existence of department stores did much to make it respectable for women to venture out on their own for a day on the town. One of the earliest was begun in London by William Whiteley, who expanded his drapery business to include many other services and opened a hairdressing salon in 1876.[42] Women were able to purchase a wide range of hair products, jewellery, accessories, and hairpieces in all colours.[43] In 1894 Harrods department store decided to set up a hairdressing

Lavishly appointed hairdressing cubicles in Harrods hairdressing salon, circa 1900

Picture courtesy Harrods archives

venture in what had been its Oriental tea-room and in 1898 opened its Ladies Hairdressing Department with a staff of nine, including a departmental junior. The latter reminisced 50 years later that one of his jobs was to procure pints of beer from the nearby Buttercup public house for the men to drink during their morning break.[44] From these relatively humble beginnings the new business prospered and a decade later Harrods was able to claim that its recently renovated Ladies Hairdressing Courts were 'unquestionably the finest in the world', boasting 33 richly decorated hairdressing, manicure and chiropody, and relaxation lounges that included such features as Rose Castile marble, polished satinwood, oak parquetry, Egyptian style carving, silver-plated fittings and Turkish carpets. In the adjoining sales room the customers could purchase wigs, transformations, fringes, combs, manicure sets, tails of human hair, hairpins, nets, and similar requirements.[45]

One distinctive feature of Harrods' special service was its provision of an all-inclusive package to prepare their clients for presentation at their majesties' court. The mysteries of court coiffure were naturally part of the package. 'Harrods have an expert staff of hairdressers ... who know to a nicety all that there is to be known concerning the manipulation of hair to suit the latest style of arranging the regulation plumes and veil – a detail of utmost importance that may, and often does, make or mar the whole general effect of many a court *toilette*.'[46] All this exclusive pampering paid off. By the mid 1930s the store offered a gorgeous modern streamlined beauty salon with 72 private rooms covering half an acre. Its facilities gave the cream of London society lots of amenities well beyond basic hair care. It offered foam baths, massages, and slimming treatments in addition to manicures and chiropody, all set amongst avant garde décor, fresh flowers, and luxurious furnishing 'so that my lady may recline with the greatest of comfort'.[47] The *Morning Post* reported in 1936 that in each individual beauty booth 'an ivory telephone is at your right hand awaiting the calls you may wish to make to friends. A tray for tea, writing or reading swings into place on your left.' [48]

Other department stores (such as Lewis' in Manchester, Birmingham, Liverpool and Leeds)[49] offered similar, if less grand, hairdressing salons with modern décor, scrupulous cleanliness, and specialised services. Most also included barbershops and children's salons. Barbara Barter remembered being taken with her sisters to have their hair trimmed at Selfridges in the 1930s: 'Children were not pandered to in those days! However, children who were good and sat still were rewarded afterwards by being given a ride on one of the beautiful rocking horses, which were stationed between the high chairs. This was the high spot of the occasion and all was over too soon.'[50] Harrods' juvenile hairdressing salon also offered a hobby horse and a room for the children to run around, cleverly located next to the toy department![51]

Of course, Britain's elite had always expected the finest in personal services. What was much more novel was the emergence of salons and services geared to the needs and incomes of

Cedarholm Beauty Parlour, Spokane, Washington 1929
Picture courtesy Northwest Mueseum of Arts and Culture/Eastern Washington State Historical
Society, Spokane, Washington L871.40117-29

middle-class and lower-middle-class women. Here was a part of the trade that featured women as both providers and consumers. High street or home-based shops were sometimes identified by in directory listings by a single name – Deirdre, Doreen, Anne, Violet. Other hairdressers, who were not always listed in trade directories (they might work casually), attended to women in their own neighbourhoods, working hours to suit themselves and their clients. Still more had 'mobile' businesses that served remote communities, rural residential schools, hospitals and nursing homes. It seems to have been common for young hairdressers to 'go mobile' after marriage, visiting first a clientele based on former salon customers who were now young moms, the elderly with limited mobility, and others not readily served by public transport. Some were self-trained; others took formal courses; and the remainder had been assistants or junior stylists in someone else's salon.

The way mobile businesses were conducted was highly variable – and still is. The *Daily Express* in 1928 suggested to its women readers that the two girls who toured the country in a motor car, offering their services to schoolgirls, students, and nurses in country colleges and hospitals, had a 'career with prospects'.[52] An upmarket girls' school or seniors' residence might offer a fully equipped salon that the hairdresser visited once a week or more frequently. In August 1977 eleven North Lancashire women held a reunion to remember their days in the 1920s as hairdressers. 'We were beauticians as well,' recalled Edith Monkhouse, who

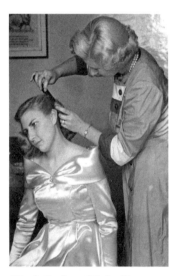

Wendy Parker of Oxford in 1951 having her hair done for her wedding by her cousin, Sheila Jennings, who ran the Gainsborough Salon in Reading and who used Wendy in an advertisement to attract other brides. Sheila had dyed Wendy's hair blonde in 1948 when Wendy was 15

worked at Madame Mensforth's salon, 'and our clientele came from a wide area around Lancaster. We even went out to boarding schools at Arnside and Casterton to do the girls' hair – everyone [there] had very long hair and it was a full day's job. Remember there were no hairdryers, we had to rub it dry.'[53] Other mobile hairdressers expected patrons to greet them with newly washed hair that they cut and/or set, and sometimes dried, combed out and lacquered. Many a time a newly dyed head was rinsed over the family bath-tub. If this seems strange to some readers, consider that in the economic downturn of late 2008 moonlighting hairdressers gave low-priced cuts at hair parties, sometimes conducted in the host's garage.[54] Today mobile hairdressing is often mutually beneficial. It aids the busy professional who can have her hair done on her own premises and at a time convenient to her, while it helps another professional (male or female) manage a complicated life and avoid the need for a lot of fixed capital investment.

How did one become a hairdresser? And why? The explanations are complex. Any combination of desire, natural aptitude, and the time needed to serve as an apprentice could play a role. The Lancaster retirees mentioned earlier earned a wage of three shillings per week as an apprentice after the Great War, which could rise to thirty shillings per week after a four-year apprenticeship. Young women may have enjoyed the glamour of new styles as well as the independence of a freely chosen trade and the ability to use their skills and not punch a time-clock. Other women took up the profession when times were tough in their usual line of work or to furnish a living for themselves and their dependants when a husband left or died. It is likely that hairdressing often provided the same sort of tenuous livelihood that taking in laundry had done for an earlier generation, though perhaps it yielded more social and artistic satisfaction. Lancashire mill girls, it was said, often became hairdressers. A leading Bolton hairdresser noted that, in addition to manual dexterity, former mill girls' powers of concentration were honed by the close watching of machinery; the majority 'are girls of a very high and reliable type, the hairdressing trade is gaining at the expense of the cotton trade'.[55] Less kindly, a woman in 2001 thought that her aunt, who began hairdressing in the mid-1930s, 'probably picked it up as she was too good to work in the mills which offered very little skilled labour to women then, only scummy jobs like bobbin-tender and doffer. Hairdresser is at least a skilled sort of job for women.'[56]

Another version of the durably fashionable waved bob: Ivy Longstaff in the 1930s

Across the country, ordinary women without any particular training but with an aptitude for hair care set up businesses to serve their neighbours with a bobbed cut, a shampoo, and a little personal attention.

As well as training through apprenticeship, women were also being trained in schools. New classroom-based forms of training catered to the growing demand. Both public educational facilities and private enterprises (the latter usually marketing their proprietary processes) began to establish courses to replace or supplement the onerous apprenticeship system. One of the first of the former was the London County Council's Barrett Street Trade School for Girls, which opened in 1915. By the late 1920s nearly one thousand girls had been trained there and it was reported in 1927 that they had no difficulty in obtaining work after their two-year programme, which covered both boardwork (dressing false hair on a board or wig form) and salon practice.[57] Soon many Barrett Street graduates were employed in prominent West End salons, with several holding managerial positions.[58] Miss A M Tracey, the school's longstanding senior instructress, had herself been the first forewoman in Harrods' hairdressing department.[59] She and the school's head, Miss Cox, well understood the workings of the fashionable world and ensured that their charges, many of them girls originally from the East End, were carefully selected and trained for work in the capital's fashionable milieu. Miss Cox cunningly arranged for students to graduate in March (as would girls trained in couture and millinery), at the beginning of the London season, when their services would be most in demand.[60] Trade schools introduced common standards of training, which often concluded with examinations under the City and Guilds system. This thorough and rigorous system provided graduates with a solid foundation and still is, in the words of one industry expert, 'the Rolls Royce of training organizations'.[61] Sometimes school-based training was combined with shorter periods of apprenticeship.

But not all members of the trade were convinced. 'The "mass production" hairdressers, turned out in rapid quick succession, are a serious danger', warned one editorial in 1925. For this writer the real remedy lay in a 'revival of the apprenticeship system'.[62] In contrast, Gilbert Foan in 1931 endorsed the new approach. 'Never before have young entrants into hairdressing had the opportunities and consideration they enjoy today. They owe a big debt to the far-sighted men and women who have fought so long to establish recognized standards.'[63] Perspectives taken by established hairdressers depended on several factors: attitudes toward women, the role of trade credentials, and assessments of economic prospects. For some hairdressers women were seen as a threat because they were generally paid less – fine if they were your employees, not fine if they were your competitors – and were deemed to undercut men because, it was said, they didn't really need the money (the ancient 'pin-money' argument).

The more enlightened took a strategic view of what some labelled 'the sex problem in hairdressing'. 'The war [1914-1918] did more than all the suffragette propaganda to give woman the freedom she has long demanded', wrote one commentator. 'Before the war there was a fair proportion of women engaged in hairdressing, but in the absence of men ... women developed a skill and capacity in regard to the so-called higher branches of the profession that made them quite indispensable in countless establishments throughout the United Kingdom.'[64] As late as the 1920s some hairdressing bodies would not let women compete in the hairdressing competitions: one noted female hairdresser set up the Ladies Hairdressing Academy in 1923 specifically to provide women with a way to enter competitions abroad because they often were not able to enter them in England on the same terms as men.[65] Some organisations were progressively inclined. The Eugene Permanent Wave competitions held at Royal Agricultural Hall in London in 1927 boasted identical £40 first prizes for both men and women. The same company also sponsored a golf competition with one silver cup for ladies and another for gentlemen.[66] It is no accident that the Eugene Company had its own training facilities and a great many of its students were women.

Patricia Martin in her youth: a feisty lady, according to her daughter, who was always 'making waves' in her life

Another major point of contention in the 1920s and 1930s was the emergence of cut-rate providers. 'It would seem that there is much price cutting going on in the more lowly establishments where shingling is performed at prices that would – and do – make the establishment hairdressers blench with horror', one report asserted in 1927; allegations of price cutting led some hairdressers' organisations, such as that in Bradford, to try to fix minimum prices for ladies' work.[67] Informal training and low prices were considered by at least one hairdressers' advocate, Gilbert Foan, as a species of 'blacklegging' that was 'a dishonourable practice and one that should be stopped forthwith'.[68] Foan's rhetoric was probably informed by his background as a member of the Independent Labour Party and two-time Labour candidate. This was a minor issue for others, who saw the low-priced services as simply meeting the needs of new clients. More business was being done than before the Great War in established salons and new clients were seeking services affordable enough for them. The market was segmenting in a natural way. Inevitably, not everyone was happy. One West Yorkshire correspondent complained about a fifteen-year old girl practising 'alleged hairdressing' in her family's council house, 'one of the ordinary Corporation living-room and scullery homes, with no sanitary or other equipment suitable to such work', and urged his colleagues to expose such practices, which were often in violation of local bylaws prohibiting business enterprises in council flats.[69]

While most years in the 30s were good to hairdressers, 1937 was spectacular. For 1937 saw the coronation on 12 May of King George VI and his Queen, Elizabeth. This great event brought publicity beyond what advertising could buy and afforded plentiful opportunities for hairdressers to ply their craft at its most extravagant. Trade journals and the popular and fashion press devoted oceans of ink to the upcoming coronation. Hairdressers offered illustrations of elaborate hairdressings to be worn with tiaras and coronets in high society and encouraged special hairdressings for the countrywide celebrations of lesser mortals. 'Regal hairstyles are the order of the Coronation season', gushed *Woman and Beauty*, 'hair swept back from proud brows, heads crowned with curls.' 'Jewellery is going to be in the limelight, so take out the family jewels and wear them in your hair.'[70] The popular Queen and her two young daughters were a hairdresser's dream: they were well known by everyone, well-liked, and short-haired. The princesses were presented as modern girls who wore short, up-to-date styles at a time when many girls were kept in long hair until they finished school. Moreover, the princesses' hair was just long enough to permit some artful work by their hairdressers. George VI's attractive wife and daughters were as much fashion trendsetters as was the present Queen's famous late daughter-in-law, Princess Diana. Few subjects could afford the lavish costumes of the royals but they could, and did, try to emulate their hairdos. For hairdressers, 1937 was a very good year.

Irene Rouse of Coventry,
pictured in 1933 aged 17.

It is likely that Irene's girlhood
ringlets did not last much longer

References

1   Vera Lee Pettibone, *Bobbing Days* (1924), British Library, VOC/1924/Pettibone.

2   My Beauty Shop (1929), British Library, VOC/1929/AKST.

3   Albert E Langley, 'From Lather Boy to Shop Proprietor', *Hairdresser and Beauty Trade,* 20 January 1933, 43.

4   *Hairdressing*, November 1913, 1219.

5   Diana Athill, *Yesterday Morning: A Very English Childhood* (London: Granta, 2002), p. 89.

6   *Hairdresser and Beauty Trade*, 20 August 1938, 10.

7   MO Directive, April 1939, Personal Appearance, Respondent #1459.

8   'The Present and the Future', *Queen*, 9 January 1933, 33.

9   For a description of the original method see Gilbert A Foan, ed. (New

edition edited by N E B Wolters), *The Art and Craft of Hairdressing :A Standard and Complete Guide to the Technique of Modern Hairdressing, Manicure, Massage and Beauty Culture* (London: Sir Isaac Pitman and Sons, Ltd.,1950), pp. 217-219.

10   *Harrods Catalogue*, 1895, 1295; *Beauty and Hairdressing*, Madame, 27 March 1897 n.p. (clipping held at Harrods archive).

11   Victoria Sherrow, *Encyclopedia of Hair: A Cultural History* (Westport, Connecticut: Greenwood Press, 2006), pp. 257-8.

12   *Hairdressers' Weekly Journal,* 1 August 1908, 1143 as quoted in Caroline Cox, *Good Hair Days: A History of British Hairstyling* (London: Quartet Books, 1999), p. 141.

13   *Hairdressers' Weekly Journal*, 13 March 1909, 435.

14   Sherrow, *Encyclopedia of Hair*, pp. 303.

15   *Hairdressing*, September 1912, 869.

16   Cox, *Good Hair Days*, p. 147.

17   *Hairdressing*, November 1913, 1240.

18   Sherrow, *Encyclopedia of Hair*, p. 303.

19   MOA, Diarist no. 5353.

20   *Hairdressing,* 15 March 1926, 16.

21   *Hairdressing and Beauty Trade,* 24 October 1941, 7.

22   Langley, p. 12.

23   *Woman and Beauty*, May 1936, 20, and January 1937, 12.

24   *William Bull, 'A Prosperous Business Built in Seven Years', Hairdresser and Beauty Trade*, January 1933, 10.

25   Bruce Warmington, *Woman's Crowning Glory* (London, 1933), unpaginated pamphlet.

26   Bull, 'Prosperous Business', *Hairdresser and Beauty Trade,* January 1933, 11.

27   *Hairdresser and Beauty Trade*, 4 November 1933, 30.

28   *Hairdresser and Beauty Trade,* 16 October 1936, 41.

29   *Hairdressing*, March 1925, 306.

30   '"Permanent Waves" Ramp Exposed', *Daily Herald*, Thursday 5 May 1932, 9.

31   *Hairdressing*, February 1925, 247; Sherrow, *Encyclopedia of*

Hairdressing, p. 304.

32   *Hairdresser and Beauty Trade*, 20 August 1938, 10.

33   *Woman and Beauty,* April 1932, 48.

34   See for example, *Woman and Beauty,* March 1931, 52; June 1931, 52; October 1932, 42; April 1934, 46; September 1937, 38, November 1938, 51.

35   *Women and Beauty*, May 1930, 44.

36   *Hairdressing*, May 1925, 5.

37   As quoted in Corson, *Fashions in Hair* (1965), p. 620.

38   *Woman and Beauty*, January 1932, 32-33. See also *Spring 2001 Directive* (Mass Observation Archive, University of Sussex): the responses of women old enough to have experienced hair care in the 1930s largely confirm this view.

39   *Hair Tinting and Beauty Culture*, March 1, 1926, 7.

40   Cited in Charles Berg, *The Unconscious Significance of Hair* (London: Allen & Unwin, 1951), p. 4.

41   These statistics are drawn from the following directories: *Lancaster, Morecambe & Suburban Directory, 1934; Blackburn, Burnley, Preston, Barrow & District Trades Directory, 1937-38; Kelly's Directory of Hampshire and the Isle of Wight. Wiltshire, Dorsetshire & the Channel Islands, 1939; Kelly's Directory of Bournemouth, 1935; Kelly's Directory of Brighton and Hove, 1936;* and *Kelly's Directory of Sussex, 1938.*

42   R S Lambert, *The Universal Provider: A Study of William Whiteley* (London: George Harrap, 1938) as quoted in Bill Lancaster, T*he Department Store: A Social History* (London: Leicester UP, 1995), pp. 21 & 74.

43   As quoted from *Whiteley's Illustrated Catalogue and General Price List for 1885,* in Lambert, *Department Store,* 181.

44   *Harrodian Gazette,* November 1948, 154.

45   *The Fashions at Harrods, 1907-8*, c.1907-8, p. 39.

46   *Harrods Catalogue*, 1912, 1521.

47   'Women's Hairdressing Department, Typescript, 9 June 1937. Held at Harrods Archives.

48   As quoted in Sean Callery, *Harrods Knightsbridge: The Story of Society's Favourite Store* (London: Ebury Press, 1991), p. 125.

49   *Hairdresser and Beauty Trade*, 16 September 1933, 16.

50   Gordon Honeycombe, *Selfridges: Seventy-Five Years, the Story of the Store, 1909-1984* (London: Park Lane Press, 1984), pp. 211-212.

51   *Harrods News*, 11 October 1926, unpaginated leaflet.

52   *Hairdressing*, May 1928, 5.

53   *Lancaster Guardian,* 5 August 1977, 7.

54   'Get Bobbed but don't get clipped, *New York Times*, Thursday, 10 December 2008, E1&10.

55   *Hairdresser and Beauty Trade*, 18 August 1933, 5.

56   Mass Observation Archive (University of Sussex), *Spring Directive 2001* [A1292].

57   *Hairdressing*, January 1927, 565.

58   *Hairdressers' Chronicle*, 25 May 1928, 15.

59   *Hairdressing and Beauty Trade*, 14 April 1933, 11 & 35.

60   Personal communication, Katherine Baird, London School of Fashion.

61   www.cityandguilds.com/cps/rde/xchg/cgonline/hs.xsl/20486.html, 20 October 2008.

62   *Hairdressing*, June 1925, 33.

63   Gilbert Foan, *The Art and Craft of Hairdressing* (London: New Era Publishing, 1931), p. 7, as quoted in Cox, *Good Hair Days,* p. 80.

64   *Hairdressing*, January 1924, 613.

65   Ibid, 620; and *Hairdresser and Beauty Trade,* 14 April 1933, 11.

66   *Hairdressing*, January 1927, 573 and 576.

67   *Hairdressing,* June 1927, 33, and January 1925, 229.

68   *Hair Tinting and Beauty Culture*, 15 March 1926, 17.

69   *Hairdressing*, July 1927, 79.

70   *Woman and Beauty*, April 1937, 24.

4

HAIR IN WAR AND PEACE

'Your first thought must be your hair. Perms have to be arranged far ahead these days, and if you are having a new one you'll want to book it for at least a fortnight before your wedding day.'

(Woman's Magazine, June 1944, p. 62)

'I have decided I can fight the Second Front better with curly hair.'

(Helen Lloyd, manuscript diary, 5 June 1944, Surrey History Centre, Woking, Surrey)

By the mid 1930s hairstyles were generally longer than those of a decade before: hairstyles evolved incrementally and often with considerable variety. Fashion journalists might commend long upswept styles one month, switching to the desirability of hairpieces the next, and even occasionally endorsing the return to radically short hair for the daring few. Hair 'this year', according to one beauty expert in 1936, 'is definitely longer than last, soft about the face, curled over the head, softer in line at the neck'.[1] Both long bobs and shoulder length hair lent themselves to sometimes elaborate styles. Hair in the later 1930s was usually embellished with curls – curls had been reinstated in importance and might be shown on any part of a woman's head – and hair was commonly stiffened into a no-hair-out-of-place bandbox smartness. This look was most often topped off with a fetching hat or evening hair jewellery that might have come out of a real bandbox.[2] These pre-war styles needed frequent care, a perm for those not naturally endowed with curls, an expert hairdresser, and (not least) discretionary funds.

Fashionable hair had become refined and domesticated – proper and certainly not rebellious. Mothers no longer tried to emulate the hairstyles of their daughters. Fashion and the hairstyles that went with it called for a mature, controlled femininity, and these feminine ideals were influenced as much by high society as by the screen glamour of actresses who wore jewels and furs to complement their coiffures. This intensely feminine look was a rejection of the sporty, spirited androgyny of the flapper of the 1920s, and perhaps of her feminism as well.

By 1940 long hair was being championed by most of the voices and faces that had influence. 'There is no denying', wrote one beauty columnist in that year, 'that longer hair gives infinite variety. Film stars and Model Girls know this, so most of them have hair to the shoulders – a length that can be arranged to give many effects.'[3] Longer hair, she added, could be set at home. This was important because hairdressers, along with everyone else, were starting or soon to enter the armed forces. In addition, there was a more carefree glamour about long hair; it didn't need the careful precision of shorter fashionable hairstyles to look smart. Long hair gave women choices, a message that beauty columnists had been preaching for years. Individuality was the objective – every day a different look. In January 1941, *Woman and Beauty* illustrated what it called the 'Four-in-One', a cut that allowed a woman to have four different styles in a day (morning, afternoon, evening, and 'that special occasion').[4] Few real women, except perhaps the Duchess of Windsor, ever achieved such daily extravagance.

Ann Seymour, a prominent beauty columnist in the 1930s and 1940s, consistently championed the desirability of regularly changing one's hairstyle. She urged her readers to watch the photographs of smart actresses and note that they did not keep the same hairstyle month after month and year after year, as less adventurous women did. Her message would have resonated particularly well with those young women who dreamily followed every nuance of their favourite film stars. 'If your features are similar to theirs,' urged Seymour, 'take the photograph along to your hairdresser and ask him to copy it exactly, and you may discover in yourself a new and unsuspected beauty.'[5]

Left to their own devices, lots of young women in the late 1930s and early 1940s would have happily given their hair a joyous toss and worn it long and hanging free. Real glamour came from Hollywood. Vivien Leigh, with her long luscious locks, became a major star with her appearance in the 1939 film, *Gone with the Wind*, which played for three years at the Ritz, Leicester Square and in almost all parts of Britain during the early 1940s, drawing in audiences in the millions, the majority of them women. She became a role model for tens of thousands of women. Rita Hayworth's long seductive hair, Marlene Dietrich's dangerous-looking elegance, Barbara Stanwyck's sophisticated glamour, Jean Harlow's seductive blonde-haired siren look, Katharine Hepburn's gorgeous red hair, and many more, introduced glamour via the silver screen into the most humdrum of lives. Veronica Lake's long, curled, peek-a-boo hairstyle, with a long strand hanging seductively over her right eye, attracted untold numbers of young women. For a short time Lake was a major box office draw, particularly following her appearance in a 1941 hit, *I Wanted Wings*, in which she and her remarkable hair upstaged the rest of the cast. 'I never did cheesecake; I just used my hair', she is quoted as saying.[6] She looked undeniably sexy; young women's mothers with stiff hairdos and respectable hats did not.

In Stepney in 1940, a Mass Observer reported that Hollywood's influence was much in evidence. Younger women, in particular, almost always permed their hair, usually wore it long, dyed or bleached it frequently, arranged it in contrived styles often with numerous curls both piled high over the forehead and cascading waves or curls at the back, and commonly adorned their hairdo with coloured or diamante clips or other hair jewellery. Only the very poorest, this observer noted, left their hair straight and unadorned.[7] One of the few influential cinematic exceptions to the long-haired look was Ingrid Bergman's short tousled cut for her role alongside Gary Cooper in the 1943 film adaptation of Hemingway's famous novel, *For Whom the Bell Tolls* – but this was later in the war, when more utilitarian values prevailed.

Films were a major purveyor of cutting-edge hairstyles, and their audiences were huge. After long hours at factory, school, or other work, including housework, the cinema was a key recreational outlet. By 1939, on the cusp of war, 23 million people attended a cinema each week, and some 990 million tickets were sold in the year. Most tickets were modestly priced – as little as twopence or threepence for matinees and the best evening prices were around a shilling.[8] In 1935, The New Survey of London observed that the 258 cinemas in greater London were capable of accommodating a quarter of the whole region's population on one day.[9] It was not uncommon in wartime for young women – often with money in their pockets for the first time and few opportunities to spend it on clothes, shoes, or cosmetics – to go to the cinema several times a week. The already robust trend of the 1930s was reinforced as wartime conditions made many homes cold, grim, even damaged, while the local cinema was large, warm, cheerful, and offered up to three hours of distraction (a main film, B movie, newsreel, and cartoon or 'short') and sometimes the agreeable companionship of a soldier, sailor, or airman. One working-class woman recalled that her diary revealed that she had made 141 cinema visits in 1941 alone.[10] Throughout the war cinemas remained packed, with audiences increasingly reluctant to leave their seats to seek shelter during air-raids. The images of big-name actresses and their choices of hairstyle were inevitably on the minds of millions of women, and women's magazines usually idealised the choices in fashion and hairstyles of these Hollywood stars.

✂ ✂ ✂ ✂

Hairstyles became more prominent subjects of discussion in the 1940s, for the demands of wartime impinged on almost all aspects of life, including hairdressing, and compelled adaptations and innovations. Changes in women's hair during the Second World War reflected, symbolically and in reality, the dramatic shifts in the opportunities and constraints in women's lives and the new attitudes towards women's roles. War was bound to have an impact on fashion and how it could be expressed – and also on the practice of personal hygiene.

Up until the second half of 1941, however, the implications of war for hairdressing were not particularly profound; after 1941 they were. Indeed, there is some evidence that commercial hairdressing was actually flourishing in 1940-41. According to the trade journal, *Hairdresser and Beauty Trade*, in 1941 women in the North were becoming more appearance-conscious and 'are spending more on hair and beauty treatment than before the war', a trend that this journal mentioned again with satisfaction in June, when, it was noted, many holiday makers in Lancashire 'had taken the precaution, before going away, of having their hair attended to'.[11] At that moment economic realities were favouring hairdressers. 'Perhaps one of the best reasons for the great increase in the Trade is the fact that women have more money and less to spend it on. Usually they would buy clothes, but with the rationing they turn to hair and beauty treatments as an outlet for their spending ability.'[12] Occasionally new salons appeared, and not always for the well-heeled: in early 1941 the Middlesbrough Co-operative Society opened one with nine cubicles that included up-to-date systems of permanent waving.[13] In Coventry in 1939 a twenty-year-old girl set up a hairdressing business near a small factory estate where more and more girls were taking over men's jobs; soon she was so busy she needed an assistant.[14]

Some of war's social changes were partly responsible for the hairdressing industry's prosperity early in the war. 'Very few girls of 15-17 could afford to spend much at the hairdresser's prior to the war. Nowadays their services are in great demand', observed a columnist for *Hairdresser and Beauty Trade* in February 1942.[15] Not only had young women more to spend at earlier ages and more freedom from home rules, older women and women in isolated areas were also making more use of hairdressers. Older women were getting about more than they had in peacetime. They had become active volunteers, going to knitting-for-the soldiers meetings, serving at canteens, and facilitating provisioning of all sorts through Women's Institutes and the Women's Voluntary Services: 'Feeling they must look their best, they are now paying regular visits to hairdressers. Previously these visits were reserved for special occasions.' Another explanation for the boom in hairdressing, the same correspondent thought, was related to people being evacuated from cities in danger. 'With people evacuated in growing numbers from fashionable places, local hairdressers in the receiving areas are finding business brisk, and the smart heads of the evacuees are tempting the locals to pay more frequent visits to the hairdresser', according to *Hairdresser and Beauty Trade* in March 1941.[16] Some women, of course, like the middle-aged and comfortably-off Barrow diarist Nella Last, already had 'a fixed appointment every other Thursday'. 'A dirty or greasy head is not only uncomfortable but gives one a feeling of inferiority – even a cat keeps its fur clean', she noted in a response to a directive from Mass Observation.[17] Outside the larger Northern towns, however, the weekly or fortnightly visit to the hairdresser had never really caught on, but in the early 1940s local hairdressers began to hope for record business.

Prior to mid-1941 hairdressing was in some ways affected by war, but not yet seriously. Hair imports (mainly for transformations and wigs) were stopped in 1940; hairpins and combs (many of the latter had come from France) were less and less available by 1941. Perhaps the most striking changes occurred in those cities that were heavily bombed from September 1940, for there – notably London – hairdressers and their clients were sometimes obliged to decamp to safer quarters. Some hairdressers took to going underground with their business. A few buried their businesses in the deepest cellars in town, some of which were located in posh hotels. As a writer in *Vogue* put it in late 1940: 'At the Dorchester, business booms, especially in the basement, where everyone spent the "alert" being shampooed and set, and manicured, and massaged, and foam-bathed'.[18] Another hairdresser working in Barking in the autumn of 1940 said that she would often take clients down to the Anderson shelter backing onto the salon and complete her work there. Large department stores rushed to be able to serve their clients in underground shelters, while Peter Jones was one of the first establishments to adopt the new perms that needed no complex electrical equipment and could be carried on in shelters, at least in those equipped with hair dryers.[19] Bentall's in Kingston on Thames, reassured clients: 'Bentalls Hairdressing and Beauty Services carry on in a normal manner from the sounding of the Alert until All Clear. When the ex-anti-aircraft spotters on our roof advise that danger is imminent, customers are evacuated speedily to a temporary salon in the basement shelter. Here a permanent wave or manicure is continued until danger is past.'[20]

It was only from around the middle of 1941 that new pressures forced major changes on hairdressing and the ways it was practised. There were two main reasons for these changes. First, hairdressers and their assistants were being called up or volunteering for war service, leading to many businesses closing. Second, supplies were declining. Some of the chemicals used in shampoos and dyes were needed for war materiel and to supply the Forces. On 14 January 1943, *The Times* reported a Board of Trade Order which prohibited the manufacture of 'certain hair preparations made wholly or partly from petroleum'.[21] A photograph at the Imperial War Museum shows a young woman (at 16 too young to join the Services) mixing hair dye. The caption notes that hairdressers were only allowed a small quantity of dye and thus diluted it to make it go further.[22] Scanty colouring supplies did not go far, and affected the choices of a great many women. Ursula Bloom, beauty editor for *Woman's Own*, responded on 2 August 1941 to a reader's query about how to stop hair going grey: 'The trouble is that nearly all the rinses and tints are off the market because the factories [i.e. the chemicals] are needed for vital war products. At such a time I'd think twice before I started something so difficult to keep up.'[23] Later that month she took a harder line with so-called bottle blondes, saying: 'Believe me, it is only right and proper that factories should be making goods which are indispensable to the war effort. Afterwards you can go as golden as you wish, today you can't!' [24]

Magnifying these woes was the fact that hot water was less available and cuts in electricity posed a hazard to the prolonged process of perming. One previously successful business in Coventry had to be sold after the bombing of the city in November 1940 disrupted supplies of water and electricity, and the owner's assistant had a nervous breakdown following the death of her pilot fiancé.[25] Shampoos became scarce as did curl papers used for perms. Fancy hair ornaments and false hair virtually disappeared, though members of the elite, the greatest users of false hair, largely abandoned evening dress and the accompanying elaborate hairdos for the duration of the conflict.

Professional hairdressers had to respond to these constraints and often anticipated them. They reacted to the challenges in a variety of ways. Some, especially those with large salons and suitable storage, hoarded precious materials such as perming chemicals and paper sachets, curlers, and hairpins. Bleaches, tints and hair-setting lotions were all scarce but shortages of shampoo, essential for virtually all hairdressing, were particularly troublesome. 'Good perfumed shampoo was hard to obtain', a Dorset hairdresser remembered, 'but the customers always liked to think they had the best... One trade secret was to make shampoo out of soft green soap ... to which we added verbena essence and the customers thought they were getting a very expensive hard-to-get shampoo.'[26] Plans were made to try to keep equipment such as perming machines in good working order for as long as possible. In some cases the relatively new Sartory system replaced dependence on the cumbersome electrical machines. This system involved chemical pads that created their own heat after immersion in water and eliminated the agony of sitting under a perming machine for hours.[27] When conditions in bombed-out areas were really rough, some intrepid hairdressers carried on with tin basins and kettles, boiling water on oil stoves, and, lower on the social ladder, asking patrons to bring their own towels.[28]

As young hairdressers entered war service, older women often filled their places. Retired female hairdressers were sought out to replace staff lost to the war effort, and many middle-aged women did return to their old jobs. One large salon in the north of England had employed fifteen assistants with an average age of 23; by December 1941 there were twelve, with an average age of 43 and one over 50.[29] Even with such help most salons were not staffed adequately to respond to walk-in trade or requests for service within a few hours. It was said in September 1942 that 'Selfridges, where the hairdressing department is always busy and appointments now have to be made four days ahead, are now trying to get in touch with as many of their former assistants as possible'.[30] Persuasion was sometimes needed to convince these women that they could do the job even if they felt themselves a little out of date. If more coaxing were needed, *Hairdresser and Beauty Trade* noted in the same month that working conditions had improved over the last 30 or 40 years; modern premises were designed for hygiene and comfort, hours and working conditions were better, and training systems had attracted 'a better class of young person to the Craft'.[31]

Some hairdressing businesses simply ceased to operate as their owners closed up shop when they themselves signed up for military service. The ranks of hairdressers were further thinned by the internment of enemy aliens; and a few hairdressers who had imitated suave European manners and accents and thus, even if actually Cockney, were sometimes taken for the enemy, also quickly signed up or, if too old for call-up, dropped their fake names and accents, retired, or took up other businesses. Members of the trade lobbied to be able to provide hairdressing services on military bases and in military facilities, to have their work recognised as an essential service, and to be allowed to provide hairdressing to women working in munitions factories and other war-related facilities. A trade journal in 1941 argued that women hairdressers in their twenties should not be conscripted to work in munitions. The author cited three girls who, like many thousands of hairdressers, were working twelve to fourteen hours a day, looking after the hair of clients. 'They are, in fact, as one works manager has said, giving the war workers confidence and "pep" by virtue of smart coiffures they devise for their discriminating clientele.'[32] This case found little favour in Whitehall.

War meant that many women were on the move in ways they had never been before – living away from home, commuting to industrial works, serving on military bases, or being evacuated from a city in danger to a region of safety. Uprootedness became a new norm. It was reported in May 1940 that in Coventry 'a trained hairdresser offered her services for WVS work. She is now touring the reception areas around Coventry giving hairdressing service to evacuees.'[33] This unprecedented female mobility forced changes as to how and where hairdressing was carried out. Some factories came to recognise the importance of having hairdressers on site. Long and awkward hours, combined with fatigue, the blackout, and poor transport, made it very difficult for women in munitions industries to get to a hairdresser. By July 1942 qualified hairdressers had been appointed to the staff of several war factories in the North West. This action had been taken on the recommendation of watch committees, who clearly viewed on-site hairdressing as a positive measure – for health, safety, and morale – for hundreds of young employees.[34] Other institutions arranged for women to have hairdos during breaks in their long shifts. This service could take the form of authorised breaks or it could be completely unofficial, as when girls did each others' hair on lunch breaks. Other factories ran hairdressing clubs; women paid a small sum, and used a lottery system to determine who would enjoy an inexpensive perm or set that week.[35] Productivity did not suffer as a result of these arrangements. In mid-1944 it was reported that Morris Motors in Oxford 'estimated that since they opened their own works hairdressing saloon 500 production hours have been saved weekly'.[36]

Many hairdressers were able to ply their trade in wartime,

though they often had to be adaptable, taking on formal work assignments, volunteer work in officially sanctioned salons, or providing casual services to other women. In 1941, at an RAF operational station in Scotland, a WAAF with beauty training started a hairdressing and beauty parlour in a disused hut, with apparent success.[37] While it seemed that few of the Services at that date officially employed women as hairdressers, it was reported that girls with civilian beauty training, in the ATS and elsewhere, were encouraged to undertake the hair-care of their colleagues.[38] When visiting ATS units in Scotland, HRH Princess Mary, the Princess Royal (only daughter of George V), toured a beauty parlour staffed by women who were, in many cases, hairdressers in civilian life and another similar hairdressing shop in the South-East Command.[39] A photograph in the Imperial War Museum shows Miss Irene Ward MP, Conservative Member for Wallsend, near Newcastle, chatting with ATS members 'who are getting a professional "hair-do" without leaving the camp'.[40] Trade magazines encouraged business owners to be flexible in booking appointments for women in the Forces or war industries, to recognise their clients' shortage of time, and to be tolerant of occasional difficulties in making appointments precisely on time or of last-minute cancellations. Frank A King, writing in 1942 of 'The Hairdresser at War', counselled hairdressers to watch for the dates of Services' dances and other functions for which the 'the girls will require special attentions', and to schedule civilian clients for times when the service girls are on duty.[41] In February 1943 a young Wren reported her hairdressing prowess in a letter to her fiancé: 'Have had an amusing time this evening designing glamorous hairstyles for the little stewards who are going out tonight with their Canadian Tommies. They're all so excited with their new-found beauty and are longing to see if the boyfriends notice anything. "Ow, Maureen, make me beautiful too!"'[42]

Women's organisations also tried to establish hairdressing services for women doing war work or joining the Services. In July 1942, by which time the demand for hairdressing much exceeded the supply of full-time professional hairdressers and their salons, the WVS in Burnley, Lancashire, sought volunteers with hairdressing experience. Since equipment was also scarce, the WVS also issued an appeal for 'any public-spirited person to kindly offer or sell, at a reasonable price, a hair-dryer'.[43] Another source noted that 'any girl who joins the WRNS' – it was thought by many women to be smartest women's branch of the Forces – 'with a sound knowledge of hairdressing will soon find her services are greatly in demand. Particularly when a dance is to be held, every rating will want a shampoo, haircut, and dressing.' Across the country, the writer further observed, 'there are innumerable instances of girls in uniform, who have set up salons where their colleagues can have hair attention and beauty treatment'. The official proviso was that payment could only take the form of a present from one girl to another.[44] By October 1942, *Hairdresser and Beauty Trade* reported that members of the WAAF could have free haircutting and shampooing monthly at hairdressing shops being established on RAF stations for which airwomen skilled as hairdressers had been recruited.[45] In late 1942 the WVS in Gainsborough, Lincolnshire, set up a social club for young women who had been conscripted to work there in the munitions industry, and tried to make the building as attractive as possible: 'We have now purchased a hood dryer, and engaged a new hairdresser, a Mrs. Cook, who will take 50% of the taking and hand over 50% as we shall have all overhead charges to pay for, including heating, electricity, gas, towels, etc.' This 'Liberty Club', with its 'very nicely fitted up bathroom', 'excellent cubicle for hairdressing, with basin, geyser, electric dryer, etc.' and 'a room for setting and waving etc.', in the words of the WVS County Organiser who inspected it, reveals the importance that women of all ages – most WVS members were middle aged and older – attached to appearances, and to conveniences that would allow women a certain kind of self-respect.[46]

Britain's allies also recognised the need to provide hairdressing services to women in uniform. At an American Nurses Club in 1942, a ladies' hairdressing salon was installed. It was staffed by skilled civilian hairdressers recruited in Great Britain. 'All the salons are properly equipped and vary in size according to the size and needs of the individual club', according to one writer.[47] Some military authorities were certainly aware that

Wynfryed Susan Williams pictured in 1944 when she was a plotter with the Royal Observer Corps attached to Fighter Command in Exeter. The photographs were taken to send to a boyfriend on active service in Ceylon. Above shows her hair when off-duty; below how it was brushed back when in uniform, though then it would have to be above her collar

attractive grooming was a major concern for women in uniform. In Canada the women's branches of the forces routinely provided their own hairdressers. Cecil Gill, who was at one time with the well-known house of Louis and Bernard in Manchester and for fifteen years was proprietor of a beauty salon in Toronto, had been made sergeant hairdresser in the Royal Canadian Air Force. He was put in charge of hairdressing at an RCAF (Women's Division) Department where he designed 'suitable service styles for the girls, with due regard for simplicity and smartness'.[48]

✂ ✂ ✂ ✂

The realities of wartime strongly favoured shorter, and somewhat simpler hairstyles. Hair had to be kept tidy and above the collar when worn with a uniform; it had to be off the face and above the shoulder for safety reasons in munitions and other war industries; and, for all women, shorter hair was easier to wash and keep hygienically free of lice, dandruff, and other hair and head problems. 'At present page boy bobs and masses of artificial curls are common and give the wearer considerable trouble when worn with the service hat, or "cheese cutter"', noted *Hairdresser and Beauty Trade* in November 1941.[49] The disappearance of a wide range of haircare supplies further encouraged change. Hairdressers' best strategic business decision by far was to promote a new, short hairstyle. Shorter hair could help improve their increasingly permless business, do away with the need for many hairpins, and ease the shampoo shortage. It benefitted servicewomen by readily meeting military dress codes, and for all women it was relatively easy to care for. Short hairdressing also became patriotic.

The new hairstyle of choice was the Liberty Cut. 'Goodbye to the Greta Garbo raggle-taggle locks to the shoulder,' trumpeted one fashion writer in May 1942, 'they never did make you look your best, even if you think they did. There is today a new haircut called the Liberty Cut, and your own hairdresser can do it for you.'[50] It was a short cut that could be styled in many different ways to fit in with the 'above the collar' dictates of the military and yet – at times – be quite attractive. On 10 April 1942, *The Times*, under the heading 'War-time Hairdressing for Women', reported on a trade meeting at the May Fair Hotel introducing the Liberty Cut. Women were being urged, it reported, to adopt short styles 'in the interests of hygiene and as assistance in the spread of possible serious epidemics', and added that the style was devised by the Guild of Hairdressers to meet the demands of those in factory or civilian life who needed to wash and set their hair themselves. The name of the cut was clever, referring both to the objectives of the war and the freedom of styles the cut was alleged to make possible.[51]

Leading hairdressers advertised the style heavily. They emphasised to reluctant colleagues both the artistry and the profitability of the new cut, and reminded them that they were 'doing a national service by cutting hair shorter'.[52] 'Make full use of the opportunities presented to you by the introduction of the Cut, but for goodness sake don't kill the goose that lays the golden egg', remonstrated one editorial in 1942.[53] Industry leaders also enlisted the support of the fashion press, sought the endorsement of senior Services personnel, and pitched their product directly to the women of Britain through radio. In April 1942, the BBC featured a programme advocating the Liberty

Cut, with Mr E L Gifford, of Truefit & Hill Ltd of Bond Street, London, speaking as its advocate.[54] When asked if a woman's local hairdresser would know about the cut and how to do it, Gifford replied that 'we've sent the technical details of the Liberty Cut to most hairdressers throughout the country, and they have appeared in all the trade papers', and noted that the response had been 500% more than for any hair fashion they had ever advertised before.[55] Business need and military necessity had found powerful common cause.

A beauty expert for one of the London magazines, Mary Embrey, was interviewed by the BBC for its series 'Women at War' in 1942 and supported the Liberty Cut on the highest possible authority – what she called the 'high ups' of each of the three Services, the WRNS, ATS, and WAAF. According to her, 'all were agreed on one point ... the unsuitability of the long bob when the wearer was in uniform ... unsuitable because it looked untidy under a service cap, because it was unhygienic, and because it detracted from the smartness of a girl's appearance.'[56] The main target audience for the Liberty Cut, women in uniform, was huge. It included civilian service organisations like the

WVS, nurses, and ambulance and bus drivers, as well as to women in all three military services. But Embrey, as a style journalist – no doubt to the delight of the hairdressing profession – cast the case for this short style even more broadly. She suggested that it could be worn beautifully by many ages and faces and could be 'adapted with equal ease to the charm of youth and to give poise and sophistication to the mature'. [57] The cut could be set in many styles, needed less attention than longer or more complex styles, required a fine cut only every

Gwendoline Batchelor of Coventry in 1942. High-piled curls were a popular look for wartime dances

Roma Gallop, a proud WAAF with a Liberty cut
Picture courtesy Alison and Trevor Hancock

three months, and could be well cared for at home by any woman. However, as was common in most fashion magazines, the fairly curly style illustrated in her article would likely have been beyond most women who lacked the time to visit their favourite hairdresser and the means to pay for his or her services.

Another beauty columnist linked fashion and practicality. 'Long hair is out-of-date', she said; 'spend something on the new Liberty cut, and save on hairpins which are very hard to get. Remember that a good hair cut is always an investment, and perms are difficult and very expensive.' She concluded with a salvo in favour of Home Front initiative: 'We had come to rely too much on the hairdresser and now we've got to rely on our own brushes and combs, and our fingertips.'[58] Women in wartime were unusually busy – some with paid employment (and in wartime there were a lot more of them), others as volunteers, housewives contending with long queues and rationing and other domestic inconveniences. Consequently, since women often did not have time to visit a hairdresser, home hair care started to be endorsed and declared practicable by beauty writers, with short hair having obvious advantages.[59] Vigorous hair-brushing was thought to improve hair's health and delay the need to wash it. 'If the hair is well brushed nightly with a clean brush it remains quite clean even after several weeks', testified a factory worker interviewed on the BBC in February 1943. More pragmatically, on the same programme short hair was endorsed by a doctor as a deterrent to lice or even more serious medical conditions: 'In the event of typhus or any other epidemic of that kind, it would be the greatest help to doctors in combating it if everyone – men and women – kept their hair as short as possible.'[60]

✂ ✂ ✂ ✂

Women throughout Britain, as civilians or members of the Forces, all faced constraints in dealing with their hair. Simple hair-washing at home could sometimes be difficult. Hot water was troublesome when fuel was not to be wasted or was even unavailable. When bombs burst watermains, water itself became a serious issue. Visits to the hairdresser were already for many women a cherished luxury, not least because hot water was cumbersome to come by in a great many homes even before the war, including in many country houses. When the servants who had heated and carried water in large houses left for war work, hair-washing might become every bit as tedious for a member of the gentry as it was for her working-class counterpart. Shampoo became ever scarcer and women relied on shredded soap boiled in water, ordinary laundry soap like Persil or Rinso,[61] men's shaving soap (which remained unrationed), and the longstanding, generations-old stratagem of dry shampoo. One of the discoveries during the recent renovations of Horace Walpole's house, Strawberry Hill in Twickenham (it is currently on display there) was a packet of soapless shampoo from 1943. 'Oatine', as it was called, had been licensed by the Ministry of Food, contained edible material and, it was claimed, 'produces wonderful high lights and glints in the hair, and gives new life, beauty and luster to even dull or faded hair' – the language of advertising changes little over the years. Talc, household starch, or orris root was sprinkled on the head, left for a few minutes, and then vigorously brushed out to remove oil and dirt. No wonder, then, that a bottle of Drene (a pre-war soapless shampoo) brought from abroad by a relative or a beau would probably have been repaid with a grateful kiss, hoarded, and eked out over months. Even famous role-models had to make compromises about their haircare. Marlene Dietrich, for example, when travelling to entertain the troops, took with her three months' worth of cosmetics, labelled in huge letters for dressing by torchlight, and she had had her hair soap specially made to lather in practically no water.[62]

Hair assumed for many woman enormous importance in wartime. Here was a rare area where 'Make Do and Mend' could serve attractiveness and self-esteem. A good hairdo bolstered a woman's morale. For at least a few, great hair was valuable enough to take risks for. One woman recalled that she had a perm during the war that was a frightening experience. She reported that her hair had just been rolled into a great overhead machine to begin the perming process when the air raid signal went off. She decided to stay put; and, after signing a form accepting personal responsibility, thought to herself, 'the chances of my being bombed are very much less than that of my hair being ruined'. She subsequently reflected that it 'was the last perm of that calibre I ever had!'[63] In 1940 a Mass Observation researcher asked at a beauty shop in Peckham if women feared having perms lest they were caught under electricity in a raid and was told emphatically NO.[64]

On the eve of the Blitz, one Mass Observer found that almost everyone, of every age and class, took pride in her hair.[65] But achieving off-duty glitz or even ordinary respectability became a challenge. Girls had great trouble finding bobby pins, usually known by their brand name as Kirby grips. One day in 1943 the manager of a government office, perhaps himself the father of daughters, released his female staff early because there was

Grips were an indispensable aid to a good hairstyle,
but were in short supply during the war

a rumour that the then very rare hair-grips were available in town.[66] One man recalled that his mother would pay him and his brother a penny for every Kirby grip they could find. Soon, as clever children will, he and his brother 'saw the good sense of buying them by the packet to sell to her individually every time she ran out'.[67] A nurse in a Liverpool hospital recalled being 'absolutely heartbroken when her box of hairgrips fell on the floor', while an eighteen-year old Ilford waitress one day received as a tip a packet of hairclips 'for your lovely hair'.[68]

Advertising, public and private, told women that 'Your Duty is your beauty',[69] and there is lots of evidence that British women (at least of marriageable age) did their best to comply. Substitute hairpins, often made of cheap plastic or soft steel, were deemed much inferior; they didn't spring back to their original shape and constantly fell out. Even more important was the lack of combs. Pre-war products, often made of what today would be labeled 'endangered' species like tortoiseshell, had disappeared from store shelves. Purchase taxes, introduced in October 1940, added insult to injury: hairnets, hairpins, and curlers attracted a 33 percent tax (in contrast to 16 percent for most garments and footwear). From October 1942 coupons were needed to purchase towels, further explaining why women often needed to take theirs with them to the hairdresser. Ingenuity was a wartime virtue. A few women received combs made of aircraft aluminum; others got combs of poor materials, still others from prisoners of war who had carved them and then traded them for a few cigarettes or other comforts. One desperate young Land Girl cycled several miles to obtain her solitary comb, which was 'large and green, resembling a garden rake'.[70] When basic utensils were so scarce, it was no wonder that many beauty experts and public officials took the time to admonish women about the hygiene dangers of sharing haircare implements.[71]

✂ ✂ ✂ ✂

Wartime demanded flexibility, including changes to what women placed or omitted to place on their hair. Pretty hats were an early casualty of war. According to one report in 1942, the President of the Board of Trade, recognising that hats were becoming scarce, wrote to the Archbishop of Canterbury asking him to announce that church attendance without a hat was not improper.[72] As one author put it: 'Before the war no well-dressed woman went out without a hat but within a few months to wear one almost became regarded as a sign of unpatriotic frivolity.'[73] This was only partly true. On many heads patriotism was signalled by touches of military style, with headgear styled to closely resemble military caps. Other hats sported military symbols, a badge or pin in remembrance of a friend or relative, or simply to show solidarity with the boys. As rationing began to pinch, a military look gave an air of authority to an outfit necessarily of slim cut and sparse and disciplined in trim. A smart hat, at least in the hands of the skilled milliners photographed by the great society photographer, Cecil Beaton, could even make 'utility' clothing look glamorous.[74]

The government at one point tried to treat hats as an unnecessary luxury, even making a misguided attempt to suppress the historic Luton hatmakers in 1942 (irate hatmakers, armed with scissors and hatpins, marched on Whitehall).[75] But it was really supply shortages, in the end, that constrained the industry. Hats remained unrationed but raw materials quickly dried up: straw from Italy, braid and velour from Austria or Switzerland, and feathers and furs from even more exotic places. Two plain, wool felt hat designs were authorised as 'utility' wear (and even the authorities appeared not to expect women would like them much); any others were uncontrolled. Women with fine bits and bobs of dressmaking trimmings hidden in their closets or work-baskets could hire a clever milliner to update their headwear. Others used scraps of pre-war fabric to create their own, sometimes eccentric, headgear.[76] Part of the 'Make Do and Mend' culture included instructions on how to update headgear in inexpensive ways that took a modicum of special skill. One advertisement encouraged women to add gay little bows to their plain felt hats by using very small lengths of ribbon cunningly disguised to look like something much more lavish.[77]

Jane and Judy Milliners, in a fashionable London locale (Wilton Place, SW1), boasted of the magic they could work with a man's disued silk hat.[78] Most women adopted simpler solutions – notably wearing their own old hats for years.

For many women as the war went on, headwear was a necessity for most of their waking hours: if they worked in the military (the Naval forage cap was considered especially smart); in ancillary roles as members of the ATS (the organisation the young Princess Elizabeth joined); or in munitions industries where hair covering was essential for safety reasons. Military caps may have varied but rules about how to wear the hair under the hat – clean, tidy and off the collar – were reasonably straightforward. In 1942 the *Book of the WAAF* added more practical advice. It advised an expert haircut to avoid elaborate hair settings; washing the hair once a week with soft green soap boiled up in water; and never using another woman's comb, to avoid dandruff.[79] 'I wore my hair long and rolled it round a piece of tape just to sit nicely round my cap with my hair off my shoulders as we all had to do', recalled one veteran.[80] Another had less luck with military authority. Before an inspection, a WRNS member had carefully used some of her small wage to have her hair cut, only to be told by the commanding officer that it was not short enough! So it was back to the hairdresser to have a bit more taken off, a significant expense on her small pay.[81] Canadian authorities enforced similar prohibitions on hair below the collars and no elaborate hairdos but, fearing a backlash, one RCAF recruitment film assured the viewer that hair could be beautiful and still meet regulations.[82] Enforcement of standards was flexible for some. A beautiful photograph of Princess Elizabeth in 1943, in uniform as honorary colonel of the Grenadier Guards, shows her lovely hair almost grazing her collar top. But then her regimental badge was a diamond brooch given to her by the officers and men.[83]

Away from work regulations, hatlessness became common. Photos of women in public in 1939 show most with hats; in such photos from 1945 hats are much less commonly worn, and then mostly by older women. And for most women, a headscarf, either casually tied beneath the chin or elaborately pleated or folded, turban style, became a part of everyday life. Certainly it was more practical when riding a bicycle, walking, and standing in endless queues in all weathers. The turban or headscarf became ubiquitous, and it was sometimes given a little pizzazz by a pair of sunglasses, not themselves a necessity in the British climate, but providing a look that could lend a little glamour to the wearer. Government authorities, too, tried to make hair coverings in regulated workplaces look a little less utilitarian and convey an appealing fashion statement. Women were sceptical and a few were defiant, although most conformed in the interests of avoiding scalping in a factory with many moving parts. One woman who did not conform came to grief in a munitions plant in Croydon on 5 November 1942. According to another woman who worked there, 'Rachel Thurgood, one of our new turners, going behind one of the lathes got her hair entangled with a revolving rod of metal'. The lathe was quickly turned off and her hair cut free but 'it had taken the greater part of the hair off one side of her head and also left a completely bald patch about the size of a 5 shilling piece just above her forehead'. Her workmates, it seems, were not particularly sympathetic. 'Actually, we are not very surprised that there has been an accident as Rachel has obstinately refused to tie her hair up in a scarf and only wore a stupid little chenille fishnet which was no protection at all. She has now caused retribution to fall on all the machine operators as the decree has gone forth that we are all to wear the hateful khaki convict hats with a peak. And pretty good frights they looked today, even the young and pretty ones.'[84] According to a BBC programme, in 1941 there had been 179 accidents due to hair getting tangled up in drills and spindles.[85]

The headscarf was practical headgear designed for convenience, often concealing what a woman did not care to have revealed, such as curlers or unwashed hair. One woman recalled: 'I can well remember running down the lane to catch the 6.20 a.m. train, munching a dried egg sandwich, with my hair in curlers but tucked under the triangular scarf – "turban" which was quite the vogue then.' 'We used to wear them all the time', another woman commented, 'because in the war we had to go to work at 8 o'clock in the morning and sometimes we didn't finish till 8 at night – if there was any special work on we used to have to stay till a particular batch had gone through so you didn't always have time play around with your hair.'[86]

Land Girls endured even more beauty challenges that most women. Many were conscripts who had never been away from their inner-city homes, and they now worked hard to grow Britain's food. Ever resourceful, they found ways to look after their hair even when working in the cold and muck. Some used coiled scarves over their heads to roll their hair over and covered it with the ubiquitous headscarf. When scarves were too dear, others bought surgical slings (which were unrationed) at a chemist's to achieve a similar look or used the top of old stockings to the same effect. Sometimes Land Girls who did not adequately cover their locks were horrified to find

Gladys Carney from Gosforth, aged 18, in 1944 when she joined the Land Army and was stationed at Haydon Bridge near Hexham. The secret of her hairstyle, she said, was to cut the top off a lisle stocking and roll it up, using it as a pad to roll the hair around

that thistledown turned their young heads prematurely grey or filled them with chaff when working in a farmer's field.[87] Worse, girls who had left a fashionable little bang or roll exposed at the front of their hair might find it bleached by the chemical spray used in orchards.

We cannot know the full weight of British women's efforts to achieve good-looking hair with Hollywood glamour. But we do know that even the government came to recognise that looking good was a key part of morale and that a fetching hairdo in a pinched, grim world was no small thing. We also know that many of the women who worked so hard to put on a good face – and present a good head of hair—were eager to find sweethearts, many of whom would be far different from the men they had known as youngsters. War brought not only rationing but also a great deal of freedom to young women, as well as higher wages than they or their older sisters had ever known. Who knows what comfort a small photo of a Hollywood look-alike in the jacket pocket of a battledress may have given a young soldier? Subsequent British and American films have made this link to home very significant indeed – and it probably was.

Women worked hard to achieve glamour, or at least decency. One woman remembers having 100 pipe cleaners in her hair – they took the place of curlers – worn under her headscarf all day, which she then painstakingly removed one by one and wound each curl around her finger. 'I was very proud of my curls!' she recalled years later.[88] A more common style adopted by many long-haired British women was to roll straight hair into arrangements such as those described by beauty columnist Ursula Bloom in 1942. 'Hair is easier to manage dressed in long upward sweeps and tucked into neat rolls', she advised. 'Learn to shape a roll properly. Brush straight up with a spot of brilliantine, then curl round a tail comb, pin one end securely, and then train the other end to come towards the face almost like a curl. Fashion with invisible pins.'[89] Another approach was what was sometimes called the Victory Roll, which involved hair rolled up tightly around the head, sometimes with a large curl formed at the front. However their hair was dressed, beautifully coiffed women on dance floors were wooed by men in uniform, from home and abroad. Some became war brides, destined to spend much of their lives in foreign lands or follow their husbands all over Britain. Others still became unwed mothers, sometimes of dark-skinned half-American children. For many, war claimed the lives of fiancés and new husbands. Few, one imagines, ended up with much in the way of Hollywood glamour.

Some young girls, often taking their first job in wartime, took a while to come to grips with their hair and the style that best suited them. One fifteen-year old copied the adult fashion of snoods. They were ornamental pouch-like nets to hold long hair at the back of the head, quite common in the nineteenth century but restored to fashionability by Parisian standards and by Vivien Leigh's appearance wearing one in *Gone with the Wind*. For some factory officials, the most successful and safe hair covering was a snood with a peaked cap at the front, though many women, it was thought, refused to cover completely their alluring forehead curls.[90] Some women had a variety of coloured versions but one teenager chose a simple hairnet. 'It was a quick and easy way of keeping hair tidy, but I was persuaded out of this by my family who said I looked like an "old woman" (I did). Then I chose a page boy, an easy style copied from a film star by finger rolling the hair and fixing it with Kirby grips ... Curly hair ruled out other experiments except bangs or leaving one side falling over my face à la Veronica Lake.'[91] For other youngsters, wartime, even evacuation, could mean a welcome reprieve from their mothers' relentless efforts to turn their straight-haired daughters into a curly-topped Shirley Temple, the child film star. For many children of the 1930s and 1940s, a neat short bob was popular and fuss-free, with, perhaps, a barrette or hair-slide on one side. For other little girls longer, straight hair with an Alice band and sometimes a fringe was an easy choice. Naomi Mitchison, who was able to shed her long hair before the war began, recalled it was a nuisance and she was 'always losing hairpins' from her upswept hairstyle.[92]

For older girls at boarding schools, wartime brought more complex sartorial aspirations, even if neither mum nor a hairdresser was close to hand. Reminiscing in 2001 for Mass Observation, one woman recalled that all the girls wanted to resemble the heroines of *Picturegoer* magazine such as Margaret Lockwood, Veronica Lake or Patricia Roc, but that over the course of the term the most ambitious hairdos began to deteriorate – unless one had naturally curly or wavy hair. Perms done in the holidays became ever frizzier and limper during term, while a few girls struggled with curlers and corrugated wave-clips. Managing one's hair was a crucial part of growing up. The girls washed their hair themselves (a new experience for this informant), and then dried it in front of one of the few gas fires, in pairs, on a rota basis, the latter a delightful chance for shared confidences with a congenial fellow student. As with all schools, not all learning took place in the classroom. Former students, no older than their early twenties, might return for Old Girls' Day with peroxide bleached locks, a source of shock and envy.[93]

While high wages for women in wartime meant solid returns for some hairdressers, photographs from the Home Front show many with dowdy headscarves and sometimes even worse hats. The famous 'Make Do and Mend' did not always work, as Gladys Langford, a particularly acerbic London diarist, noted in January 1945. 'She [Miss McKeeves] is middle-aged, musty smelling, and wears a carroty "switch" of hair held in place with a greasy green ribbon, and the "switch" contradicts the iron-grey of her eyebrows.'[94] Elsewhere she noted sad-looking wigs and grubby rolls for upswept hair which, one presumes, in wartime their owners were in no position to replace. More generally, she noted that the new hairstyles were a serious impediment for fellow concert-goers. 'A new style of hair-dressing is becoming popular among women. It is very artificial – the front hair is apparently scragged up over a huge pad several inches above the scalp so the person is a pest in a picture house or theatre, no one sitting behind can see a thing.'[95] This affront to Gladys, an inveterate theatre- and cinema-goer, was a variant on the Liberty Roll, the long-haired response to the commercial patriotism of the Liberty Cut. It was high and rolled up on top, and also rolled up from the neck to meet the requirements of uniform dress.

Women who had to perform in public were bound to be hair conscious. One daughter of a singer reported that her mother's hair had turned bright orange after a henna rinse. She also noted that for women in the public eye, long hair was very important and that leaving it grey was not an option.[96] Some patriotic articles declared that appearances were not important – but clearly they were. Well-cared-for long hair and a slash of red lipstick made a woman look better, and, it was thought, made those around her (men in particular) feel more buoyant and optimistic, which of course was deemed vital to the war effort.[97]

When the Allies eventually won the war, everyone cheered this victory, not least women and their hairdressers. In 1945 the magazine *Queen* recognised that the wartime Freedom or Liberty cut was still in vogue but suspected that most women yearned for post-war lives free of uniforms and mandatory off-the-collar hair and unwelcome restraints. No sooner had peace been declared than the magazine began advocating longer hair, the addition of switches, and the glamour of elaborate upswept hair, sometimes with elegant topknots, none of which would have been compatible with wartime headgear.[98] In one post-war photo of women in a queue, almost all of them hatless, rather dowdy looking, and lacking posh hairdos, there stands Margaret Roberts, later Thatcher, wearing a flamboyant, attention-demanding hat – in later years to be replaced by her helmet of hair.[99] Hair – and whatever else might be on a woman's head – has always made a statement.

May Day Festival with lively post-war hair, late 1940s Ymir, British Columbia
Picture courtesy Ymir Arts and Museum Society

References

1   Ann Seymour, *Woman and Beauty*, March 1936, 52.

2   A bandbox was decorated box in which millinery was kept. In casual parlance the term came to be used to denote something very neat and smart.

3   *Woman and Beauty*, September 1940, 20.

4   *Woman and Beauty*, January 1941, 22-23.

5   Ann Seymour, 'Newest Ways to Do Your Hair', *Woman and Beauty*, June 1931, 52.

6   Bloomfield, Gary L; Shain, Stacey L *Duty, Honor, Applause: America's Entertainers in World War II* (2004), p. 409 as quoted in http:// en.wikipedia/Veronica_Lake.

7   Mass Observation Archive (University of Sussex), Topic Collection 18, Box 1, Folder 1/F.

8   Martin Pugh, *'We Danced all Night': A Social History of Britain Between the Wars* (London: Bodley Head, 2008), p. 229.

9   H Llewelyn Smith ed., *The New Survey of London Life and Labour* (Vol. IX) (London: P S Kim & Son, 1935) p. 8.

10 Langhamer, *Women's Leisure in England, 1920-1960* (Manchester: Manchester UP, 2000), p. 59.

11 *Hairdresser and Beauty Trade*, 27 June 1941, 5.

12 *Hairdresser and Beauty Trade,* 21 November 1941, 12.

13 *Hairdresser and Beauty Trade,* 28 March 1941, 10.

14 Norman Longmate, *How We lived Then: A History of Everyday Life During the Second World War* (London: Hutchinson, 1971), p. 273.

15 *Hairdresser and Beauty Trade,* 6 February 1942, 9.

16 *Hairdresser and Beauty Trade,* 7 March 1941, 5.

17 Mass Observation Archive (University of Sussex), Directive, Personal Appearance, April 1939, Nella Last.

18 Carolyn Hall, *The Forties in Vogue* (London: Octopus Books, 1985) p. 8.

19 Longmate, *How We Lived Then*, p. 274.

20 *Surrey Advertiser,* 19 October 1940, 8.

21 *The Times*, 14 January 1943, 2.

22   Imperial War Museum, Photographic Collection, D 18217.

23   *Woman's Own,* 2 August 1941, 13.

24   *Woman's Own,* 22 August 1941, 6.

25   Longmate, *How We Lived Then*, p. 274.

26   As quoted in Longmate, *How We Lived Then*, p. 275.

27   Carolyn Cox, *Good Hair Days: A History of British Hairstyling* (London: Quartet Books, 1999), pp. 149-50.

28   Hall, *The Forties in Vogue*, 37.

29   *Hairdresser and Beauty Trade*, 19 December 1941, 12.

30   *Hairdresser and Beauty Trade*, 4 September 1942, 5.

31   *Hairdresser and Beauty Trade*, 11 September 1942, 16.

32   *Hairdresser and Beauty Trade*, 24 October 1941, 6.

33   *WVS Bulletin*, no. 7, May 1940, 11.

34   *Hairdresser and Beauty Trade,* 24 July 1942, 18.

35   Maggie Wood, *We Wore What We'd Got: Women's Clothes in World War II* (Warwick: Warwickshire County Council), p. 64.

36   *The Times*, 19 July 1942, 6.

37   *Hairdresser and Beauty Trade,* 21 February 1941, 5.

38   *Hairdresser and Beauty Trade*, 21 February 1941, 5 and 24 July 1942, 18.

39   *Hairdresser and Beauty Trade,* 24 October 1941, 6.

40   Imperial War Museum, Photographic Collection, D 15355.

41   *Hairdresser and Beauty Trade*, 23 January 1942, 6.

42   Maureen Wells, *Entertaining Eric: Letters from the Home Front, 1941-44* (London: Imperial War Museum, 1988), p. 77.

43   *Hairdresser and Beauty Trade*, 24 July 1942, 4

44   *Hairdressing and Beauty Trade*, 24 October 1941, 4.

45   *Hairdresser and Beauty Trade*, 23 October 1942, 7. The same report mentions that ATS salons were also being set up.

46   WRVS Archive & Heritage Collection, Devizes, Wiltshire, Narrative Reports from Gainsborough, Lincolnshire, later 1942, mainly 'Mrs. Ridley's Personal Report' of October 1942 and Mrs. Boys' report of 2 December 1942.

47   *Hairdresser and Beauty Trade*, 27 November 1942, 5.

48   Ruth Roach Pierson, *"They're Still Women after All": The Second World War and Canadian Womanhood* (Toronto: McClelland & Stewart, 1986), pp. 155-6; and (for Cecil Gill) *Hairdresser and Beauty Trade*, 11 January 1943, 9.

49   *Hairdresser and Beauty Trade*, 21 November 1941, 5.

50   *Woman's Own*, 29 May 1942.

51   *The Times*, 10 April 1942, 2.

52   *Hairdresser and Beauty Trade*, 24 April 1942, 11.

53   *Hairdresser and Beauty Trade*, 1 May 1942, 3.

54   *Hairdresser and Beauty Trade*, 24 April 1942, 4. The script for this broadcast is held in the BBC Written Archives, TX 24 February 1942. I am indebted to Erin O'Neil, Archives Researcher, for this reference.

55   BBC Written Archives, TX 26 April 1942.

56   Mary Embrey, 'The Liberty Cut', *Woman's Magazine*, July 1942, 15.

57   Ibid.

58   *Woman's Own*, 17 July 1942, 9.

59   Jean Barrie, 'Set it Yourself', *Everywoman*, October 1942, p. 49, and 'Hairdressing at Home', *Everywoman*, September 1943, pp. 22-23.

60   BBC Written Archives, *The World Goes By*, 24 February 1943.

61   Longmate, *How We Lived Then*, p. 275.

62   Hall, *The Forties in Vogue*, p. 52.

63   Wood, *"We Wore What We'd Got"*, p. 64.

64   Mass Observation Archive, (University of Sussex, MO) Topic Collection 18, Box 1, report dated 8 August 1940.

65   Ibid.

66   Longmate, *How We Lived Then*, p. 271.

67   Robin Bryer, *The History of Hair* (London: Philip Wilson Publishers, 2000), p. 122.

68   As quoted in Longmate, *How We Lived Then*, p. 273.

69   See Icilma Hair Powder advertisement reproduced in Jane Waller and Michael Vaughan, *Women in Wartime: The Role of Women's Magazines, 1939-45* (London: Macdonald Optima, 1987), p. 100.

70   Longmate, *How We Lived Then*, p. 273.

71 For example, *Woman's Own*, 29 May 1942, 10, and *The Book of the WAAF* (1942), 29.

72 Wood, *We Wore What We'd Got*, p. 65.

73 Longmate, *How We Lived Then*, p. 271.

74 Collin McDowell, *Forties and Fashion* (London: Bloomsbury, 1997,) see for example, pp. 86-7, 90.

75 As reported in Longmate, *How We Lived Then,* p. 272.

76 For an example see McDowell, *Forties Fashion*, p. 83.

77 Wood, *We Wore What We'd Got*, as reproduced, p. 67.

78 Wood, *We Wore What We'd Got*, p. 6.

79 *Book of the WAAF (1942*), p. 29.

80 Wood, *We Wore What We'd Got,* p. 43.

81 Mass Observation Archive (University of Sussex), Spring 2001 Directive, D 1697, woman, 77, living in a village north of Glasgow.

82 Pierson, *They're Still Women After All*, pp. 155-156.

83 Hall, *Forties in Vogue,* p. 21.

84 Sue Bruley, ed., *Working for Victory: A Diary of Life in a Second World War Factory* (Stroud, Gloucestershire: Sutton Publishing, 2001), p. 90.

85 BBC Written Archive, TX 24 February 1943.

86 Wood, *We Wore What We'd Got*, p. 45.

87 Wood, *We Wore What We'd Got*, p. 46.

88 Wood, *We Wore What We'd Got*, p. 45.

89 *Woman's Own*, 4 September 1942, 18.

90 'World Goes By', Script held at the BBC Written Archives, TX 26/04/1943.

91 Mass Observation Archive (University of Sussex): Reply to Spring 2001 Directive, J1890, married woman, 69, living in Hull.

92 Mass Observation Archive (University of Sussex), Directive, Personal Appearance, April 1939, Naomi Mitchison, #1534.

93 Mass Observation Archive (University of Sussex), Spring 2001 Directive, N1592, Retired Social worker, Hebden Bridge.

94 Diary of Gladys Langford, Manuscript in the Finsbury Library (Islington Local History Collection), 13 Jan 1945.

95 Gladys Langford, 10 March 1945.

96 Mass Observation Archive, University of Sussex, Spring 2001 Directive, C 1878.

97 See http://www.bbc.co.uk/history/british/ britain_wwtwo/women-at-war-04.shtml, 12/13/2008.

98 *Queen,* 16 May 1945, 36.

99 *Memory Lane: A Photographic Album of Daily Life in Britain 1930-1953* (London: J M Dent, 1980), Photograph 316.

5

ANYTHING GOES

'Combing through the London couture collection [of] hair styles, the evidence is that anything goes. It's the feminine look, OR the masculine look. It's curly curls, OR the smooth made with the slim-lines. There are hairstyles falling well over the face, and hair styles swept back to the nape; heads made to look oval and nut shape, and heads cut to look square cut to form boxes.' (Hairdressers' Journal, 29 January 1965, p. 3.)

Once the guns fell silent, blackout curtains were torn down, uniforms were abandoned, and families were reunited (albeit missing some loved ones), most women sought to get back to some kind of normality. It was a normality that was initially quite constrained. Austerity and scarcity outlasted the conflict; belt-tightening persisted and in some respects got worse; rationing did not end entirely until 1954; and enormous national debts would not be repaid until decades later. Post-war life was tough. The future was menacing; it held threats of nuclear war and/or Soviet domination. Young men faced mandatory National Service and younger children of both sexes (of whom there were many) learned about atomic shelters and 'duck and cover' routines meant to protect them from radiation. Women were all too well aware of these demons. But they also wanted a little 'self-care' and luxury in their daily lives.

That luxury could take the form of New Look fashions from Paris, with extravagant volumes of fabric in the longer skirts,

The Stars set the style: the cover of Hairdressers' Journal, September 1949
Picture courtesy London School of Fashion

closely corseted wasp waists, and high-heeled shoes – all of this was a whole different world from 'Make Do and Mend' and Utility garments, climbing into vans or tractors, and all things practical and multifunctional. In 1949, two years after the first New Look collection was introduced, 'the House of Dior accounted for a full 5 per cent of France's export sales, mostly made up of exquisite handmade dresses'.[1] Relatively few women could emulate the New Look at home, even if a handful like the nimble fingered Nella Last were capable of helping their friends reconstruct garments to achieve a dropped-waist longer skirt. But most women could emulate the hairstyles that went with the New Look.

These styles were feminine and formal and reflected a conventionality dictated, for the most part, by the fashion-forward elite, the mature and sophisticated, and their hairdressers. Mary Wingfield, in the January 1949 issue of *Woman's Magazine*, advised her readers that 'all smart women are having their hair cut short'. Hair, she noted, was nowhere more than six inches long and a 'great many of the new styles are actually a softer, prettier version of the "bob" that swept the country in the 'twenties. The length is the same at the back, but the added softness is in the cutting. The ends of the hair are tapered now, so that they turn up in tiny feathery curls.' [2] Wingfield knew that Mayfair stylists led the way in promoting these new styles and that small-town and suburban stylists and their clientele were more cautious. But she had confidence in what might now be called the 'trickle down' impact of elite culture and felt able to decree firmly that long, loose glamorous curls were no longer in fashion but that neater, more controlled haircuts were.[3]

Soon even the conservative and wary were taming their locks to a neat bun or French roll – a new look characterised by a tidiness and formality that had been found rarely in food queues or on canteen duty in wartime. 'Short', during these years, when applied to hair, was an elastic term and did not usually mean what it had meant in the 1920s. While embracing an element of practicality, the new version of short hair was intended convey glamour, even gravitas. As one writer put it in 1952, 'short hair on the over-forties can look most attractive, but it cannot afford to be windswept and curly – it must be moulded into dignified and sophisticated lines, but retaining the softness that is essential for the older face'.[4] A rigid rather than an exuberant or casual look was what women were told to favour. These, after all, were not easy-going times.

Hairstyles were closely linked to fashions in clothes and hats, and for several years these fashions were incompatible with long hair. Readers of women's magazines – and with the end of paper rationing these magazines had a wider distribution and more readers – encountered articles in which style leaders lauded long full skirts and dainty hats, both of which suited short hair.[5] The 're-introduction of long hairstyles,' according to one leading stylist in 1949, 'apart from the fact that the Craft doesn't want it, depends to some extent on the milliner and dress designer. And until the cap-shaped hat and long skirt are outmoded, long styles will not be needed – short hair and short skirts do not go well together.'[6] The following year he returned to the theme that the 'new look fashions, which brought with them the short cut, achieved sudden popularity only because they provided a welcome change from austerity fashions'.[7]

Of course, most women were not yet liberated from austerity. While the clientele of fashionable hairdressers adopted short styles with alacrity, the rest of the country was slower to adopt styles that required more frequent hair appointments and thus more money spent on hair care. But hairdressers had other strategies to nudge reluctant clients. In 1950, short hair's main weapon, said Joy Hathaway, who was a prominent voice in the field, was 'its practicality and comfort... The staidest client comes round to a fashion trend in the end'. She noted that 'older women especially are partial to the neat, tidy appearance of the short cut. The very youthful appearance shorter hair gives them is also a stronger argument. And this applies to a large age range, since everyone responds to a friend's flattering remark, "You look years younger".'[8] If this weighty consideration were not enough for a woman, Hathaway suggested that a hairdresser wait until summer to 'introduce to your clients a new style. It is the season when most women feel that they want to smarten up their appearance, especially their hair... The client will be looking for something practical, suitable for bathing and an open-air life.'[9]

On the whole Joy Hathaway's pronouncements were widely accepted. A great many women had their hair cut short. And all those short hairstyles – often augmented by a perm and a frequent shampoo and set – was a hairdresser's good fortune. As the editor of the *Hairdressers' Journal* enthused at the end of the fifties: 'Phenomenal is probably the best adjective by which to describe the post-war development of the hairdressing craft, not only in Great Britain, but throughout the civilized world'.[10] The post-war years were a time of strict 'rules' about deportment, demeanor, and appropriate social behaviour. There was the rule that a woman over 40 should not wear her hair below her chin line (unless worn up in a bun or the like). There was also the rule, particularly severely applied to the expanding number of teachers, librarians, and office

Margaret Carr of Stanley, County Durham, aged 13 in 1953 (top) and aged 15 in 1955 (bottom)

workers, that hair must always be tidy and carefully in place. Hairdressers and the manufacturers of hair products were among the chief beneficiaries and promoters of these rules. A survey of over 1600 women in 1949 revealed that well over half of all women between 16 and 60 had their hair cut at a hairdresser's and around a third went to the salon for permanent waves either regularly or occasionally.[11] It was only the oldest women who were relatively immune to the lure of the beauty salon, many of them presumably retaining their long, rarely cut Edwardian hairstyles.

A smart hairdo was relatively expensive, but it was an indulgence that was becoming increasingly routine. In July 1950 a 62-year-old Mass Observer who said she had previously never paid any special attention to her hair reported that she had had her first perm three or four years previously, 'and this has been followed by others and by [a] fortnightly "shampoo and set" which is now my regular routine and my only "personal" extravagance'.[12] That same summer, Barrow housewife Nella Last, who considered professional hair care her sole personal indulgence, spent three hours at her hairdresser having her yearly perm – this was in addition to her normal fortnightly visit. Mrs Last, a very careful budgeter, put aside money for her hairdressing expenses but was delighted on this occasion when her husband unexpectedly gave her money for her perm.[13] Less fortunate women lamented their inability to meet what had become widely accepted standards of hair care. 'If a shampoo and set didn't cost so much', said an unemployed 28-year-old, 'I should have my hair done much more often instead of doing it myself, and this I am sure would make me feel better groomed and I might dress with more care as a result'.[14] Hair-consciousness was on the rise, and few women were happy with the prospect that they might be out of step with or unable to conform to the standards of their time.

The shortest fashionable styles may have required only a haircut, but these cuts had to be frequent in order to keep hair looking smart, and the most striking of these cuts were set in tiny curls, a most profitable procedure for the hairdresser. They required careful cutting, sometimes a perm, gobs of setting lotion, lots and lots of pin curls and later rollers that felt like pinecones, and a combing out by the stylist followed by a good thick layer of lacquer. All this specialised care was a normal expectation. During the 1950s, on both sides of the Atlantic, the 'standing appointment' every week (or perhaps every second week) became a regular part of many women's routines. In the 1970s in Ontario I was friends with an Englishwoman in her forties who still maintained this practice, which she had adopted years before. She was a superb university teacher and researcher but apparently never washed or styled her own hair, and she barely altered her set, rigid hairstyle throughout her adulthood. Might memories of breaking ice in the washbasins of her frigid girls' boarding school have added to the appeal of a warm salon, I occasionally wondered?

The 1950s and early 1960s were glory years for hairdressers. A consequence of this briskness of business was a proliferation of salons. In the United States the number of beauty shops more than tripled between 1938 (the country was then still deep in the depression) and 1953; most of them were owner-operated small businesses.[15] In the middle of 1948, according to the author of *Ladies Hairdressing as a Career* (1965), there were 54,000 hairdressing employers in Britain, while fifteen years later there were almost 108,000, 'barely enough', he remarked, perhaps with slight exaggeration, 'to meet the needs of a society in which the entire female population, from the age of fifteen and below to the age of seventy-five and above, goes to the hairdresser on an average of once every ten days… Some young women think nothing of having their hair professionally tended as often as twice a week.' While this must have been at the extreme end of the spectrum – the author's mission was partly to show what a flourishing trade this was for a person to enter – the thrust of change was undeniable. 'One of the most striking features of this revival of hairdressing', he went

Isabel Mahone of County Durham in 1957

Isabel's sister, Nancy Mahone, in 1949, aged 16

on to claim, again, more or less truthfully, 'is its classless nature, which is quite new.' He wondered if in any past age 'comparable importance was attached to the arrangement and manipulation of hair by qualified experts.'[16]

In post-war England hairdressers were usually doing well, in part because the demand for their services was penetrating further into the lives of labouring people. Growing numbers of working-class women were among their customers – and the working class was easily the largest social class in the country and the one that had the potential to generate the greatest number of new customers. It was claimed – almost certainly correctly – that women of modest incomes were spending more on their personal appearance, including their hair, than ever before.[17] The English poor and near-poor of the early 1950s were better off than the poor of a generation before – the welfare state and full employment were partly responsible – and women of this class were now able to indulge in occasional mini-splurges on themselves. A visit to the hairdresser in a factory town was one way to put some sparkle into life, to be a bit celebratory, to mark a special occasion. In South Lancashire the annual Wakes week was traditionally the time for a seaside

Pat Maggs, top left, aged 18 and her sister Janice, top right, aged 20, pictured in 1958. Along with these other Coventry girls, they were entered as models in a local hairdressing competition

holiday, which, according to one observer in that county in August 1951, brought the 'usual rush of business to the salons' as women prepared to be festive; hairdressers in towns like Bolton reported that they had been 'rushed off their feet' on the eve of the holiday, though once a town's holiday week was over and savings were depleted hairdressers experienced a 'severe temporary slump'[18] (working-class patterns of spending were notoriously irregular). In December 1951 this correspondent reported on the organising of 'hairdo clubs' by Lancashire factory operatives. 'The mill girls pay one of their number a nominal sum of either a shilling or half a crown a week towards the club, and as the festive season draws nigh, they use the money they have saved on a perm. Members of the craft in busy industrial towns such as Ashton, Oldham, Rochdale, Bury and Bolton have not been slow to realise the potential clientele which might be developed as a result of what might be called this "perm as you earn" savings system and during the last two or three weeks quite a few salons have been busy catering for the requirements of the "girls from t'mills".[19]

Not all hairdressing occurred in salons. Women experimented with the new home hair perm kits, which were widely available from the late 1940s, even though they often smelled vile, had uneven results, and frequently sent users back to their stylists for a polished look. It was probably fairly common for a woman to perm her own hair but still go regularly to a professional to have it set, styled, and lacquered. The easier-to-use products coming on the market for perming, shampooing, lacquering, tinting, and colouring stimulated a do-it-yourself hair care revolution. A typical home hair-care adventure may have been something like this. 'Ettie came because we are perming each other's hair this weekend', wrote Alice Haines, a woman in her mid-thirties, one Saturday in 1945. 'Edna has lent us her drier, and we got through the first stage this evening, which is to thoroughly clean the hair.' On Sunday they 'got the hair permed up in Endura curlers and [had] dinner by 2 o'clock, which we thought quite good. Then they had to cook (these curlers) for six hours. The time flew. At ten past six Ettie's time was up, and I set her hair and dried it. Then at 8 o'clock it was my turn! I set my own hair. Very satisfactory perm so far.'[20] Home hair-care was facilitated by the increasing number of houses with inside bathrooms plentifully supplied with hot water (an obvious necessity) – hundreds of thousands of new homes were constructed in the 1950s – and such technological innovations as the aerosol can, the propellant of hairspray, which was essential to sustain the beehives and bouffants appearing from the mid-1950s.

Some hairdressing professionals worried that their livelihoods would be threatened by home hair-care products, but this alarm was unwarranted. With growing prosperity from the mid-1950s, there was money to go round. Wages were increasing; there were more possibilities for discretionary expenditures in working-class budgets; and more families were moving up to enjoy middle-class standards. So, overall, women continued to patronise hairdressers even as they took more active steps to manage their hair at home. Some professionals came to realise that the heavy expenditure on advertising by the manufacturers of hair-care products was actually to their advantage, for these advertisements helped to make women more hair-conscious and more sensitive to how they 'should' look, and thus more inclined to seek out the services of experts. Advertising helped, too, to make the colouring of hair more widely acceptable – 'You owe it to yourself', 'I'm worth it', 'Live life as a blonde' – but since colouring was almost always best done by a professional hairdresser, beauty salons and their proprietors continued to prosper.

Bouffant, 1960s

After the war the hairdressing industry was beginning to target a new market – teenagers. This trend was particularly pronounced in America. Lillian Blackstone, who owned a salon in Brooklyn, New York, was able to boast in 1948 that her entire business was teens, something that would have been unheard of a generation earlier. With a clientele made up of high school and college

The bouffant co-existed with wartime styles for many years. Right: Avril Morgan from Newcastle Upon Tyne, pictured in 1968

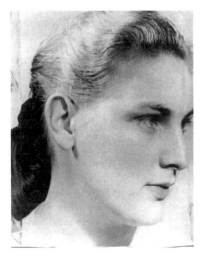

Marguerite Lowder of Morpeth pictured in the 1950s (top) after having her first perm; at age 17 in 1958 (right); and at age 20 in 1961 (bottom). She suffered a brain haemorrhage when she was 20 and had to have all her hair removed: when it grew back she wore it short

students, she advocated advertising in school newspapers to attract new beauty patrons.[21] In England a few years later, in 1954, the trade journal *Hair and Beauty* stressed the importance of the young client, 'the young Miss or Teenager. No emphasis is too strong to put on this type of business – after all, it is the business of tomorrow.'[22] If, as one source put it, the American beauty shop was 'Growing faster than the Dark Roots on a Platinum Blonde', teenage girls had a lot to do with it. By the 1950s they were spending unprecedented sums on hairstyles, cosmetics, and clothes. In 1956 Elaine Budd, beauty editor of *Seventeen* magazine, noted that the country's eight million teenagers had money of their own to spend – some four billion dollars of it.[23] Spending money, whether from parental allowances or part-time jobs, mostly went to support an adolescent's social life – dates, records, visits to snack-bars, clothes, cosmetics, and hair. Few school or college dances were complete without a trip to the hairdresser. If some teenage girls wore swinging, casual, low-maintenance ponytails, at least as many endured sleep disturbed by uncomfortable rollers, done to create the perfect hairstyle, quite often a stiff flipped-up hairdo well secured by hairspray. And the ponytail itself was often welded into elaborate 'updos' for special occasions.

While American culture was a powerful influence on Britain's youth, post-war austerity meant that the practical uptake of American fashions was constrained. American youth culture was fuelled primarily by wealth, of which Britain still had little. In the immediate post-war years, ready-made clothes were too expensive to be casually purchased, while home dressmaking was still the norm in many girls' homes (this was a near-universal skill at the time). Some of the most desirable clothes – notably blue jeans in women's sizes – were not widely available in Britain before the mid-1960s. Consequently, fashion-conscious teenagers turned to hair to make the best of their looks despite their often modest budgets. Some peroxide, a cheap perm, and sometimes a few colourful Woolworth's hair ornaments could make a working-class girl attractive to the lads – and make her appear older too. 'You get dates early if you manage to look older', commented one woman in her early teens to a social researcher.[24] Despite the slump in the Lancashire cotton industry in 1952 and the consequent cutbacks in working class expenditures, women workers, many of them young, were not inclined to neglect their hair; 'several hairdressers report that clients have told them they prefer to cut out visits to the cinema rather than cancel perm appointments', and home perms were being ever more widely adopted in the district.[25] Middle- and upper-middle-class teenagers were better able to spend money at salons, and their hairstyle choices usually reflected the sort of restrained glamour that their mothers favoured (who were also likely to pay their daughters' bills) at least as much as the assertiveness of American youth culture. 'Arthur of Baker Street' was that rare British hairdresser who especially courted a teenage clientele: in 1952 he converted the basement of his premises into an 'Under 21' salon with appropriate prices and advice.[26]

For the young, the hair culture of the early 1960s was still dominated by the backcombed edifices of the beehive or the bouffant – styles that could be either models of propriety or a bit outrageous if one's desire was to flaunt convention. These were hairdos often done at home. They were also sold to the well-heeled by the society hairdresser Raymond, widely known as Mr Teasy-Weasy for his heavily teased or backcombed styles. Raymond, a vigorous self-promoter, made himself and his styles household words, in part through

A business-like beehive with bow, mid-1960s

Picture courtesy Pat Reid

annual shows at the Café de Paris at which he unveiled his newest variations on the bouffant, such as the Champagne Bubble Cut. Backcombed styles became ubiquitous, partly because they could be done by anyone. They permitted – with the support of large quantities of hairspray – extravagant personal statements, such as those later celebrated in the stage play and film *Hairspray* (1988). This musical send-up of the bouffant continues to draw audiences in part, I think, because it is an engaging and hilarious take on young womanhood, and mocks the tyranny of fashion. In the early 1960s there were bouffants for everyone. There were permed, modestly bouffant styles for mature matrons and sleek, take-me-seriously versions for aspiring young professionals. The latter look could be found on virtually every woman pictured in my 1966 Canadian university yearbook and followed most of us into our first jobs.

Denise Bridle of Shirley, Southampton, in 1967: she took great pride in her beehive hairstyle

Hairdressers were busy people. Many were keen entrants into hairstyle competitions, where they used lashings of lacquer as well as feathers, jewels, and other sparkly gewgaws to create fantasy

Mandy Laming of Gosport, Hampshire, with her backcombed beehive hairstyle

styles meant to cement their reputations and demonstrate to the world that they were artists. Many British hairdressers

Sheila Chambers from Tyne and Wear in 1965, aged 16

became famous – Freddie French, Raymond, Trevor Sorbie, Joshua and Daniel Galvin and, of course, a young Vidal Sassoon. Sassoon, a keen competitor in the 1950s, described the 'competition fever' that gripped young stylists: 'In those days three or four hundred hairdressers would turn up to watch the competitors at work, despite the fact that the results – particularly the fantasy styling – might never be seen in public.'[27] Photographs from the time show lacquered monuments rising above a model's head that had little to do with either the model or her clothes. A futuristic boat might sit on a young woman's carefully coiffed head.

John Steinberg, later to become a celebrity stylist in Canada, has described the clientele he worked for in the early 1960s in a working class area of London, which was 'rather unromantically called Crouch End'. His clients were a varied group that included 'senior citizens, strippers, gangsters' girlfriends, art students from the Hornsey College of Art – and ladies of the night'.[28] Early-week specials lured seniors in for a cut, perm, shampoo and set, while later in the week, to the strains of modern jazz and lounge music, 'we imitated the styles of famous British pop stars, usually exaggerating them to keep the clientele happy'. Delivering this happiness might include radical haircuts for the arts students, 'provided it was teased afterwards', and flaming red or highly bleached blonde for prostitutes, either set in an updo or an exaggerated flip. 'As part of the fixed price they paid, they could return mid-week for a comb-out, which consisted of dismantling and reconstructing their "do" (which their customers were forbidden to touch)'. When they later returned for a full shampoo and removal of all the hairspray, which was a regular requirement, they were given 'a rinse in nail polish remover'![29] All this meant, among other things, that hats were worn less and less often in most social settings since a firm helmet of hair had usually replaced them.

✂ ✂ ✂ ✂

When I first visited England as a teenager in 1961 it was still definitely stuck in the 1950s – lots of rules that few of us flouted very much; proper jackets and ties for the boys, almost always skirts – often quite stiff ones – for the girls (we wanted to seem suitably grown up and not all that different from how our mothers looked); stiff underclothes and awkward garter belts for women; and of course stiff and carefully coiffed hair. When I returned to live in London in early 1967 it was – at least to me at the time – a different world. Rules were being jettisoned right, left and centre. Old norms were going up in flames. Style, especially in personal appearance, was undergoing a radical transformation. The term that was so often used to describe this time – the 'swinging' sixties – seemed apt, given the decidedly unswinging character of the 50s, despite a handful of mods and rockers and a few angry intellectuals.

Change came rapidly from the mid-1960s, mainly for a whole generation born at the end and just after the end of the Second World War, most of them members of the baby-boom generation. Their numbers and wealth created markets; and their rebellion against authority shook the status quo – and sometimes inspired their elders. The rebellion in hair was to change a whole industry and become a visible marker of the gulf between the young and the not so young. The year before Bob Dylan released the album with the song that was to become virtually the anthem of a generation – 'The Times They Are A'Changin'[30] – Vidal Sassoon developed the geometric cut that was to make his the most famous name in hairdressing. He also changed the direction of the industry. He updated the bob, pioneered the asymmetrical cut, and developed the five-point cut. All these styles depended on accurate and precise cutting, required no rollers, sets, or perms (though the latter was later used in some variations), and did not rely on being frozen into position with hairspray. 'I felt hair should swing along with fashion', Sassoon mused in his 1968 memoir *Sorry I Kept You Waiting, Madam*, adding that for him 1963 would 'always be the year of the happening' (a contemporary term for status-quo shifting events).[31] 'Women were liberated from weekly trips to the salon for a shampoo and set and backcombing their lacquered locks by Vidal Sassoon', noted the *Hairdressers' International Journal* in a 2007 supplement celebrating 125 years of the industry and their publication. He 'revolutionized the industry with his high impact, low maintenance cuts with more than a nod to the Flapper cuts of the 1920s'.[32] It was a very modern look. The hair felt free. With a good toss of the head it fell back in place. And it had the added advantage that it worked beautifully with the modern clothing of Mary Quant in London or the designer André Courrèges in Paris. Earlier stylists had sometimes emphasised the importance of a good cut but, unlike Sassoon, they usually meant it was a cut that readily accommodated several settings of rollers or pin curls for different looks. Sassoon's breakthrough was to encourage a more logical, functional relationship between the head and the hair on it. Some observers called this a modernism with links to the 'form follows function' aesthetic of the Bauhaus.

These sleek uncluttered styles were extremely appealing to young women, if sometimes startling for their companions. A Canadian anthropologist (born in 1951) remembers 'seeing my girlfriend in the five-point cut. I thought she was the strangest creature I had ever seen. Wisely, I kept this to myself. And I pretended not to notice when entire families would stop in the street and point at her as we passed. I grew to like the look. But it was the end of our relationship. She was suddenly worldly and sophisticated, and I was, just as suddenly, shambling and awkward and twelve. The Sassoon cut had transformed us both.'[33] An even more radical hair statement at this time was pioneered by Twiggy (Lesley Hornby), the gaunt teenager who was catapulted to stardom by a haircut. Her hair, a new interpretation of the severe 1920s Eton crop, was ultra short and pressed close to the head; it made her the 'face of 1966', according to the fashion editor of *Daily Express*, Deidre McSharry.[34] Her haircut was deceptively simple, reputedly having taken stylist Leonard Lewis of Mayfair and colourist Daniel Galvin a whole day to create.[35] (This was an era of celebrity hairdressers and their widely influential styles: Trevor Sorbie and his wedge cut, Toni and Guy, whose hairdressing business opened in London in 1963, John Frieda, and others created stylistic buzz in 60s' London – a buzz that did not take long to spread around the English-speaking world and find followers in countless communities.)

The fashionable heads of the later 1960s were sleek, shiny, mobile and chic – but they were not always free from artifice. For there was another revolution at play – a boom in wigs, postiche, wiglets, and hairpieces of all kinds. In contrast to past practice, flamboyance was key. Expensive supplementary human hair was a status symbol, and synthetic hair was often as blatantly false and eye-catching as costume jewellery. Part of the point of both was not just to wear a wig but to be known to be wearing a wig.[36] One could be a sexy platinum blonde on Saturday night and a demure brunette in the office on Monday morning. Falls (long partial wigs) of long European hair could be costly (as much as $600 US) but a similar synthetic product was affordable on a working girl's wages at around $10. Small hairpieces or wiglets were used to give a flirty special occasion look while packets of hair strands could be attached to create instant streaks without the cost and tedium of a more permanent process. So-called 'fun wigs' were widely worn to change one's image in an instant. The invention in Hong Kong of machine-made, washable nylon and acrylic wigs led to a flooding of the market and made the dream of being someone else for a few hours affordable, achievable, and fun. So many women enjoyed these new space age accoutrements (new products of the laboratory were welcomed) that, according to one estimate, a third of all European women wore what hairdressers termed a 'wig of convenience'[37] and the figure in North America, with its greater wealth and larger black population (long used to hair transformations), was probably higher. In India, where hair was commonly given up as part of religious rituals, the government set up a processing factory in Madras 1966 which, by the end of the 1960s, was reported to be turning out some 12,000 wigs a month.[38]

The embrace by the young of change and novelty, the rejection of conformity and the enthusiasm for playfulness are particularly evident in hair colouring. A combination of advertising and technical improvements made hair dyes increasingly acceptable – and desirable – in the post-war era. Hair colour is often the first thing that is noticed about a person's appearance. For centuries people have coloured their hair to draw attention to themselves or to project a certain image. In 1960 an article in the *Lancaster Guardian* suggested to women in that smallish northern city that they might have a little fun by trying rainbow colouring, 'the latest contribution which hair makeup has to offer the fashion scene'. For this effect, it reported, 'several "fantasy" colours can be included in the same coiffure – deep pink, flame, green, bright yellow. And there's no need to be afraid of what the boss or the neighbours will say during the week for the colours can be washed out quite easily!'[39] Spray-on glitter, another temporary enhancement, was already in use at this time.

The wonderful malleability of hair colour gave rise to a new hairdressing profession – the colourist. This new specialty developed from a combination of the virtually infinite range of colour combinations made available by the latest dyes and the increasing public prominence of the hairdresser's work on the fashion runway. Before the middle of the twentieth century most models prepared their own hair before a fashion shoot. But soon fashion designers asked for hair that mimicked the colours used to dye fabric, and thus hair was expected to match the clothes on display, and eye-popping colours were often the result. These trends then spread beyond the fashion stage and the practices of highlights, low-lights, and hair with two or three colours became a regular aspect of many women's habits of hair care. As someone once remarked, starting to bleach or colour one's hair is the beginning of a long-term and costly servitude to one's colourist. In 2007, a trade journal, *Focus on Pigments*, featured an article that estimated that annual worldwide spending on hair colourants was approaching $4 billion.[40] Colouring is yet another example of crossovers in fashion – from the runway and high society to the high street, and from kids experimenting with their identities to their mothers wanting to avoid looking frumpy.

All these generalisations fail to acknowledge one key development from the mid-1960s – many women started to let their hair grow long and sometimes did not patronise a hairdresser at all. Long hair, brushed but not 'done up', became one dominant style of the late 1960s and early 1970s. This was another way that youth displayed rebelliousness and claimed freedom from constraint. Long hair, freely flowing down a woman's back (if it was naturally straight), often falling well below her shoulders, was the antithesis of the approved fashions of recent years, the 'set', very orderly hairstyles. Young women's hair was no longer expected to have to endure such stiff, formal presentation. One woman who came of age at this time recalls the changes vividly. Hair, she thinks, 'really defined the mood of the time. People were just beginning to grasp that hair was a part of our identity, so why straighten it' – if you were a black American – 'or curl it or do anything but display it.' While young blacks might adopt Afros, 'white guys were letting their hair grow long, and girls were no longer using curlers or orange juice cans to straighten their hair, but were just letting their hair "do its thing".'[41] To be natural, in hair as in so much else, was seen in the years around 1970 as a very good thing.

The hippie rock musical, *Hair*, which premiered off Broadway in October 1967 and thereafter spread like wildfire on stages around the world, put into words these new and unprecedented ideals. Hair should be any way you want it to be. There was, too, a bias towards hair 'as long as God can grow it'. This was a pop-culture proclamation that made hair a key aspect of how a person showed himself or herself to the world. The best presentation of hair would be free of artifice, and uncontrolled except for plaiting, twisting or beading or, best of all, adorned with flowers. These were highly visible ways of making a statement in favour of freedom, rebellion, youth and love.[42]

It was not long before (let us call it) hippie hair influenced the mainstream of fashion. By the 1970s women in their millions were letting their hair grow long, sometimes ironing it if it was not straight enough for their taste. Liberated from perms, rollers, and hairspray, they could stay away from hairdressers for long periods, perhaps only making infrequent appointments for a trim every few months or to have a few streaks added that would take quite some time to grow out. Younger women – there were a lot of these baby boomers – found that long hair had much to recommend it. It was usually attractive, especially when better groomed than matted hippie hair. It was perfectly acceptable at the office or in other professional workplaces. It could easily be wound into an updo, if mood or circumstances called for change, or given waves by the now readily available and easy-to-use heated rollers. Moreover, the natural look was not only popular, it was also warmly endorsed by the makers of hair products, who now saw fit to extol the merits of their natural shampoos. And, from a business point of view, even if visits to hairdressers by the young ceased to be de rigueur, older women, many with increased wealth, continued to value their services, so the industry continued to prosper.

✄ ✄ ✄ ✄

One of the significant cultural crossovers has been between Britain's black community and her white population. A great many black women came to Britain from the Caribbean committed to English values – photographs of them arriving in Britain in the 1950s and 1960s, in careful, conservative dress and painstakingly coiffed hair, spoke of what they knew of the previously distant 'mother country'. In their first decade or so in Britain, Afro-Caribbean women tried assiduously to achieve 'good hair' – that is, hair that was smooth, sleek, and tidy, and thus very different from what nature had given them. This look was costly to achieve, both in time and hair products, but it conferred respectability and was widely regarded within the black community itself as the ideal of beauty. Justine Henderson recalled that, growing up black in the 1950s, 'you always knew that it was not a good thing to have nappy hair. You always straightened it. One of the first things you learned about taking care of your own hair was how to straighten it … I always knew once you washed your hair, until it was straightened, you put a scarf on it.'[43] This view was widely shared throughout the black diaspora; in America hair that appeared straight had long been approved of in the black community and was thought essential to getting any kind of professional employment. It was in the USA where products for straightening, growing, and managing black hair was the foundation of some black-owned businesses and widely credited for the creation of America's first female millionaire, Madam C J Walker. Walker advertised her hair growth and management products in black newspapers and magazines, set up a mail order business, initiated a hair-care training program, and developed the so-called 'shampoo-press-and-curl' method of hair straightening that became the foundation of the black beauty industry. All these developments were influential and in existence about four decades before black women emigrated to Britain in any numbers.[44]

The black immigrants to Britain who at first emulated the 'motherland' were finding their own distinctive style by the 1970s. And what style it was! It was a hirsute voice of pride, flamboyance, and affirmation – or perhaps just a small bit or joy and fun in a strange land where making a living and earning acceptance was often hard. Whatever was meant, Afro-Caribbean hair-care became a significant part of British coiffure, both in the salon and imported as hair-care products. At first, black women used products that were either homemade or developed by relatively small black-owned businesses. Wigs, extensions, and other hair pieces were also sourced primarily from within the black community. But soon enough, and perhaps inevitably, the mainstream hairdressing industry took notice. In February 1980 *Hairdressers' Journal* devoted a spread to what it called 'Afro Hair', though the styles pictured were hardly that. There was an intricate design of smooth coils for special occasions; a relaxed (chemically straightened) hairdo that had been set on rollers and shaped into a mainstream bouffant; and a somewhat more ethnically referential style in which the hair was slicked up to the top of the head, wreathed in a plaited coil and accentuated by a second (and presumably false) plait of hair threaded with ribbons.[45] Five years later, the same journal devoted a full issue to black hair, advising that 'hairdressers of the progressive mid-eighties can no longer afford to ignore one of the most rapidly expanding areas of their craft, and could continue to miss out on the potential clients they could attract if their working knowledge of Afro hair techniques was up to standard.'[46] Advice was offered on relaxers, hair treatments, and the use of tongs and hot rollers on black hair, which was often sensitive both because of its nature and the damage that had often been done to it by harsh chemicals and the over-use of hair extensions.

Here, then, was a new and important market. It did not take a degree in business administration to recognise that hair was critically important to black women and that, on average, they spent more time and money on their hair than did white women. After the 'fun wig' fad of the late 1960s, it is likely that only a minority of younger white women had a wig – but large numbers of black women owned a wardrobe of wigs and hair extensions. Black women were also much more likely to change their look regularly and were prepared to spend the money – lots of it – needed to achieve this.

The evidence of cultural crossovers in hair fashion is obvious from the 1970s. Approximations of black hair fashions were found on the heads of daring white women. For example, the Jheri curl and the California Curl were essentially chemically relaxed hair that maintained the curly textured look of natural Afro hair but simulated shiny, soft, tamed curls and resulted in a look widely imitated by non-black women. The latter adopted long loose perms that were allowed to dry naturally and were often scrunched up with a dab of gel to enhance the shine and curl – a strikingly similar look to the Jheri curl. Hair extensions, which were particularly popular with black women, became widespread in all segments of a hair-conscious world as women worried that their own tresses could not deliver the look they really wanted; and some white women yearned for the striking appearance that came from complex braiding, often ornamented with ribbons and beads, that was the heritage of women of African backgrounds. Conversely, there were non-black women who shared some of the characteristics of nappy hair and sought out effective techniques to tame it. Diane Simon, the kinky-haired daughter of straight-haired parents, so regretted her 'Jewish Frizz' and the stigma of being the 'the only one with frizzy curls in a class of twenty sleek-haired girls' that she eventually wrote a book about her own and other people's hair anguish.[47]

Black conceptions of beauty came to embrace a wide range of looks. The May/June 1986 issue of *Black Hair and Beauty* demonstrated just how far hair fashion had come from the smooth and managed propriety of the 1950s and early 1960s. One picture showed a conventional European bob that was pumped up with highlights applied to the front and pushed up into an edgy quiff. An Afro-punk style was adapted on untreated natural hair by cutting fan shapes across the top, cropping the hair very short on the back and sides with a 'V' shape shaved at the back, and then painted in to coordinate with the model's clothes (gold in this case). A spiky 'Egyptian' look was created with hair weaves, innovative cutting, and lots of hairspray and hair gloss.[48] There were, as well, lots of conventional big-hair looks that became common among women of all hair types and colours on both sides of the Atlantic in the wake of the wild popularity of such American television series as *Dallas* and *Dynasty* and the prominence of celebrities such as the singers, black-skinned Diana Ross and white Dolly Parton. Their looks required lots of care, wigs and extensions, and plenty of confidence. Big hair could convey a wide range of social messages – wealth, glamour, power, or trashy 'in your face' chutzpah.

Rather than imitate European coiffure – although lots of them did just that when they felt like it – black women by the 1970s (and a small minority before then) felt confident enough to do their hair their own way, as they liked; and many, following in the footsteps of Madame C J Walker, set up their own businesses to serve other black women and black men, as well as mixed race and white clients. Since then, salons have come to cater for a wide range of styles and ethnicities. Marlene, the Trinidadian owner of Camden Locks, a salon at the eponymous Locks in north-central London, specialises in 'Afro-Caribbean styles, European dreadlocks, highlights, relaxers and extensions' as well as body piercing and tattoos. Her clientele was in 2011 as diverse as the city in which she works and her background in hairdressing eclectic. Trained in Trinidad, she worked in the Harvey Nichols department store and in Camden Locks market before opening her own business around 2000.[49] Bridging the cultural and gender gaps in a racist and sexist world would always be a challenge, she admitted, but she loves what she does and deems it worthwhile. Her ethnically diverse clientele with their taste for dreadlocks, piercings, and tattoos are young, self-consciously fashionable, and perhaps employed in entertainment or artistic professions.

But what of the more typical black hair customer? The American comedian Chris Rock's documentary film, *Good Hair* (2009), provides ample evidence that the notion of 'good hair' as straight or gently waved and shiny still has immense popularity – and profitability. Inspired by his young daughter, who wished aloud for 'good hair', Rock's documentary focuses on the vast amount of money that black women are prepared to spend on gorgeous hair (an estimated $9 billion annually in the US) – hair that no-one is allowed to touch and hair that has to be carefully protected from rain.[50] One black receptionist, who was complimented on her 'freshly done, magazine-ready hairdo, which had been chemically straightened, tinted light brown, and augmented by shoulder-length human hair that had been tightly woven to her scalp', observed that to preserve this very costly hair-do she had trained her boyfriend not to touch her hair while they were making love.[51] A contrary view was expressed by Assante Infantry, a journalist who reviewed the film in a Canadian newspaper. 'I have great hair,' she said, 'What's not to love?' she said of her closely cropped natural style. 'It's weatherproof, takes two minutes to style, and is maintained by a $30, 30-minute haircut every six or so weeks.' But she did confess that she had not always appreciated her current style's beauty and simplicity and in elementary school had pestered her mother to get her hair chemically straightened, like most of her classmates, and subsequently had spent 14 years addicted to 'creamy crack', a common term for the compulsive use of hair-straightening chemicals.[52]

Black women in the English-speaking world now appear to be able to do whatever they want with their hair. Michelle Obama, the wife of the American president, in 2011 wore the smooth style that speaks of power and control, a look not unlike that adopted by many a corporate lawyer, but she left her young daughters' hair natural. In the US a woman's hair is often judged before her ideas, as the white-skinned Hillary Clinton sometimes observed, and her brown hair and headband have long been replaced by blonder tones and a style that is

Black women today are able to do whatever they want with their hair: foreground left to right: Adeola Ezekiel, Uki Francis, Juliet Olasiyan, Linda Isa Ashuma and Joy Ewujowoh

both serious (no fussy curls for her) and a colour light enough to stand out in a sea of tall men in their dark suits. In Canada, Michaelle Jean, the country's Governor General for five years (the Queen's representative and technically head of state) and a woman who is Haitian by birth, was not at all intimidated by her vice-regal role, presenting a smooth, disciplined head one day and an uninhibited natural Afro the next. After the devastating earthquake in Haiti and Jean's own appointment as a UN ambassador to that struggling country, her empathetic Afro was even more in evidence.

What do today's black women in Britain think? An inspection of the October/November 2011 edition of *Blackhair* shows an enormous variation in looks. There are elaborate advertisements for hair extensions in many colours, styles, degrees of curl or straightness, and lengths (some extravagant), and descriptions of hairstyles in which even an exceedingly close cropped 'natural' style requires moisture treatments, cutting, and dyeing to a deep black – and hours of preparation. One article suggests that natural hair is becoming more prominent. In another there is a profile of a salon in London that offers 'the unrivalled styles and professionalism you would expect in the heart of the capital without the heart-stopping price tag'. The client interviewed is thrilled with her Keratin or Brazilian blowout treatment (a recent chemical straightener that has given rise to health concerns in various countries) and seemingly untroubled by its £250 and upwards price tag. 'My hair now has body, movement and a lovely shine ... Also I would never consider washing my natural hair at the gym, because it would shrink to at least half its pre-washed length. However, though the curls did return when I washed my hair, they were looser, and as such my hair is easier, and quicker, to wash and style.'[53] Five women interviewed on the street give a picture of the range of contemporary Afro-Caribbean styles; all of them relied on hair extensions, all their styles were long, and only one used added hair to pull up into retro 1940s rolls. Sally wore her hair in a natural Afro but added four rows of Brazilian curl clip-ons for volume and what she called 'slightly rock chick mixed with elegance'. Vanessa used Peruvian extensions for her wavy locks. Jackie affected a chick-punk style with long hair extensions and a funky cap. Nicola had a simple yet feminine style with long smooth waves. And Natalie, who said she was forever trying different things with her hair, was sporting the wide rolls of what she called an old school African hairstyle (it looks much like the hairstyles of white women in the Second World War). If these five women are any indication, 'anything goes' was – and no doubt still is – very much the norm in the world of Afro-Caribbean hair.

✂ ✂ ✂ ✂

The title of a book published in 1998 – *388 Great Hairstyles* – was a sign of the times; such a title with such a big number would have been virtually unthinkable a half century earlier. Big numbers when applied to available – and feasible – hairstyles are typical only of recent times, for since the 1960s hair has been seen, increasingly, as a part of the body to which almost anything can be done, and perhaps done frequently. Some hairstyles that began as manifestly outrageous – punk, for example – later became, with modifications, fairly mainstream. In the past generation there has been a kaleidoscope of styles: some extravagantly feminine, others aggressively androgynous, and many in between. With globalised communications, a new style appearing in one place is likely to be adopted almost immediately somewhere else. New technology has been applied to hair to ensure that personal choice has become virtually unlimited.

Diana Clay of Coventry on her 21st birthday in 1962, with her 'cottage loaf' hairstyle

In 2009 Elly Jackson, singer for La Roux, described to *Observer Woman* the experimentation in hairstyles that led to her short, flaming red coiffe gelled to a pointy spike: 'Until a couple of years ago I had hair down to my chest. Everyone said I looked like Joni Mitchell [the Canadian folk singer]. I'd had enough. So I kept cutting it until it got to my ears and started experimenting with it. From then on I started to look more and more like Rick Astley. [I] like to think it echoes Young Americans-era David Bowie.'[54] While youth culture has, of course, been most open to this I'll-try-anything attitude, older women have also become finely attuned to a constant and rapid flux in hairstyles.

Hair colour is now pretty much whatever and whenever you want it to be, in whatever combination desired. Wild colours, at least on the young, are so commonplace that they now draw little notice. The bleached blonde, regarded as rather shocking and arousing censorious comment some decades ago, has become so normal, in all sorts of shades and on women (and some men) of all ages, that one brunette journalist, after trying out a blonde wig for a day, concluded that most blondeness was a tedious attempt to be blandly inoffensive, or to fake youthfulness, or just to fit in to a society where blonde highlights, lowlights, and under-lights had become ubiquitous.[55] Around 1980 blondeness still meant something – according to anthropologist Grant McCracken, a woman could reinvent herself in accord with any one of a number of celebrity blonde images, from the bombshell (Marilyn Monroe or Diana Dors) through cool (Grace Kelly) to sunny (Doris Day), most of them attempts to be someone else, guided by 'the extraordinarily transformational powers the good hairdresser has'.[56] Today any of us can be some kind of blonde: the late Princess of Wales and former Prime Minister Margaret Thatcher pioneered the current mode that seems to reflect the thinking that, 'if in doubt, tint it a bit blonder'. It probably worked for them. The blonder her hair, the more readily a woman is likely to catch the camera's eye. Early in the second decade of the twenty-first century blondeness may have lost a bit of its lustre and may no longer make the firm statement it once did. But that may merely be a consequence of the vast colour range that is now deemed acceptable. Moreover, a lot may depend on where you live or what your business is. Few middle-aged women appear on television in their natural grey hair. In Southern California women of a certain age are vastly more likely to be blonde than grey. By contrast, in the small mountain city where I live, Nelson, British Columbia, which is well-disposed to alternative lifestyles and things thought natural, grey heads are everywhere, so much so that one hairdresser I knew remarked that, given that colouring was so important to a thriving business, it was hard to make a good living in this town.

Hairstyles have shot off in all directions, and various strange things have happened, including on the fashion catwalk. Enormous effort has been put into making models look more or less like you and me. In one season the 'bedhead' look was featured, to be followed by the apparently artless ponytail; later still one saw a lot of the slicked-back minimalist look. None of this was either artless or easy. One catwalk stylist described the complexity of his efforts to make 50 models look like the girl next door. It took a lot of time and skill to make scores of incredibly beautiful women look sort of ordinary – only taller, thinner, and with much better cheekbones than anyone else. Back on the High Street, there have also been noteworthy developments. One has recently seen lots of power haircuts and high-maintenance big hair, both with modern origins in the 1980s, as well as the long, luscious and wavy styles that prevailed in the 1990s. All these cuts have been shown in whatever colour or degree of curl the individual (or her hairdresser) considered flattering.

Of course, what no-one can control is the weather. And the English weather can be the bane of many a woman's existence. 'Others battle with drink or drugs, but my

A mature, tinted, tanned and tamed Florida look, circa 2003
Picture by Don Jackson, courtesy Gail Wells

demon is frizzy hair', wrote one woman in 2010. 'It looks good when it's straightened, but it turns into candy floss in even mild humidity. I can only imagine what it would be like to camp at Glastonbury, I shall never visit Hong Kong and I always take a hat with me if it looks like rain.'[57] This woman, in company with thousands of others, became captive to a new tool of hair technology – the ceramic flat iron, which came to outsell hairdryers. This device was not so much about fashion as self-management. It was a tool to help a woman better manage her hair and present the face to the world that she wished to present. Maybe that is what – despite all the advertisements – hairstyle has always been about.

Take a glance at the magazine rack at your local newsagent's or convenience store and you are likely to find a clutch of publications depicting dozens – even hundreds – of hairstyles for the consumer to try out for herself or take to show her hairdresser. In 2010 one journal, *Hair Gallery*, compiled more than 900 styles, including Hollywood hair, wedding hair, the sexiest combinations of cut and colour, and a vast array of everyday and special-occasion glamour looks. The seemingly endless selection of hair products and devices appears to make virtually anything possible. Colouring products, gels, mousses, hairsprays, keratin treatments, weaves and extensions, as well as ever-more sophisticated tools to smooth, wave, and straighten, mean that experimentation, creativity, and fashion statements are constrained only by the limitations of a woman's hair type, finances, free time, and sense of adventure.

But underpinning these seemingly limitless variations, there are – at least to my eyes – essentially four key haircuts, albeit with plenty of subtle or not so subtle variations. (I exclude here kinky or Afro/Caribbean hair.)

The first of these is the short, layered cut. It can be an exceedingly short cut, and at various times has been dubbed the pixie, Italian boy, or Eton crop. It is probably best worn by young women with fine features and fabulous bone structure. It can take the form of the casual layered look widely seen in shopping malls and on High Streets. It is a cut that takes readily to striking colour, transforming applications of gel, or such funky personalisations as an unexpected tiny braid or tendril gracing a cheek or dropping down behind an otherwise trim neckline. The enduring popularity of this cut is due largely to its ease of care. It is a wash-and-wear cut that requires no special care on a daily basis beyond, if its wearer chooses, a dab of styling mousse or gel.

The second cut is the now classic short bob. It is done in hairdressing salons from Beijing to Boston Spa. It is largely a blunt cut but takes well to variations such as a fringe, layering to shape the neckline, or the sharp lines of geometric or asymmetrical cuts made popular in the 1960s. The style endures for several reasons. It suits most ages and facial types. Many seniors wear it as well as children. It is a cut within most women's comfort zone. It can be both high style and utilitarian. And it is relatively simple to care for but has enough length to permit variations for special occasions while still being short enough to blow dry conveniently at home. It takes well to do-it-yourself trendy trappings like jewelled hairclips or a few pinned-on feathers (the latter was a global fad in 2011). With a fringe and no parting, the style can also readily accommodate a wig. From its once radical roots in and just before the 1920s, the short bob has become the staple of hairdressing in the early twenty-first century.

A third fundamental style is the long bob, a cut that may be as long as shoulder length or a bit more. This style can be curved under the ends in a traditional pageboy, or flicked out in soft waves (especially if tapered a bit) or a classic flip. Here is a style open to lots of variations, from the smooth controlled look popular in boardrooms and other business settings to romantically curled or waved presentations. It is also often long enough to accommodate an updo, or at least a partially pulled back demi-ponytail or loose curls. It looks best well-tended but can still work satisfactorily with fairly widely spaced visits to the hairdresser.

Finally, there is long hair. There will always be a place for it. It signals luxuriant vitality. It is enduringly popular with most men. (But don't wear it if you're beyond a certain age.) It is readily transformed in a large variety of ways to suit different moods and circumstances. And it is closely associated with celebrity, from the aristocratic elegance personified by, say, the Duchess of Cambridge to the big-haired glamour of many models and rock stars. Long hair is also associated sometimes with the carefree insouciance of free thinkers. And, if desired, it can easily be pulled back into a practical ponytail or a simple plait or braid, or wound into a twist or bun (as in Edwardian times).

A woman can, then, appear to be whatever she wants to be. Our hair is that malleable. It can also be a source of much anxiety, even self-loathing. If eyes are the mirror of the soul, perhaps hair is an expression of our aspirations – or maybe a distraction from wobbly self-confidence.

Lydia Sharman aged 15 with her
Goth look, 2011
Picture courtesy Lydia Sharman

References

1   'Couture Clash', *Atlantic,* January/February 2008, 110.

2   Mary Wingfield, *Woman's Magazine,* January 1949, 52.

3   *Hair and Beauty*, July 1952, 17.

4   *Hair and Beauty*, January 1952, 22.

5   *Hair and Beauty,* November 1952, 22.

6   Xavier Wenger, *Hairdresser and Beauty Trade*, 30 December 1949, 10.

7   Xavier Wenger, *Hairdresser and Beauty Trade,* 1 September 1950, 8.

8   Joy Hathaway, *Hairdresser and Beauty Trade,* 4 August 1950, 8.

9   *Hairdresser and Beauty Trade*, 9 June 1950, 8.

10   Foreword to J G Flitman, *The Craft of Ladies' Hairdressing* (London: Odhams Press, 1959), p. 7.

11   Mass Observation Archive, File Report 3184, November 1949, 6.

12   MO Directive on Appearance, July 1950, Respondent no. 1041.

13   Nella Last, manuscript diary, 7 June 1950.

14   MO Directive, July 1950, #1246.

15   Julie A Willett, *Permanent Waves: The Making of the American Beauty Shop* (New York and London: New York University Press, 2000), p. 135.

16   John London, *Ladies Hairdressing as a Career* (London: W & G Foyle, 1965), p. 11.

17   Geoffrey Browne, *Patterns of British Life* (London: Hulton Press, 1950), p. 62.

18   Granville Hinchcliffe, in *Hair and Beauty*, August 1951, 49.

19   Granville Hinchcliffe, in *Hair and Beauty*, December 1951, 49.

20   Haines Papers, University of Sussex Special Collections, Alice Haines Papers, Box 3, Diary, 10-11 February 1945.

21   Gillian Blackstone, "My Entire Business is Teens", *American Hairdresser*, September 1948, 62, as quoted in *Permanent Waves: The Making of the American Beauty Shop* (New York: New York University Press, 2000), p. 136.

22   *Hair and Beauty*, January 1954, 7.

23   As cited in *Permanent Waves,* p. 136.

24   As quoted in Adrian Horn, *Juke Box Britain: Americanisation and Youth Culture, 1945-60* (Manchester: Manchester University Press, 2009), p. 143.

25   Granville Hinchcliffe, in *Hair and Beauty*, August 1952, 51.

26   *Hair and Beauty,* September 1952, 14-15.

27   Vidal Sassoon, *Sorry I Kept You Waiting, Madam* (London: Cassell & Co., 1968), p. 59. Illustrations of these fantasy styles can be found in Cox, *Good Hair Days*, pp. 104-110.

28   John Steinberg with Alexandra Innes, *Follicles: 50 stories of life and the art of hairdressing* (2008)[self pub, online print on demand, seemingly reworked from articles on Salon Magazine, so no publisher or place of pub listed], p. 6.

29   Ibid, 7.

30   This song was issued as an album in 1963, as a single the next year, and rose to the top 10 singles in the United Kingdom.

31   Vidal Sassoon, *Sorry I Kept You Waiting, Madam* (London: Cassell & Co., Ltd, 1968), pp. 98, 120.

32   *Hairdressers' International Journal*, November 2007, Supplement, 83.

33   Grant McCracken, *Big Hair: A Journey into the Transformation of Self* (Woodstock, New York: Overlook Press, 1996), p. 53.

34   As cited in Caroline Cox and Lee Widdows, *Hair and Fashion* (London: V&A Publications, 2005), p. 11.

35   Ibid, 11.

36   *Hair and Beauty,* January 1967, 7.

37   Cox and Widdows, *Hair and Fashion*, p. 77.

38   Bryer, *Hair*, p. 136.

39   *Lancaster Guardian and Observer*, Friday, 26 February 1960 , 6.

40   'World Spending on Hair Colorants approaching $ 4bn per annum', *Focus on Pigments*, Vol. 2007, No. 9, passim, 7 pgs.

41   Catherine Gildiner, *After the Falls* (Toronto: Knopf, 2009), p. 266.

42   Eric Grode, *Hair: The Story of the Show that Defined a Generation* (Philadelphia: Running Press, 2010), p. 31.

43   As quoted in Cox, *Good Hair Days*, pp. 178-9.

44   See Ayana D Byrd and Lori L Tharps, *Hair Story: Untangling the Roots of Black Hair* (New York: St Martin's Press, 2001), passim.

45   *Hairdressers Journal*, February 1980, 31.

46   *Hairdressers Journal International,* 12 July 1985, 10.

47   Diane Simon, *Hair: Public, Political,* Extremely *Personal* (New York: St Martin's Press, 2000).

48   *Black Hair and Beauty*, May/June 1986, 40, 52 &53.

49   www.camdenlocks.com

50   'There's billions in straight hair', *Toronto Star*, Friday 16 October, 2009, E, 4.

51   As cited in Cherilyn "Liv" Wright, 'If you let me make love to you, then why can't I touch your hair?', in Juliette Harris and Pamela Johnson, eds.,, *Tenderheaded: A Comb-Bending Collection of Hair Stories* (New York: Pocket Books, c.2001) p. 163.

52   'Good hair starts at the roots', *Toronto Star,* Friday 16 October 2009, E, 1.

53   *Blackhair,* October/November 2011, 80.

54   'How I Get Dressed' *Observer Woman*, September 2009, N. 45, 8.

55   Polly Vernon, 'Ooops, I bleached it again: How a nation went blonde by mistake'. *Guardian Woman*, September 2009, 5. 7.

56   McCracken, *Big Hair*, p. 187.

57   www.guardian.co.uk/theguardian/2010/mar/20/women-fighting-frizzy-hair

Large flower arrangement (45 cms high) made of human hair,
housed in a walnut showcase and dating from 1871
Photo courtesy of Museum Tot Zover, Amsterdam

6

HAIR BOUGHT, DONATED, ADORNED AND CRAFTED

'As a commercial commodity, hair is of vast importance.' These words were written in 1880. The writer, C Henri Leonard, went on to assert that 'fashionable Paris alone, and London much more, consumes annually over one hundred thousand pounds of human hair in the manufacture of her chignons and wigs, an amount that would load down, from its bulk and weight, twenty of our largest freight cars'. The buying and selling of hair was a trade with many beneficiaries. 'Thousands of people', he said, 'from the wealthy wig-seller, whose customers are of royal birth, down to the poor peasant girl who grows her locks to be shorn – for the girls of the Brittany and the lower Pyrenees repair annually to their fairs in droves, each in turn surrendering her rich long hair, hanging down to her waist, to the buyer's shears – make a fair amount of their living from traffic in this material.'[1] A visitor to a fair at Collinée in Brittany in the summer of 1839 described the scene: 'In various parts of the motley crowd there were three or four different purchasers of this commodity, who travel the country for the purpose of attending the fairs and buying the tresses of the peasant girls. They have particularly fine hair, and frequently in the greatest abundance ... We saw several girls sheared one after the other like sheep, and as many more standing ready for the shears, with their caps in their hands, and their long hair combed out and hanging down to their waists. Some of the operators were men and some women. By the side of the dealer was placed a large basket, into which every successive crop of hair, tied up into a wisp by itself, was thrown.'[2]

Writing of the hair market in Morlans, a journalist for the *Hairdressers' Weekly Journal* told his readers in 1882 that 'Morlans is a small town in the old Land of Bearn, now a portion of the lower Pyrenees. It is unknown to the rest of the world, save, perhaps to Paris where it has a reputation as the seat of the great market in hair. This market is held every other Friday. Hundreds of trafficking hairdressers then throng to the little place from far and near, in order to buy the hair of young peasant girls fresh from the head. The dealers wander up and down the long narrow high-street of Morlans, each with a pair of bright shears hanging from a bright leather strap around his waist, while the young girls who wish to part with their hair stand about in the doorways, usually in couples. The dealing is carried on in the best room of the house. The hair is let down, the tresses combed out, and the dealer names his price. This varies from three to twenty francs. If a bargain is struck, the dealer lays the sum in the open palm of the seller, and in a minute the long tresses fall on the floor. The purchaser rolls up the tresses, places them in paper, and thrusts them in his pocket. The writer says it is very rarely that a maiden can contemplate her fallen tresses disappear into the dealer's pocket without a gush of tears; but she consoles herself by exclaiming, "Well, it will grown again," and by looking at the money in her hand.'[3]

The hair of peasant girls from the poorest regions of France, as well as from Germany, Romania and Russia, was valued by buyers for several reasons. Traditional attire in many rural areas included headdresses that covered all the hair and was thought to protect it; peasant lifestyles meant hair was unlikely to have been curled, bleached or dyed; and these women's diets, rich in beer and cider, were thought by some to make hair thicker.[4] Rural France, specifically Normandy, was deemed by the author of *The Art of the Wigmaker* (1767) to be the source of the best quality European hair. 'It is only Villagers and Countrywomen who furnish good hair, because it is always protected by their caps, since the less it is exposed to air the better', he asserted, adding that men's hair should never be used because it was too dry and brittle and that 'Ladies' hair and that of Ladies of the Town is equally unsuitable'. He also deemed hair from hot countries to be 'dry and hollow and consequently of inferior quality', a prejudice that continued for more than a century and was reflected in lower market prices for Asian hair.[5]

The fairs of Brittany, Normandy and the Auvergne were perhaps the most famous places where hair was bought but throughout Britain and Europe merchants attended agricultural and hiring fairs to purchase the tresses of domestic servants and peasants girls straight from their heads. Notwithstanding prejudice against it, a vast quantity of hair was imported from China, Japan, India and other parts of Asia. More than a little racism was associated with negative attitudes to non-Caucasian hair but it was also true that the shape of the hair was different from European (more cylindrical than round), harder to curl, and had to bleached and processed to remove the original colour before it was dyed to whatever shade was currently fashionable. In the words of the *Hairdressers' Weekly Journal*, 'hair imported from these countries is almost invariably black, and fails utterly to harmonize with the auburn and golden tints that so well befit a northern complexion. It has therefore been found necessary to boil the hair in diluted nitric acid to deprive it of its original colour and it can then by dyed to the tint most in vogue. This operation, however, has been attended with considerable danger to the workmen engaged in this new handicraft. Severe coughs, bronchitis, and other accidents were the natural results of nitrous vapours escaping from the cauldrons used for boiling the hair.'[6]

The buying and selling of hair has been widespread for centuries, and has sometimes been practised on a large scale. The trade was also a major source of revenue for the hairdressers of the elite – and yet another way for the poor to serve the wants of the rich. It was a trade with a long history. Ancient Egyptians shaved their heads and wore wigs (not always of human hair); Roman matrons sometimes cut the hair of their slave girls to augment their own coiffures; Queen Elizabeth I resorted to a vast collection of wigs as her own hair faded and thinned; and European women and men of privilege in the later seventeenth and much of the eighteenth century favoured powdered wigs, some of truly fantastic, monumental proportions, which required that the wearer's own hair be significantly augmented by hair from elsewhere. This fashion then waned. The upheavals associated with the French Revolution and other democratising ideologies of the late eighteenth century, along with an English tax in 1795 on hair powder, served to undermine the appeal of truly extravagant headgear. (The tax brought more than £200,000 into the English treasury in its first year and helped to end more than a century of powdered wig-wearing.)[7]

While the market for full wigs may have shrunk by the nineteenth century, it was more than offset by a new demand, mainly from women, for hairpieces, postiches, braids, switches and extensions, all smaller and specialised items of false hair. Fashion was rarely fully satisfied with what nature alone provided; consequently, full and partial 'transformations' – as wigs were often called in the later nineteenth and early twentieth centuries – appeared in increasing volume to meet the ever-changing tastes in fashion that preoccupied women with lots of money, or even merely some money. Hair in all its guises served a growing middle class – a middle class with wealth enough to support its social pretensions. A country parson's wife might wear 'imperceptible hair coverings' to mask her thinning hair or perhaps add a discreet ringlet or two to peep fetchingly beneath her sedate bonnet; the solicitor's good woman could appear in public with a frisette (curled fringe) and chignons or plaits at the back of her head in

A variety of hairpieces - plaits, chignons and a frisette

order to look good for her husband's business associates; even lowly schoolmistresses might experiment with a modest embellishment or two. And certainly countless women and their daughters could argue that any little deception was justified in the marital sweepstakes – as a devoted reader of Jane Austen will surely know. One Edwardian hair supplier advertised his transformations as 'so graceful and natural as to absolutely defy detection'.[8] An aggrieved Coelebs Smith wrote to the satirical journal, *Punch,* alleging that a woman who snared a spouse with added hair was guilty of obtaining matrimony with false pretences. 'Conceive', he said, 'the horror of a husband at finding that his wife took off her hair every night, together with her earrings... this is really what is meant by the wearing of a chignon.'[9] Whether this particular deception was remarkable in a culture in which most respectable women wore constricting corsets and bustles or crinolines to disguise their actual figures is not self-evident.

The range and variety of devices to enlarge and enhance a woman's coiffure were at one time truly astonishing. A glance through the late-Victorian and Edwardian catalogues intended for hairdressers and wigmakers, as well those of department stores, reveals choices of human hair in all colours and lengths; several qualities; tapered or clubbed (that is, blunt cut); straight or curled; waved or in ringlets; loose or braided; in frisettes and ringlet fronts – and many more. A customer could buy human hair from virtually anywhere in Europe or the Far East, or she could economise by using horse or yak hair or even imitation hair; non-human hair was particularly useful if a woman wanted to add volume to her coiffure, which would then be covered with purchased human hair or her own tresses. To build an elaborate dressing, there were also many frames and pads on the market. These might include – to cite the offerings on a single page of one 1912 catalogue – side or puff frisettes, pompadour rolls, curved horsehair pads covered in human hair, a so-called Marie Stuart shape, Coronet frisettes in sets of three, Roll frisettes, and oval or round coil frames, mohair or fibre covered, most available in a variety of sizes, quality, and choice of human, animal or imitation hair.[10]

Respectability made many demands upon women, and hair was one central expression of social standing that fuelled the market for certain consumer products. Tons of hair were sold on the open market. London's huge St Katherine's Dock recorded charges for the coopering, tarring, and inspection of casks or cases of over a hundredweight of human hair around 1870 on a page that also shows fees for hams, hats, harmoniums and Hellebore root as well as hair from pigs, horses, and camels.[11] *The Times* reported in 1865 that 11,000 chignons (prepared hair lengths usually worn at the back of the head) were imported from France along with enough raw, unprocessed human hair for a further 7,000 chignons to be made up in England. Hair imports from France for chignons alone were valued at over £45,000, excluding the raw material for other kinds of hairpieces.[12] Some sources recorded annual imports of human hair into the United States of nearly 200,000 pounds in weight in 1860 (a figure that would triple in six years); and of 80,000 kilograms reaching the French market in the 1880s, doubling between 1902 and 1906 when they reached a third of a million tons.[13] In Limoges, France, there was a huge auction each year at the city's Bourse aux Cheveux to which hair merchants and wigmakers flocked from across Europe to buy the hair taken from the heads of European peasants, which then travelled to New York, London, Paris and other metropolises, where it soon appeared on the heads of women of fashion.[14]

Hair was big business, even in this period that is more often associated with iron and steel than with service sector commodities. It was imported from around the world and very widely advertised, but brought few riches to its primary producers – the young women on whose heads it grew. The Victorian tourist, T Adolphus Trollope, hoped when he wrote about Brittany's annual hair fair that the young women whose hair was cut might be able to use the proceeds for a 'little dowry'. He was shocked to learn that 'the highest value given by these abominable hair-merchants is twenty sous, and the more usual consideration by far is a gaudy, but trumpery, cotton handkerchief, of which these gentry carry about with them a stock for the purpose.' 'The profit thus netted by these hairmongers', he concluded, 'must be enormous.'[15]

Whether the hairmongers' profits were enormous or not – and there is some evidence that many itinerant haircutters were not much more affluent than the women whose hair they purchased – it is clear that wholesalers higher up the marketing chain were not inclined to generosity. Mr C J King, a Holborn 'Human Hair Merchant', whose warehouse seemed to have 'hair enough to make wigs for all creation', asserted in an interview with the trade journal, *Perruquier*, in 1878 that women would willingly part with their hair 'for a comparatively small sum, or even for a common shawl, or other wearing apparel, or a piece of imitation jewellery'. They were, he reflected complacently, 'used to it' and it was a crop like any other.[16] Another writer concluded that 'it is seldom that as much as five shillings is given for a "head"' which might have taken as much as seven years to grow. When the interviewer asked a merchant how much hair he was likely to use in a year when business was brisk, he answered that he thought it would be 'about *four tons* – the result of about sixty-five thousand clippings'.[17] How many stories there must have been from the former owners of those sixty-five thousand heads of hair! Almost all, of course, were shorn without being recorded.

The suppliers of much of the finest hair were not only usually anonymous but, far too often, paid nothing at all. Their hair was taken by, or on behalf of, those who cared for them, usually without their consent. Orphans, unmarried mothers, women involuntarily housed in religious facilities as wayward or unruly – all these enriched the church's coffers with their hair, as did postulant nuns (the latter were, one presumes, willing donors). 'Convents usually furnish a large amount of fine, luxuriant hair for the French, Spanish, and Italian markets, and it is known to the trade as "church hair"', one writer observed.[18] Prices for hair, which had fallen with the short styles of the 1920s, were rising with the longer styles of the 1930s. 'Human hair comes to England from abroad,' according to an authority in 1935 – Soho in London was the centre of the trade – 'and is collected at the numerous hair fairs held on the continent... The greatest and most regular sources of supply are the many convents in France and other Catholic countries. When novices enter a convent their hair is shorn and sold at good prices. In some establishments the nuns are encouraged to promote the growth of their hair by the use of oils and massage, so that a regular "harvest" is repeated from time to time.'[19] Faith and fashion served each other. Ringlets made riches for powerful institutions and sometimes unscrupulous people.

Writers have left us with many stories of poor women who sold their only possession of value out of economic need or for love. We remember Jo, the feisty heroine of Louisa May Alcott's *Little Women*, who sold her hair to help her family. To my mind one of the most moving portrayals of a hair sale in fiction is found in Thomas Hardy's *The Woodlanders* in which Marty South makes the painful decision to stave off economic ruin by selling her beautiful hair in order to satisfy the ambition of a wealthy neighbour to display a more lavish coiffure. Of course, few women who sacrificed their tresses knew on whose head they would end up. Hardy's story is both sensitive in its depiction of the heroine's emotional struggle over the pain of giving up her hair and accurate in the precise account that the barber gives of cutting and packaging the hair – it was bound together in the direction it grew to make things easier for the wigmaker. Hardy's description is evocative of the emotional, symbolic, and sexual importance that Victorian society attached to hair.[20]

When demand for a commercial product is high, less than scrupulous practices can be always be found. Animal hair might be passed off as human. 'Wigmakers deceive themselves and their Customers by using white goat's hair in place of bleached natural hair', recorded one observer of the trade, 'even though this hair is soft, without body, apt to become yellow, breaks and, in a word, is no good at all.'[21] Other sellers, sometimes called 'kennel-rakers' or rag-pickers, were said to sort hair for sale from refuse and possibly even cull it from the dead – the latter was something the diarist, Samuel Pepys, worried about when he bought a wig in plague-ravaged London in the 1660s.[22] In February 1875 *The Ladies Gazette of Fashion* warned its readers against scavengers who waded through the gutters in search of saleable hair.[23] Natural white or grey hair was usually the most expensive hair – costly because the raw product was hard to find in good length and thickness and because demand for it was high. As a physician writing put it, 'When the man or woman reaches the grey hair stage, the phase of baldness also appears. In many instances ...[it is] accompanied by both the urgent need for the headpiece and the money to pay for it.'[24] Rarity combined with demand meant it was well worthwhile for the hair merchant to pull silver strands from cuttings of hair from various heads and pass them off as a chignon or hairpiece from a single source. In 1880 it was said that 'a fine article of white hair sometimes sells for as high as five dollars an ounce', a spectacular sum at the time when a full head of harvested hair might weigh from 8 to 12 ounces.[25] In Europe natural blonde hair was also very valuable, as was thick, healthy shiny hair of many standard shades, depending on local market preferences. Many British women, for instance, favoured auburn shades of false hair to enliven their natural tresses that so often ran to mousy brown tones.

✄ ✄ ✄ ✄

In modern times the sources of human hair have remained much as they were a century and more ago. The poor continue to supply the heads of the rich. Wherever people are poor, hair is likely to be for sale. There are still willing and unwilling donors, scrupulous and unscrupulous dealers, and some religious bodies still grow wealthy on hair. And there is an apparently insatiable demand for hair extensions and wigs, fed by a celebrity culture, an increased interest in elaborate ethnic hairstyles, and an unquenchable desire for a youthful

*'Fun' wigs were all the rage in the 1960s: here 14-year-old
Amanda Field and her cousin Christopher pose with the wig that
Amanda's mother has just bought*

appearance.

In the 1960s huge attention was paid to hair. Often it was grown very long by the young of both sexes. The decade also introduced a widespread interest in wigs, both human and synthetic, and hair extensions. Many women of all ages bought 'fun wigs' to change their look, not even trying to pretend the hair was theirs. Women of Afro-Caribbean heritage around the world began to take renewed pride in their heritage and with it lavished unprecedented care on their hair, recreating the elaborate styles of their African ancestors – frequently with the help of multiple hair extensions. Soon women of other ethnic backgrounds were found imitating these striking and beautiful styles. (It is now commonplace for pale skinned travellers to return from holidays in sunny destinations with bead-embellished cornrows.) A few years later Bo Derek, a lovely though not particularly talented actress with a skillful publicist/partner, was deemed the most beautiful woman on the planet – a '10' out of '10' – and brought corn-rows into popular culture with her widely photographed hairstyle. For many women, the proliferation of hair pieces on the High Street gave the opportunity of changing one's looks without making a long term commitment.

By the late 1960s Hong Kong had become the wig capital of the world, thanks to low wages, new machinery, and a plentiful supply of long hair – not to mention synthetic hair, which was widely available from the 1950s. In 1969 there were over 300 factories on the island, exporting over $100 million worth of wigs.[26] Wigs had become mainstream fashion in Western societies. In 2001 many Mass Observers in Britain remembered owning wigs around this time, usually as an amusing diversion. One American company sold nearly six million dollars' worth of wigs in 1968.[27] Some of these purchasers were, as they had long been, traditional Jewish women, for whom wigs might be a religious necessity (married Jewish women were often required to cover their own hair in public).[28] Wigs could be costly or cheap, a serious investment or a disposable indulgence. Even my conservative mother had a grey wig, largely to be able to pop it on and not bother with rollers or pin-curls when she had to make a public appearance. But it was hair extensions that made the late twentieth-century century false hair business really take off. Weaving straight hair extensions into a head of curly Afro hair gave the wearer straight hair without the torment. Extensions conferred 'big hair' on those whose hair was thin, and when woven into natural hair they could tolerate the rain, the swimming pool, or even the ocean without embarrassing their wearer. Of course they were costly and had to be tightened as natural hair grew. But for some women it was worth the price to feel better – perhaps much better – about how one looked.

Today, perhaps the most famous religious source of raw hair is India's Tirumala-Tirupati Hindu Temple. The temple is the wealthiest in India, its riches founded on income from the sale of donated hair, hair that is shaved as an offering to the temple. The practice is based on a centuries-old story that Lord Vishnu proclaimed that devotees that offered their hair in the temple would be blessed.[29] An act of piety soon became a source of wealth as tons of donated hair, much of waist length, continued to make its way to lucrative auctions and processing factories around the busy port of Chennai (formerly Madras) and from there to Western consumers. Since most Hindus, who make up 85 percent of India's billion-plus population, reputedly have their heads shaved at least once in their lifetimes, hair dealers have clearly tapped into a lucrative market – a market that in 2005 was estimated to produce revenues of $300 million for the temple authority and its exporters.[30] Temple barbers shave the heads of the faithful in *kalyana katta* (tonsuring sheds) and the scale of the hair harvest is such that a computerised system has been introduced to track devotees, who are given tokens for tonsuring; and hair cutting takes place around the clock by 500 barbers organised into three shifts. Donated hair is then washed, deloused, and graded by quality, colour, and length before being sent to auction.[31] A search of the internet reveals many places where you can buy 'Indian temple hair' in the form of extensions, wigs, and men's toupées, in a great variety of colours and styles.[32] Companies in the industry will sell you raw hair 'direct from the temple' as well as other types of hair – human hair from India or China, synthetic hair or hair from yaks.

'Temple hair' has become extremely fashionable in the West. An Italian newspaper, *Corriere della Sera*, reported that a single company in Nepi, Viterbo Province, India supplied 'temple hair' to fifty countries, listed many Hollywood celebrities on its client list, and enjoyed an annual turnover of $10 million (US).[33] This reputedly special hair often graces the heads of footballers' wives, big-name fashion models, and high-end actresses. But how much of it really came from the temple? The London *Observer* in 2006 uncovered evidence that village women across India were being targeted for their waist-length tresses, with agents hired by unscrupulous exporters to offer men as little as $10 for their wives' hair, or even forcing women to give up their locks. Women reported being mugged for their hair or coerced by families into selling it, while others have saved the combings from their hair grooming for the itinerant hair collector. Hair pickers make the rounds of refuse heaps and pavement barbers in search of saleable hair. The Indian Minister of State for Textiles and Commerce, Tamil Nadua, asserted that only 20 percent of premium exportable hair actually came from temples.[34] Fraud in the fashion industry, though, is hardly surprising.

Hair has always had a value. During the Second World War a shop for second-hand goods in Barrow-in-Furness raised money for the Red Cross, and on 13 July 1943 one of its volunteer workers was planning to visit a hairdresser in order to sell him 'two switches of lovely honey gold hair' that had been donated.[35] In January 1937 the *Coiffure de Paris* reported that Max Factor spent $1.5 million in Europe buying up hair for use by actresses in Hollywood films, with blonde hair commanding three times the price of other colours.[36] The tresses of well-known people have been especially prized. England's King George III used to give distinguished visitors a lock of his hair – often in an elaborately embroidered folder. You can see an example of both his hair and the presentation packaging in Kew Palace, his summer residence, located in what are now England's famous horticultural gardens. Specimens of the hair of American presidents were preserved as early as the 1880s in the US Patent office, while in 2007 a lock of John Lennon's hair fetched $48,000 US at an auction of Beatles' memorabilia.[37]

Anyone's hair, if in fine condition, can earn its owner a goodly sum. The Toronto *Globe and Mail*'s Report on Business noted in February 2010 that an Ohio woman received $200 for her 'healthy blond hair' and a Californian earned $715 for over 60 centimetres of 'luxurious virgin hair'.[38] As with any object of value, theft is a risk, as Rio de Janeiro resident, Mirna Marchetti, learned when in 2007 scissor-wielding thieves cut off her waist-length hair as she rode on a city bus. Police speculated that the thieves hoped to sell the hair to a hairdresser or beauty salon which, they estimated, could charge more than 500 reais (US $320) for top-quality hair extensions.[39] Thefts of high-quality hair from beauty-supply stores in the United States are now (2011) commonplace; even in hard times the demand for hair remained buoyant. Jamelia, a UK pop star, who made a documentary about the sources of hair for wigs and extensions, noted in 2009 that 'people pay up to £2,500 for a weave with Russian hair but the women at the other end don't benefit much from it. They were selling their hair for £100 at the most, and some would sell for £4.' Adding that she herself no longer wore wigs or extensions in everyday life, Jamelia admitted that she sometimes did so professionally.[40]

✂ ✂ ✂ ✂

Hair can be a gift – a gift that anyone can give – and women have for long been aware of its value. In 1942 in Surrey, England, when money was being collected to support the nation's war efforts, 'a woman wrote that the only thing she had to give for Sutton and Cheam's Warship Week was her hair, over a yard and a quarter long, which she would willingly sacrifice.' The Chairman of the Borough Savings Committee went to see her and 'found her living in a Council house and obviously in poor circumstances. He thanked her for her unselfish offer but told her that he could not possibly accept such a sacrifice.' (One can only assume that he was sensitive to possible humiliation involved in a donation from apparent desperation.)[41] Recently, as hair-losing cancer treatments have become common, hair donations have become a widely accepted gesture of empathy and solidarity. Women in their twenties and early thirties have voluntarily had their hair cut short, thereby allowing much of it to be given to charities; and university students have banded together to donate their hair for both cancer research and the making of wigs for patients enduring chemotherapy. Teenagers in one town in British Columbia gave their ponytails for 'Angel Hair for Kids'.[42] Cancer-care websites offer instructions for hair donations, because now virtually everyone knows that contemporary cancer treatments frequently result in hair loss, and hairdressing firms, such as the British firm, Toni and Guy, train staff to work sensitively with cancer patients.[43]

Children are particularly appealing recipients for hair donations. Christine, a friend of mine, when she found that she was pregnant for the first time, decided to cut off her long, lustrous hair, to help a child. She donated her hair to Locks of Love, a 'non-profit organisation that provides hairpieces to financially challenged, disadvantaged children in the United States and Canada under age 18 suffering from long-term medical hair loss from any diagnosis'.[44] Over time this has become a favoured philanthropic gesture for ponytailed young women. (Locks of Love asks for 10-inch ponytails, explaining that little girls without hair want long hair – 8 to 10 inches are needed for a chin-length wig after processing – and that boys' wigs are made from shorter hair culled from the ponytail leftovers.) The Canadian Cancer Society's website says it takes approximately '12 donations of unprocessed hair and costs about $1,200 to craft a single hand-sewn wig for a child'.[45] Marianne Kakamura, a 54-year-old artist who had not had her hair cut since the seventh grade, asked a hairdresser to cut her treasured waist-length hair very short the day before her first chemotherapy treatment. 'He braided it before he cut it', she noted, and we sent the braids to *Locks for Love* [sic]. I kept one for myself.'[46]

Generosity in the donation of hair is closely associated with our own fear of hair loss. For many of us our hair is a vital part of our identity. An article in an online Seattle women's magazine was titled 'Losing Hair – Losing Identity', while a web search shows Identity Hair or something like it to be a fairly frequently occurring name for a hairdressing business in the United Kingdom, the United States, and Australia.[47] There are many causes of hair loss, or alopecia, ranging from aging, stress, and auto-immune disorders through the side-effects from treatments for cancer and other illnesses. There is also something called traction alopecia which is caused by tightly bound hair or, more commonly, by the over-use of hair extensions. The supermodel Naomi Campbell has often been snapped by the paparazzi with large bald patches at her hairline from years of wearing long hair extensions.[48] According to the American Cancer Society in 2006, 662,000 women alone in that country are diagnosed with some form of cancer every year.[49] So it could happen to any of us at some point in our lives. No wonder so many of us obsess about it. It's certainly way more likely than being struck by lightning.

Because cancer treatment and its common side-effect of baldness are so widespread, it is not surprising that organisations, governments, and insurers try to provide assistance. In 1992 the charitable foundation of the Canadian Cosmetic, Toiletry and Fragrance Association (CCTFA) launched 'Look Good Feel Better' as Canada's only charity focusing on helping women manage the effects of cancer treatment on their appearance and their morale. By 2010 close to 100,000 women had been helped by the charity's free workshops and publications, many of them devoted to hair alternatives from scarves to wigs.[50] Wigs themselves are not paid for by the charity and can run from an estimated $150 for a machine-made, synthetic-fibre hair prosthetic (which probably looks unconvincing) to about $1500 and up for a custom, fitted human-hair wig. The British group, Macmillan Cancer Support, estimates that 'real hair wigs can cost between a few hundred and a few thousand pounds' and are not normally available through the National Health Service (though synthetic wigs sometimes are). Wigs need regular replacement; some require careful, often professional styling and maintenance; and wearers are generally recommended to have at least two. As we have seen, some charities provide hairpieces to those in need and governments may give some assistance either via a direct grant or the waiving of sales tax or VAT. Private insurance can help too; for example, my supplementary medical insurance will cover two wigs per year up to a maximum of $100 per wig.

The emotional impact of hair loss can be at least as devastating as financial failure and it can well be a journey with many ups and downs. Jackson Hunsicker edited a beautiful book of photographs of women who had agreed to be photographed bald; she began after her own transformative experience of appearing in public wigless for the first time, and recalled her initial reaction. 'When I was diagnosed with Stage Two breast cancer, my initial reaction wasn't, Oh my God, I have cancer, I might die; it was, Oh my God, I have cancer, I'm going to lose my hair and then I'll be going around looking like one of *those* people.'[51] In the book that she produced five years later, there are photos of all sorts of women, of different ages, colours, socio-economic backgrounds and life experiences – and just about as many views about their baldness. Some reported feeling unfeminine, undesirable, self-conscious, conspicuous, or like an ugly 80-year-old man; others found their sudden physical change brought them closer to loved ones or fellow sufferers, or closer to an appreciation of what was most important in their lives. For one 36-year-old physician, her own cancer alerted her to the importance of becoming a 'squeaky wheel' patient. 'This is

Paula Jones of Park Gate, Hampshire, pictured in 2012 wearing a dark brown monofilament wig cut in a textured and layered bob. Paula wore the wig while undergoing treatment for breast cancer; her own hair has now grown back

your life! Being liked doesn't assure you're going to be treated any better. Demanding the best medicine possible is what's important.' A 76-year-old native American rights activist expressed her values by foregoing a wig. 'To get a good one, they are very, very expensive… it would be a shame to spend all that money when you could feed a large number of homeless people instead.'[52]

Most bald cancer patients, if they survive, will eventually get their hair back as will many other alopecia suffers. But some won't. Countless postmenopausal women will experience thinning hair. It seems sometimes residents of retirement complexes are largely made up of the bald, the near bald, and the unconvincingly bewigged. These facts, along with wrinkles, stiffness, arthritis, and sore joints, are part of what is ironically called 'normal aging'. For other people, it can be much, much worse. They are the unfortunate souls whose hair never grows back and often have no body hair at all. One breast cancer treatment, Taxotere, is reputed to result in permanent hair loss from 3 to 6 percent of patients, with the lower figure listed on the drug's product monograph since 2006. An Oklahoma woman treated in 2007 developed a fine peach fuzz but no real hair. 'I will never be well of breast cancer because of this. My life is not over but my life is drastically changed.' 'It's devastating', said another sufferer. 'With no hair, there is no going back to normal.'[53] For such women a wig is the least of the evils.

In his sultry short story from 1921, 'Dusky Ruth', the English writer, A E Coppard, tells of a traveller in the Cotswolds who is struck by the sight of a woman at an inn. 'She had on a pair of dainty cloth shoes with high heels, but what was wonderful about her was the heap of rich black hair piled at the back of her head and shadowing the dusky neck.' A few minutes later, after the landlord retired to bed, the traveller 'arose and stood behind her; he touched the black hair... He pulled out two or three combs, and dropping them into her lap let the whole mass tumble about his hands. It had a curious harsh touch in the unravelling, but was so full and shining; black as a rook's wings it was.'[54] Abundant hair, with its sensuous implications, has always seemed worth celebrating. Long, luxuriant hair is a sign of youth, health, vitality and vigour; and, at least in cultures that allowed it to be shown freely, it has been seen as a lily worth gilding. Whether a simple flower was placed in the hair, or a tiara of precious gems, women's hair has long been thought suitable for adornment.

In the nineteenth and early twentieth century, women's hairdressings, especially for balls and other formal events, could be made resplendent with a wide variety of decoration. Combs and hairpins of precious metals, or of common wood or tin, were temptations to be found both in the pedlar's pack as well as on the jeweller's counter. A vertical spray of real or artificial flowers or a fine feather would tremble delicately at its wearer's slightest movement, drawing subtle attention to her bearing, while a flash of jewels could do the same in a more assertive fashion. Hair, especially when elaborately dressed with the wearer's or other people's hair, cried out for embellishment. Well-to-do Victorian and Edwardian heads were commonly accented with lovely pins and combs, some of which had at least the excuse of helping long coils of hair to stay in place. Jewels for the hair could be as splendid as any other adornments.[55] Similarly, bejewelled hat-pins ensured that massive hats above extravagant hairstyles stayed in place. The generation before the Great War was the high tide of hair jewellery. But hair adornments did not entirely disappear with long hair. Short-haired flappers in the 1920s wore beaded or jewelled headbands, snug enough to stay put during lively dancing but distinctive enough to draw attention.

Hair has had many meanings. Consider the custom of clipping a lock of a baby's hair. Mothers everywhere seem to do it and tuck it away in a box, photo album, baby book, family Bible, or locket. I did it myself without quite knowing why, but was delighted I had done so when the infant whose hair I had snipped became a parent himself and we could compare those golden strands with his daughter's hair – an almost exact match. A bit of human hair has long been a token of affection or respect, a way to mark a new life or to herald a blossoming romance (young lovers commonly exchanged hair samples), or to provide a memento of a life that has ended. Separation, especially when tinged with danger, stimulated such small, readily portable reminders of home or love. The American Civil War was a major stimulus for such tokens in mid-nineteenth-century America, while in Britain Queen Victoria gave and received countless gifts of hair tokens, many memorialising her consort, Prince Albert, who died forty years before she did.

This centuries-old practice reached its high point during the nineteenth century. Victorian women across the social spectrum, but particularly those in the middle class, crafted human hair into a vast and often very intricate array of ornamental objects: brooches, lockets, wreaths, earrings, necklaces, key chains, bracelets, landscapes, flowers, portraits – the list goes on. Adornments made of hair were primarily of sentimental value, though a few tried to raise these products to the level of high art. Antoni Ferrer of Regent Street employed 50 workers, displayed his work at the Great Exhibition of 1851 and characterised himself as 'Artist in Hair Jewellery to her Majesty', while Edwin Creer of 589 Commercial Road, East London, in an advertisement in 1886 called himself an 'Artist in Hair' as well as a Manufacturing Perfumer, Hairdresser and Wigmaker.[56] Whether it was art or not, one item displayed at the Paris Exposition of 1855 caused quite a stir: it was a full-length, life-sized portrait of Queen Victoria, made entirely of human hair![57] At the Great Exhibition in London in 1851 miniatures of both royals were rendered in hair and gold.[58] Perhaps this was an appropriate enough tribute to a woman whose enthusiasm for work crafted in human hair went a long way towards making such tokens a major genre among her people, both as commerce and a home craft.

Middle-class Victorian women wiled away countless hours by their firesides weaving and plaiting the hair of family members, loved ones, and friends, living or dead, into various objects to wear or to adorn their walls. Domestic magazines and other publications supplied designs and patterns. Many business people established or expanded product lines to include the tools for the craft and the gold settings, jewellery, and frames into which to set the woven results. One of the best known promoters was Mrs Alexanna Speight, whose *The Lock of Hair: The Art of Working in Hair* provided a history of the craft along with detailed instructions and illustrations, which featured motifs that had long been part of the conventions of sentimental and mourning jewellery – hearts, tombs, weeping willows, flowers and the like. Speight, a hairworker with premises in Soho Bazaar who numbered Queen Victoria's daughter, Princess Beatrice, among her clients, could supply her readers with specialised materials or create desired objects to incorporate hair supplied by the client.[59] As the craze for hair objects expanded, it was sometimes suspected (or implied by rivals) that the hair certain manufacturers used was not always entirely what it purported to be, and that coarser, more easily worked hair might replace, say, the delicate locks of a beloved infant. Economic opportunity and mass production meant that hair curls were increasingly found in inexpensive mountings, that gilt-plating replaced fine gold wire in executed hair-work, and that tawdry clasps displaced finely wrought ones on plaited hair bracelets and necklaces. This was commerce with no claim to art or fashion. (Eventually machinery, after the 1860s, took the place of hand weaving or plaiting.)

Crafted hair items, during the decades they were in fashion, were executed with care, patience, and often love. In an age when photography was in its infancy, these creations could keep the presence of a loved one close by, sometimes very visibly, and sometimes placed inside a locket or on the obverse side of a pendant worn close to the owner's heart. One common type of hair work was created by weaving or plaiting long strands of hair into patterns of varying complexity to make necklaces, bracelets, and watch fobs, or wound into decorative brooches, earrings, and other jewellery. For some work a special form or table was used with weighted bobbins similar to those used in hand lacemaking.[60] Among the finest examples of Victorian plaiting are gossamer-light woven hair executed in tubing and stiffened with glue into beaded necklaces, openwork bracelets or brooches. These lovely, delicate objects are much less ornate than other nineteenth-century craftwork but are now rarely seen because of their fragility. Easier to find are examples of a lock of hair mounted; after cleaning, careful curling using flame-heated tongs, usually with gold wire, and sometimes adding small jewels and gluing to a mount, the hair craft was set in a pendant or locket. Initials and/or a date – perhaps of a birth, death, or marriage – were sometimes fabricated from a loved one's hair and added to the design.

Hair, then, became both genealogy and a sentimental journey. It was used to connect present and past generations, and to serve as a sort of family album before the age of mass photography. Hair flowers might be formed by 'stitching' the hair with fine wire over a rod in the shape of flowers, and each flower could be made from the hair of a different person – a member of a family, a school, a church group – and blended into a horseshoe or wreath. The horseshoe shape was often favoured both for its good luck and because the open ends permitted the addition of new flowers as, say, a family grew. Hair paintings, often called sepia paintings for the delicacy of their tones, were less common; they were done by using ground human hair as the colouring agent for the paint. Often the aesthetic outcome, given the natural colours of most hair, was rather autumnal shades and perhaps brooding landscapes, frequently with memorial symbols such as the willow, tombs or crosses – this was an era, after all, when visual acknowledgements of death were almost constantly on display. These expressions of hair craft, along with other handcrafts, commonly occupied the Victorian 'angel of the house' – or, if one prefers, its bored mistress trapped by social convention. On these matters we can only guess. (While hair work is rare in modern crafts, there are a few respected practitioners of the art.[61])

While the origins of surviving hair pieces are often unknowable, others contain meticulous records of whose hair was used in each flower and when and how it was obtained. One man recently purchased a hair-work posy made by a woman born around 1870 in Omaha, Nebraska. Upon examination the hair ornament was found to have tiny labels attached to stems deep inside the bouquet; they corresponded to a list of fifteen names, the first that of Mrs Hamlin, and two of them men. All were worked in varying shades of brown hair except for one small blossom in white.[62] The very finest examples of hairwork are to be found in the world's great museums such as the Victoria and Albert Museum, which has an extraordinary collection, much of it now on public display under controlled light conditions. Prominent museums are not the only places to see hairwork.

Images are readily found on the internet, often with specimens for sale, in antique and curio shops, and every now and again in a private collection. Leila Cohoon of Independence, Missouri, in 2010 was running her own private museum, Leila's Hair Museum, with 159 wreaths and over 2,000 pieces of jewellery made of or containing human hair, including one wreath made from hair shaved from two sisters when they entered a convent, and a homemade family history, dating from 1725, containing samples of the tresses of family members.[63]

All this testifies to the importance of hair in signifying how people, mostly women, have felt about themselves and their place in the world. For many of them hair has not been a trivial matter. Hair has been the bearer of messages that gave meaning to life, and sometimes to death as well; and hair's almost universal value has ensured that it has been seen as worth trading or donating or preserving or even transforming into a work of craft. These various transactions and fabrications have, over recent generations, entered into the lives of millions of women.

References

1   C Henri Leonard, *The Hair: its growth, care, diseases and treatment* (London: Bailliers, Tindall & Cox, 1880), p. 9.

2   T Adolphus Trollope, *A Summer in Brittany*, Ed. Frances Trollope (2 vols; London, 1840), p. 323.

3   *Hairdressers' Weekly Journal*, 8 July 1882, 151.

4   Steve Zdatny, *Fashion, Work and Politics in Modern France*, (New York: Palgrave, 2006) p. 7, fn 33.

5   Mons de Garsault, *The Art of the Wigmaker*, first published 1767. Translated & edited by J Stevens Cox, Chairman of the Hairdressers' Registration Council (St Sampson, Guernsey: Toucan Press, 1991), p. 10.

6   'False Hair', *Hairdressers' Weekly Journal,* 8 July 1882, 154.

7   Severn, *The Long and Short of It*, p. 67.

8   'The Cult of the Coiffure', *Lady of Fashion*, 12 October 1905, 542.

9   As cited in John Woodforde, *The Strange Story of False Hair* (London: Routledge & Kegan Paul, 1971), p. 86, fn 41.

10   Parton Son & Co., *Guide to the Requirements of the Hairdressing Trade* (Catalogue: Birmingham, 1912), 360.

11   St Katherine Dock. Co. – Rates and Charges (c. 1860), 106. (Held at Museum of London in Docklands).

12   As reported in John Woodforde, *The Strange Story of False Hair* (London: Routledge & Kegan Paul, 1971), pp. 85-6

13   Bill Severn, *The Long and the Short of It: Five thousand Years of Fun and Fury over Hair* (New York: David McKay Co, 1971) p. 110; Steve Zdatny, *Fashion, Work & Politics in Modern France* (New York: Palgrave Macmillan, 2006), p. 7, fn 32. See also *New York Scientific Times*, as quoted in *Hairdressers' Weekly Journal*, 5 August 1882, 218. Human hair imports were expected to be 'close to $500,000 – rare growth for a business previously relatively insignificant in America'. 218.

14   Zdatny, *Fashion, Work and Politics*, p. 7 and fn 35.

15   Trollope, *Summer in Brittany*, p. 324.

16   'A Visit to a Human Hair Merchant', *Perruquier*, 15 Jan 1878, 22.

17   'The Trade in Human Hair' *Perruquier*, 15 Feb 1878, 39.

18   Ibid.

19   W J Passingham, *London's Markets: Their origin and history* (London: Sampson Low, Marston & Company, 1935), p. 231.

20   Thomas Hardy, *The Woodlanders* (London: Penguin, 1998, first published 1887), pp. 248-9 and fn 7, 382. For a detailed discussion of hair and hair fetishism in Victorian culture see Galia Ofek, *Representations of Hair in Victorian Literature and Culture* (Burlington, Vermont: Ashgate Publishing, 2009).

21   De Garsault, *Art of the Wigmaker*, p. 11.

22   'Trade in Human Hair' *Perruquier*, 15 Feb 1878, 40; and R C Latham and W Matthews, eds, *The Diary of Samuel Pepys* (11 vols; London: Harper Collins, 1995), VI, p. 210.

23   As cited in Ofek, *Representations of Hair*, p. 9 and fn 44.

24   Harman Goodman, *Your Hair: Its Health Beauty and Growth* (Garden City, New York: Blue Ribbon Books, 1943) p. 146).

25   Leonard, *Hair*, p. 10.

26   Wendy Cooper, *Hair: Sex, Society, Symbolism* (New York: Stein and Day, 1971), p. 168.

27   Cooper, *Hair*, p. 168.

28   See Lynne Schrieber, ed., *Hide and Seek: Jewish Women and Hair Covering* (Jerusalem: Urim Publications, 2003), passim; Diane Simon, *Hair: Public, Political, Extremely Personal* (New York: St Martin's Press, 2000) ch. 5.

29   Eilund Edwards, 'Hair, Devotion, and Trade in India' in Geraldine Biddle-Perry and Sarah Cheang, *Hair: Styling, Culture and Fashion* (Oxford: Berg, 2008), p. 158.

30   Dan McDougall, 'Trade in Hair forces India's children to pay the price' *The Observer*, 25 June 2006, 30.

31   Edwards, 'Hair, Devotion, and Trade', 158 -159.

32   For example, www.ec21.com/offers/indian_temple_hair.html (9 April 2010).

33   As cited in Edwards, 'Hair, Devotion, and Trade', 159.

34   McDougall, 'Trade in Hair' 30; Edwards, 'Hair, Devotion, and Trade', 159.

35   MOA, Diarist no. 5353.

36   Zdadny, p. 8.

37   Leonard, *Hair*, 68; 'Lennon Hair Sells High', *Globe and Mail,* 13 December 2007, R, 3.

38   *Globe and Mail Report on Business*, February 2010, 55.

39   "Hair theft the unkindest cut of all', Reuters news report Jan 18, 2007 as recorded in http:www.news.comau'sto ry/0,23599,21079523-13762,00.html.

40   As quoted in Hannah Pool, 'Why Michelle's Hair Matters', *Guardian*, Friday, 6 Sept 18, 2009, 8.

41   *Surrey County Herald*, 20 March 1942, 6.

42   *Nelson Star*, 29 October 2009, 4.

43   For example, BC Cancer Agency, www.bccancer.bc.caPPI, ; www.macmillan.org.uk/cancerinformation.

44   www.locksoflove.org.

45   www.cancer.ca/newfoundland-labrador/support%20 services/hair/520donations.aspx.

46   As quoted in Jackson Hunsicker, Ed., *Turning Heads: Portraits of Grace, Inspiration, and Possibilities* (Sherman Oaks, CA: Press On Regardless, 2006), p. 100. Also Ibid, pp. 102, 78.

47 http://betweenlivingand existing.blogspot.com/2008/07/on-hairand-identity.html; www.seattlewomanmagazine.com/articles/sep07-5htm.

48 www.dailmail.co.uk/tvshowbiz/article -1290449/Naomi Campbell reveals- shocking —

49 As cited in Hunsicker, *Turning Heads*, p. 6.

50 www.lgfb.ca/content_id/92.

51 Hunsicker, *Turning Heads*, p. 6.

52 Ibid. pp.102 & 78.

53 Lisa Priest, '"It's devastating...no going back to normal', *Globe and Mail*, 5 March 2010, A, 4.

54 A E Coppard, *Adam and Eve and Pinch Me* (London: Jonathan Cape, 1921), pp. 43 and 45.

55 For example, see Shirley Bury, *Jewellery 1789-1910: The International Era*, V.II, 1862-1910*v* (Woodbridge, Suffolk: Antique Collectors' Club, 1991), Plate 431, p. 630.

56 Bury, *Jewellery,* p. 686; Advertisement bound in *Creer's Lessons in Hairdressing* (1886); held in the British Library.

57 Joanna Pitman, *On Blondes* (London: Bloomsbury, 2003), p. 141.

58 Ofek, *Representations of Hair*, p. 43 and fn 46.

59 Alexanna Speight, *The Lock of Hair: its history, ancient and modern, natural and artistic; with the art of working in hair (*London: A Goubaud & Son, 1872), passim; Bury, *Jewellery*, p. 682.

60 For an example, see *Les Ouvrages en Cheveux: Leurs Secrets* (Paris: Andreé Chanlot, 1886), p. 63.

61 See for example www.melaniebilenker.com/wk_06braid.shtml; http://jennkristen.blogspot.com/; www.hairwork.com/erika_stroy.htm; http://en.wikipedia.org/wiki/Hair_jewellery; Janice Miller, 'Hair without a Head: Disembodiment and the Uncanny', in Geraldine Biddle-Perry and Sarah Cheang, eds., *Hair: Styling, Culture and Fashion* (Oxford: Berg, 2008), p.186, and Leila McKellar, 'Hairpieces: Hair, Identity and Memory in the work of Mona Hatoum', *Ibid.*, p. 170; www.wendagu.com/installation/united_nations/concept.html; and a presentation by Wenda Gu at the conference on 'Hair Stories: Practice, Culture, Theory', sponsored by the London School of Fashion and Victoria and Albert Museum, 20 November 2009, V&A.

62 www.hairworksociety.org/wreath/wreath.htm.

63 www.hairwork.com/leila/index.html; See also http://england.prm.ox.ac.uk/Englishness-mourning jewellery.html; http://victorianhairjewelry.com/victorianhairwork.html.

7

THE MODERN
HAIRDRESSER

'I don't go to the hairdresser's very often but I always find it enjoyable. The smell of the chemicals, the gentle rubbing of my scalp as my hair is washed, the warm water. The comb going softly through my hair. Hairdressers must have special training in how to wash hair without tangling it because I can't do it at home! The conversations around me, drifting through the music from the local radio station. Listening to a hairdresser trying to explain diplomatically that what looks fantastic on an 18 year old model will not look good on Madam's 40 year old face! Holidays, little bits of the lives of total strangers that I will probably never see again.' (Mass Observer, C 2929, Spring Directive, 2001)

Hairdressers, as a matter of sound business practice, have always tried to make the hairdressing experience as appealing as possible to their customers. One way to do this was through attractive shop design. Before the emergence of mass market hairdressing in the 1930s, the trade focused on the elite, and opulence and exclusivity were crucial to attracting clients. In 1901 the exclusive house of Douglas in Bond Street upgraded its offerings to the titled and wealthy with what the *Hairdressers' Weekly Journal* described as a 'lavish hand'. The ladies' salon was, was, from the photographic evidence that accompanied this article, a space of luxury unrivalled in most commercial settings. The premises included a 'costly carpeted staircase', silk-covered settees, seventeen private boxes with marble shampoo basins, and 'three hundred towels ... always on hand, delightfully warmed and ready for use.'[1] Harrods, the famous London department store, in 1907 announced the opening of its new deluxe hairdressing court, 'believed to be the most Sumptuous the World over'.[2] It also catered to women at their own residences if they lived within a mile of the store, as many of London's wealthiest and most fashionable women did.

By the 1920s and 1930s, as we have seen, styles had changed and the hairdressing business had grown in size and social reach. It had become at least partly democratised. Harrods traded its Edwardian look for the sleek design of an ocean liner – a style of shop fittings also adopted by the thousands of new entrants to the hairdressing trade across the country. In 1937 Harrods offered its customers 'a revelation in modern design' – a new salon with a large reception lounge, pink and beige décor, enhanced by mirrors and pale pink formica (a substance, it reminded its customers, that 'looks like porcelain'); it had seventy-two hairdressing cubicles, each with telephone, clock, [and] rapid drying machines'.[3] Modernity, hygiene, and technical innovation meshed well with innovative or 'streamlined' design, often making new or redesigned hair salons among the most forward-looking shops on a High Street. From the national capital to port and industrial cities and market towns, by the 1930s hairdressing had matured and expanded as a commercial enterprise. Increasingly salons offered their growing and often younger clientele a setting with a modern look, a design that reflected not only what affluent women associated with ocean-going vessels, but what any young woman would have recognised from the architecture of her local cinema. The hairdressing salon, with sleek, clean modern design and simple curvilinear forms and using modern materials, easily became a place she could associate with good feelings about life. But whatever the design preferences of the times, no self-respecting hairdresser has wanted his or her salon to look drab, or disordered, or out-of-date. Most hairdressers' customers valued – and still do – a comfortable, cheerful, and nicely presented environment.

But space and place were not, of course, all that was intended to appeal to and attract customers. There was also the quality of the personal relationship between hairdresser and client, a relationship that has called for sensitivity on the part of the hairdresser and has often carried a degree of psychological importance for the client. Hairdressing – and this is a key fact – is inescapably a touching trade. It requires physical closeness between two people. One person lays hands on another; and the part of the body that is being treated is a part that many women attach a great deal of importance to. Clients allow hairdressers the sort of access to their person that they rarely find acceptable with other service providers, outside the field of health care, where only doctors, chiropractors, nurses, and other medical professionals enjoy similar intimacies of access. Such intimacy, of course, tends to foster, or at least assume, trust in the relationship, for the client needs to feel confident in her hairdresser's judgment and tact. And feeling confident often leads to some sort of confiding.

Ever since Warren Beatty in *Shampoo* (1975) popularised the idea that a hairdresser was a fellow who might do much more than trim your locks, the 'relationship' with one's hairdresser has become a cliché of modern discourse. 'Have

Peter Collinge Hair salon in Liverpool in the 1970s
Picture courtesy Andrew Collinge

you ever encountered a hunky hairdresser that made your salon chair smolder?' asked Johanna Lenander in the April 2011 issue of the Canadian magazine *Fashion*. 'The Hair Hunk (or HH) is', she argued, 'one of the fashion businesses's most influential characters… He charms everyone from models to editors to movie stars to housewives. He's confident and irreverent and frequently introduces groundbreaking new trends (e.g. asymmetrical bobs, razor cutting, grunge hair, buzz cuts). And he often enjoys a hopping love life.'[4] How many HHs there actually are is open to speculation. But two things are clear: the best-known Hair Hunk and the living embodiment of 'swinging London' was Vidal Sassoon who, in the 1960s, both revolutionised the haircut and made becoming a hairdresser a viable career choice for heterosexual men. The late Pino Spadafora, a Toronto hairdresser, a family man with an artist wife and two children he doted on, once told me while cutting my hair that, without Sassoon as an example, he would have chosen a different line of work.[5] Howard McLaren, now senior artistic director at Bumble and Bumble salon, got his start as a hairdresser 30 years ago in Glasgow after he realised that working in the coolest salon in town meant hanging around the city's best-looking girls. These men are creative and good with people and know that, for the client, to be pampered by an attractive and friendly guy enhances her salon experience. 'How many people touch your hair, neck or ears?' McLaren asks. 'You do feel something special, unless you're a robot.'[6] 'When someone is in your chair, they're in your hands. That's a lot of trust. You connect with them physically as well as emotionally', reflected another leading stylist, Mike Viggue.[7]

There is a desire to trust a person who touches us and from this trust has come something more. In a survey conducted by the Professional Beauty Association in the US in 2008, 88 percent of women polled said it was important to have a 'personal rapport' with their hairdressers. Clients, it was suggested, tended to 'expect – even demand – a relationship with their stylist that rivals one they might expect with a significant other'. In touching a client, says Sarah Kendell, owner of Perfect Angels salon in

Colorado Springs, 'you are breaking a psychological barrier... it's a positive neurological association.'[8] A little showmanship to go along with good looks and 'emotional intelligence' are sometimes also good skills to have, as Wendy Baldwin explained in a career manual for prospective hairdressers in 1983. As a teenage trainee from a Bristol suburb working in fashionable Mayfair in the 1950s she was able to observe another famous stylist, Raymond, who 'to my mind did more for hairdressing than anyone in those days. His exuberant, flamboyant showmanship received the publicity it deserved' and his nickname, 'Mr Teasy Weasy', became a household word. He flirted and fussed over women very publicly as he glamourised ordinary women on television with his trendy hairdos and he made a lasting impression on the profession by popularising the still ubiquitous blonde streak and by marketing obviously coloured hair as the 'in thing'.[9] Perhaps for those women who just need to get their hair cut and haven't the confidence to do it themselves, all this may be a bit over the top. Nonetheless, we do, on the whole, expect more from the person who enhances our presentation of self than from the person who, say, cleans our windows or delivers our groceries.

In these early decades of the twenty-first century, consumers seem to expect a lot – perhaps because in economic tough times, they have made decisions in favour of haircare and expect to be acknowledged for it. As Jamie Brooks, managing director of the eminent London salon, Brooks and Brooks, put it: a salon with only a battered coffee pot in a corner and perhaps one spoon in the whole place, would soon be out of business.[10] Further, only a modest percentage of salon visits are brief affairs: when your hair treatment may take several hours you expect more than a tepid tea and a stale biscuit. 'Culture affects fashion more than anything elsewhere', Jamie noted as part of our wide-ranging conversation about the high-spending, affluent late 1980s and early 1990s. Wealthy clients, especially the newly affluent, were prepared to invest in everything from a costly Brazilian blow-dry to a complex colour treatment, and certainly expected their favourite latte in a stylish cup along with it. While the latest recession resulted in a 10-20 percent drop in spending, according to Habia, the government-appointed standard-setting body for the hair and beauty industry, women made it clear that they had no intention of abandoning a part of their lifestyle of great importance to them. Looking good was a top priority, even if it meant cutting back on the number of salon visits and supplementing them with products from the corner shop. Sarah Brown at Toni & Guy's says spending on looking good is something women are loath to cut back on even in recessionary times.'[11]

Hair-care fosters a psychological boost; it makes a visible statement that, for example, a woman is ready for a posh new job (even if she doesn't have one at the moment). Good hair is proof of self-worth. And visiting her hairdresser is an experience that most women have valued highly. Some clients expect conversation; a few expect glamour and/or deference; others have confided in their hairdresser. 'People do wind up telling you a lot', according to Shane Michael, one of many hairdressers who regard listening as much a part of the job as skill with scissors and colour. 'They tell you about their relationships. About their family histories, about their health.'[12]

The listening role of the hairdresser may indeed be close to that of the attentive therapist. Hairdressers are, in part, being paid to listen, and a degree of discretion is assumed as well as a degree of impartiality. Nisal Iqbal, a stylist in a high-end London salon, has observed that 'the relationship with clients comes with experience; you learn over time where not to trespass, and never to make anyone feel guilty for not talking to you.'[13] Textbooks aimed at trainee hairdressers usually include sections on dealing with people, and on verbal and non-verbal communication, along with styling, cutting, and colouring techniques. In 1990 the writers of *Foundation Hairdressing* advised its readers on how to become good conversationalists by being well informed about hairdressing and the products and services offered by their salon, developing a wide range of knowledge 'even if only by watching television or reading a newspaper', learning to be a good listener, and keeping notes on clients' interests 'to remind yourself to ask about something next time' they come in. For its apprentice readership, the textbook went on to give hints on some safe subjects to discuss with much older clients, and the hidden meaning of gesture, posture, and eye contact, including the caution that 'if a client avoids eye contact with herself in the mirror … it could mean that she does not like what she sees and what you are doing with her hair!'[14] Hearing a whispered confessional, being an attentive audience for a lively story, or working in contented silence – all these have been and still are among the skills of a successful stylist. The best hairstylists may be called upon to serve clients ranging from a dowager duchess to a harried working mother to a fashionable girl about town, and it is good if they can 'appear to bypass the class barriers that pervade other areas of life.'[15]

Some hairstylists envision their roles in broader terms. They seek not only to make their client look good but to educate her (and increasingly often him) and, perhaps, help restore a possibly frayed sense of self. Trisha Buller, the dynamic manager of the Cienté hair salon in Berkhamsted, Hertfordshire, embraces the range of hairdressers' roles with enthusiasm. Hairdressing for her is, as well as a performance profession, also a listening, educating, and supportive one. From a combination of careful listening and educated assessment of her client's overall health and stress levels as gleaned in part from an analysis of strands of hair, she hopes that she and her associates can help their clients leave the salon both looking much better and feeling much better about themselves.[16] Buller herself has moved on from a youthful passion for hairstyling to an educated and sophisticated knowledge of trichology (the science of hair). In this way she combines her personal interest and an appreciation that a clientele, who are now more savvy, have tried so many hair procedures (some with deleterious consequences) and diets that their hair requires ever more sophisticated attention.

This kind of haircare is boosted by a nuanced customer service environment – that is, an appreciation that a person spending several hours and, not uncommonly, several hundred pounds, is due a certain solicitude – perhaps mineral water in a stemmed glass and dainty biscuits on a pleasant tray – and a degree of attentiveness in accord with her substantial expenditure. Another prominent salon owner whose establishment was rated 'three times London hairdresser of the year', told me that – at their end of the trade at least – the highest level of customer care and attentiveness was essential.[17] It is no longer acceptable to shift the client from station to station – being dragged wet-haired from shampoo to colourist to stylist – or possibly to expose her looking bedraggled in a store window. In fact there has been a modest return, for some clients, to private cubicles and an abandoning the 'let it all hang out' spirit of the swinging sixties. All this makes sense. For all the self-disclosure of the age, there is still a little discretion required when mutton wishes to be dressed like lamb. Artifice is assumed – but it should appear to be artless.

Stylists today are and have to be adaptable, and attentive to clients who just want the job done competently and a bit of quiet time. Mariella Frostrup, a well-known journalist and TV presenter in her late 40s, is one who values a bit of personal peace and respected privacy, and has no need to talk: 'I look forward to going to the hairdresser's because it is the only time as a working mother that I ever get precious "me time".' As she reported this in 2009 she was shuffling her papers, connecting with her BlackBerry, getting her hair dried, and having a manicure.[18] Another busy woman thought of time in the salon as 'short-haul in-flight time—no one can get ahold of you'.[19] A few hairstylists, especially if they charge a lot for a haircut, actively discourage chatter. Sally Hershberger, a New York Stylist who charges $800 for a haircut, even once posted a 'Silence Please' sign in her salon to help her 'focus'.[20] I, for one, would want my hairdresser to concentrate completely on the job at hand if I were foolish enough to pay that much for a haircut! In salons as a whole, however, hairdressers who 'don't want their clients to tell them their troubles are as rare as those who believe in natural blondes'.[21] In addition, many hairdressers are drawn to the occupation at least in part because of its social nature. One young hairdresser in Cobourg, Ontario, told me that after successfully completing an advanced programme in mathematics and beginning work in that field, she soon decided to become a hairdresser because she found people so much more interesting than numbers.[22]

The appeal of many popular salons rests on a mix of comfortable informal chitchat (when clients want it), stylish hairstyles, friendly atmosphere, and solid business savvy. The latter often includes steering clients to trust – and purchase – products in which the salon owner has a stake. Janet, a Canadian who takes great pride in her hair, while on holiday on the other side of the country was prepared to drive an hour and a half in each direction to have hair colour renewed by a colourist who could use a formulation identical to that employed in her home salon.[23] Such brand loyalty can be highly profitable. John Frieda, a London hairstylist who began as an apprentice in his father's salon, built a fortune on a small bottle of hair serum called Frizz-Ease that he launched in 1990. In 2002 he sold his haircare line for $450 million (£270 million). Even after the 2008 recession had destroyed many livelihoods and shrunk many portfolios, the hair product giant, L'Oreal, posted stable first-quarter sales in 2009 of €4.37 billion (£3.75 billion).[24]

Hairdressing has always been to some extent about ambience. A customer in 2012 is likely to go where she feels comfortable. But some women also want other things – perhaps a hairdresser who really understands the club 'bling ', that is, which particular hair presentation will look awesome at the clubs. The best hair salons, like Brooks and Brooks, make sure that they have enough young stylists to serve these clients (along with a stylist adept with black hair) as well as the 'county set'. In central London's salons, the young are the future. Highly profitable older clients, long loyal to a particular celebrity stylist, will still move on eventually, if only in the short term, to their country estates or their Caribbean retreats. The best salons train the young to respond appropriately to the diversity of their customers and keep on top of their tastes. And despite hard times, there is evidence that hairdressing is, within limits, especially at its highest end, fairly recession proof. A good stylist can, for example, help clients to reduce the number of appointments by amending a hair colour regime to make it easier to care for at home between somewhat less frequent visits to the salon. Stylists want to keep clients through bleak times as well as good, and most of them are smart enough to adjust properly to recessionary belt-tightening.

The notion of the professional hairdresser as confidant was firmly established by the 1950s, and often earlier, since women across the social spectrum commonly saw their hairdressers weekly or fortnightly for a shampoo and set. Many more had regular permanent waves. A Mass Observation survey in 1939 found that half of all women had their hair cut at a hairdresser's, a number that grew if older women's (64+) conservative habits were discounted. Also it was predominantly women under 50 who had permanent waves at their hairdresser's – the most costly and time-consuming service.[25] In 1949 one survey showed that over 48 percent of all British women (9.6 million) had perms and 58 percent of the 25-44 age group.[26] This was an enduring and profitable trend. 'Women between 35 and 64 years of age have more professional perms than any other age group', noted a trade manual in 1968. It went on to observe the vigour of this part of a hairdresser's market. 'Those having three or more perms a year in 1957 were 5 percent, whereas in 1967 they were 17 percent.'[27] A growing number of salons by the mid-twentieth century offered the convenience of location: women in the workforce could by then readily find a congenial hairdresser close to work or on the High Street near home, even if home was in a village.

This pattern was mirrored in the United States where visits to beauty shops had become a regular part of a woman's routine. In 1948 almost 36 percent of women surveyed frequented beauty shops, a figure that had risen to 52 percent by 1952. The next year, 1953, there were 135,000 beauty shops in the US, the majority of them small owner-operated businesses, up from 5,000 in 1900.[28] (Black-owned, small independent salons were to play an important role in the civil rights movement: their relative independence from white people as either clients or suppliers provided a less vulnerable position from which to challenge the racial status quo and remain to this day good places to reach black voters.) Of course, in earlier times ladies' maids who dressed the hair of their mistresses on both sides of the Atlantic had long been privy to the secrets of privileged employers: Eliza Potter, a black American hairdresser, was one, who wrote about her experiences in the mid-nineteenth century.[29] But it was the spread of the hairdressing salon across the social spectrum on both sides of the Atlantic in the twentieth century that transformed the industry. The weekly or fortnightly visit, which might be shared with neighbours, became a social event, a cheap form of therapy, or just a jolly hour or so away from the kids, the washing, and the dust bunnies under the sofa.

The perception of the salon as a safe and congenial place to share one's woes (or happier feelings) is well established. A visit to the salon may occur more frequently than a visit with a good friend. At the Cut Above salon in the seaside town of Southwold, Suffolk, much of the traditional beauty-shop culture remains among its clientele, mostly 'aged between 65 and 95'. 'I've probably only washed my own hair once in 20 years', confessed one client; another pronounced that she regarded the salon as a second home and thought of her 30-year-old stylist as a son; while third, a 66-year-old retired B&B owner, said it was the highlight of her week and that she 'would honestly rather eat baked beans than not get my hair done'.[30] But today this cosy reality is often diminished by social and geographical mobility (how many of us have had the same hairdresser for 20 plus years?) as well as by changing fashions in hair. The woman who has her hair cut in a salon, but uses no other services, may see her hairstylist no more than three or four times a year, and often for only a short time. To maintain a coloured head is more time-consuming but, nonetheless, requires maintenance only every few weeks for most women. Nonetheless, since her hair is so much a part of a woman's image and self-worth, her hairdresser is likely to be a person who carries weight in her life, whether or not she chooses to divulge any secrets.

There are, of course, notable exceptions to the generalisation that many women spend less time at the hairdressers than was once the case. The elaborate braids and extensions that a black woman may choose necessitate hours in the salon, especially before major events – Toronto's annual Caribana festival, North America's largest Caribbean festival, is a case in point. At Nadine's Hair Salon on Eglinton Avenue West in Toronto, 25 percent of the year's sales are made during this time. Of the mood on the night before the Caribana parade, when women can get their braids, weaves, bobs, highlights or extensions done until 3am, shop owner Nadine, explains: 'We play music, we're wearing Hawaiian colours, eating, talking, dancing, it's a ball'. These are significant time-commitments. All-year-round weaves of hair extensions, which can be glued or sewn into the hairline, are the shop's best sellers. The former lasts two weeks and the latter as much as several months.[31] On the other hand, electric flat irons can turn a natural afro into a sleek, smooth style in minutes where stove-heated hot tongs and noxious 'hair relaxers' were once needed to achieve the same effect. In fact these time-consuming processes helped to create a special comradeship in black women's beauty shops. Some hairdressers have added new services such as the 'Brazilian blowout', a chemical process designed for all races to keep hair smooth and/or straight and that can cost as much as £250. Some blow-drying salons encourage women (mostly professional women or those in the public eye) to attend several times a week in order to present a polished, almost perfect, image of themselves– all this in addition to whatever other hairdressing services they may use.

Having one's hair cut, coloured, shampooed, or styled is an aesthetic and hygienic necessity. But it is, for many women, a distinctive outing as well. The service is likely to be provided in a space away from their everyday lives – a socially acceptable sensuous experience, a time for well-deserved pampering, a slight bit of voyeurism, or a welcome escape from obligations to others. Many women took offence at some late twentieth-century advertising slogans for hair products, 'Does she or doesn't she?', 'If I only have one life to live, let me live it as a blonde', 'Because I'm worth it '. But whatever the objections to manipulative advertising and to hairdressers pushing unwanted products, a great many women have felt that they were indeed 'worth it'. 'It's worth going for the shampooing – better than an expensive massage – you come away feeling like a million dollars', luxuriated one woman: 'I just go to feel good'.[32] 'I love going to the hairdresser's, it gives me a great lift and I feel so much better all over', noted another enthusiast.[33] A visit to the hairdresser was seen by a Canadian woman as a wonderful opportunity 'to reinvent myself', to summon up enticing future scenarios that went far beyond her hair. 'I invest it with all sorts of regenerative power – way more than shopping for new clothes, say. And it's a lot easier and cheaper than going on a diet or having plastic surgery!'[34]

The role played by a successful hairstyle in a woman's self-esteem has often been noted. But rarely, perhaps, has the case been as strongly made as by the civil servant who acknowledged that well-cut, coloured, and styled hair was a visible social asset in her high-profile public sector career; it made her feel smart and business-like over the phone and gave her 'confidence even though these people cannot see me!!'[35] In the 1940s Nella Last, a relentlessly thrifty and resourceful housewife in her fifties from Barrow-in-Furness, was unapologetic about her 'one luxury' of perms and regular shampoo and sets, both during the wartime years and the following years of post-war austerity. Her one excuse for this fortnightly indulgence was that she didn't eat chocolates as many of her acquaintances did! 'I always relax and rest under [the] dryer', she said. 'I like the warmth and hum and this morning looked at a pile of *Picture Posts* I'd not seen before.'[36] At a time when homes were often miserably cold and domestic comforts few, the warmth, ease, and sociability of the hairdressing salon were hard to discount.

Another woman remembered savouring her regular hair appointment as a 'weekly escape from my children while I relaxed in one chair with a cup of tea and magazines'.[37] A young British mother living in Australia in 2001 relished the guilty pleasure of reading trashy magazines without a toddler 'trying to get in on the act. Actually it's very relaxing ... the only bit of real solitude I get and the indulgence of someone else washing my hair etc.' Indeed, the entire outing gave her a welcome respite from her usual child-centred world. Here is how she described the scene:

'The reason I chose this salon over the others is because it's a co-operative – the girls rent chairs from Laura who owns the shop and they are all self-employed – and the atmosphere is relaxed and chatty. Whoever is free mans the reception desk, answers the phone and takes appointments. And they bother to use my name –"Cath, could you shampoo C...?"...They bother to write down details on a card system – and actually refer to it. So they know what coffee I like (white, no sugar) and say sensible things like "You were going back to England last time you were here weren't you? How was it?" and "How's your baby?" I know all their kids/husbands/families and where they went on holiday last and what they think of the current government. Lots of conversations involve the entire shop – four clients and hairdressers and anyone else just standing in the doorway. ... I don't mind if they keep me waiting ... It's lovely walking home after a haircut – no hair lurking in my eyes and I always feel very "clean" and neat. Then, enter the front door and back to the realities of motherhood. '[38]

Socialised to put family needs before their own, many women have been a little defensive about lauding the value they place on the reassuring, friendly, non-judgmental comfort of their local hairdresser's. But that it is an experience that has really mattered is clear. 'I feel that any money I spend on my hair is very good value', one Mass Observation correspondent declared. 'It is not only the physical appearance but the psychological boost it gives me.' Further, she noted, 'I am always guaranteed to have a good laugh [and] ... at Christmas sherry is provided.'[39]

Some women have been quick to sing their hairdresser's praises. 'Ian, my hairdresser is very good at his job and you have to book him up many weeks in advance to be sure of an appointment', noted a Norwich librarian. 'He has been cutting hair for over twenty years and is cheerful and welcoming. I always get offered a cup of tea when I arrive, plus a goodbye kiss when I leave. We get through lots of gossip and have a jolly time. He always makes an excellent job of cutting my hair....I would hate to go to one of the snooty and horrendously expensive salons around. I know I would feel very uncomfortable, probably not get any better service and feel ripped off at the end of it. I am quite happy with Ian.'[40] In contrast, a part-time teacher and museum attendant in Cheshire said she 'would really, really love to go to one of these celebrity hairdressers to get my hair cut and coloured. That would be the ultimate treat.' She settled instead for a 'very smart' salon, which was nicely decorated, offered a decent cup of coffee, was the only place she could read *Hello* magazine, and offered a loyalty card scheme so that 'after amassing about 30 points I get a tenner off a hairdo. A brilliant idea.'[41]

There was another reason that women became more comfortable going to a hair salon as the twentieth century wore on – a reason that went beyond good service and technical skills. As it grew, the industry became ever more female. Men were – and still are – the most visible 'celebrity' hairstylists, celebrities in their own right as well as professionals making a lot of money serving even bigger celebrities in the rarified worlds of entertainment, high society, and, increasingly, the fashion runway. But by around the 1950s mainstream hairdressing was predominantly a woman's trade. The census of 1961 reported that there were four times more female-owned than male-owned salons and the number of women employed either full or part-time in the industry outnumbered men by twelve to one. One salon in three was a single-person business while one in 110 employed more than 20 people. And by 1961 hairdressers were just about everywhere, it seemed.

Eight in every fourteen hairdressing shops were for women only and another one in fourteen catered to both men and women in relatively new unisex establishments.[42] There was then about one salon (including those for men) for every 1,300 people in the United Kingdom – a number that had risen 25 percent in 15 years according to the industry's best known training manual.[43] With such a range of establishments, there was usually a size and style of salon to suit every taste and budget, at least in cities.

Salons by the 1930s looked less like domestic environments and more like professional businesses. They had also become distinctly feminine. While Edwardian women's hairdressing salons were frequently little more than slightly modified men's clubs/barber shops, many from the 1930s were already resolutely feminine. Colours were drawn from a female palette; reception areas became luxurious, often embellished with fresh flowers; window displays – often with mannequin heads adorned with the latest hairstyles – became more aesthetically appealing and market-driven.[44] The salon was also designed to provide a potential shopping experience as well as a personal service, with displays of hair and beauty products available (with the endorsement of her hairstylist) to divert the client's spending from the chemist's or the local food market. On the whole hairdressers did not do well in competition with other retailers, as the fifth edition of *The Art and Craft of Hairdressing* conceded in 1968. A 1965 survey it cited revealed that few women bought shampoos, setting lotions, tints, rinses, hair sprays or other hairdressing products at the salon; most patronised the chemist's shop instead.[45]

By the 1960s salon design and décor were reflecting broader social changes. At the leading edge they adopted sharp-edged modern design, often with lots of black or silver, and psychedelic patterns or space-aged decorative flourishes. Many of the new unisex establishments, such as the trend-setting *Sissors* in Chelsea, catered to the fashionable young – women who were among the first to adopt miniskirts and men who wore their hair long like latter day Renaissance courtiers and often wore long velvet jackets. Many a fashion-conscious young woman saved her money for a Vidal Sassoon-inspired haircut, perhaps for a sharp-edged asymmetrical style, one of the beautifully cut reinterpretations of the classic bob that made Sassoon rich and famous. Not everyone was impressed. One woman recalled that 'I had my hair cut by Vidal Sassoon himself, and I remember coming out of the salon and thinking, God, I look just like everyone else. You were just turned out.'[46] Others of both sexes left their hair long, untended, and unstyled – 'Hair like Jesus wore it/Hallelujah, I adore it', as one of the lyrics to the smash hit musical *Hair* (1968) put it.

If London, sartorially or otherwise, was 'swinging', as the cover of the American magazine *Time* christened it on 15 April 1966, most of both Britain and North America had not yet reached the degree of 'cool' that, say, Carnaby Street celebrated and its promoters insisted upon.[47] While a handful of the women in my graduating class at the University of Toronto in 1966 had leading-edge haircuts (the campus was close to some of the city's most fashionable hairstylists), most had not fully absorbed the latest messages of fashion. Their beautifully cut hair was still constrained by backcombing and weighted by hairspray but they had given up their mothers' perms and rigid curls. Very soon most young hair swung like a pendulum, as the words of a popular song about 1960s London put it. Self-expression through hair soon spread. In October 1974 the *Lancaster Guardian* announced the opening of the new 'Mr. Andrew Hairitorium in Lancaster – the fifth branch of an organisation dedicated to the fashion haircutting for both gals and guys'. Other Hairitoriums had already opened in Bury, Bolton, Chorley and Preston. The fashionably white-and-green-decorated Lancaster shop aimed 'to bring big city styling into the provinces'.[48] Post-war baby boomers were coming of age in large numbers, and in a vibrant economy they had money to spend on themselves. Hairdressers noticed – and wooed them, with hip premises, cool music, and more.

Few women have been drawn into a hairdresser's by the aesthetics alone. While not all women want to chat or confide at the hairdresser's, any savvy woman must recognise that the process of getting her hair done has its vulnerable moments. What woman looks her best with wet hair, tresses caught up in rollers, or bundles of silver paper drooping over her head? Going without your glasses for a while in busy salon can undermine self-confidence, and the smell of chemicals on your own or another's head may leave a client feeling woozy. A good hairdresser knows this and takes steps to make a client comfortable. (Hairdressers' own vulnerabilities and concerns may explain why today many try to talk clients out of having perms.) A S Byatt's character in 'Medusa's Ankles' first goes into a salon attracted by a voluptuous Matisse nude on the wall, a bit of décor the owner chose as a match to the colour scheme, but she returns for the social experience as well as the haircut rather than the décor.[49] Surely many women have had similar experiences. And almost all hairdressers know this.

One of the oldest instruction manuals for the trainee hairdresser, *The Art and Craft of Hairdressing*, first published in 1931 and subsequently reprinted in a great many editions, put great emphasis on the psychological and customer service aspects of the trade.[50] 'The best advertisement is a satisfied client, so that efficient craftsmen only should be employed', it counseled. 'But it is not only sufficient to study efficiency as merely efficiency, there is the psychological element to be considered ... Many operatives, whilst being excellent workmen, possess temperaments unsuited to the intimacy of ladies hairdressing'. 'Grousers' were to be avoided, as were those with grooming deficiencies the customer 'can leisurely observe ... in the revealing mirror over the basin'.[51] The continued relevance of this standard text was revealed by John Steinberg, a young British-born-and-trained hairstylist, who, when setting up his first independent salon in Toronto in 1977, turned to its decades-old pages. 'A smile and every indication of pleasure on greeting them (clients) is no more than they may reasonably expect', he read, along with the advice that 'irritation must never be conveyed by tone of voice or expression'. Despite its sometimes stilted language, he learned two truisms from this guidebook of hairdressing: keep your people-skills as sharp as your hairdressing tools, and 'everyone who sits at your workstation deserves equal time and, attention. No judgments allowed. Just great hair.' [52]

When asked about the future of hairdressing, prominent hairdressers and teachers of hairdressing offer a range of views. One common opinion is that the recession of the 2010s will drive out hairdressers of little skill and more dash than talent. As an example, one stylist mentioned a salon whose owner had built his business around a grand piano, while another foresaw the decline of the currently fashionable blow-dry salons which meet a transient taste and do not require cutting or colouring skills or innovative styling. Others hope for regulation of the industry, a cry for standards by the profession that has been voiced for much of the past century. Very often concern is expressed about mobile hairdressers, who are variously thought to undercut respectable businesses, or give the profession a poor name by their meagre skills and outdated techniques. One informant went on to suggest that mobile hairdressers were in particular need of regulation (no qualifications are currently required) since they often served the ill and elderly whose hair requires especially sensitive care.

A successful salon, as Jamie Brooks pointed out, has consciously to plan for the future. He employs stylists of various ages and backgrounds – between 12 and 15 people as a rule. The younger stylists usually charged less and their clients were often students at the nearby London School of Economics or young researchers from the British Library, but these were individuals who might well stay with the salon as their careers progressed. They were introduced to the salon by the young stylists and their presence helped keep the salon au courant with the latest 'club' looks. In a multicultural society that is progressively more racially mixed, a sophisticated assessment of each head of hair has become ever more important. An older clientele may be individually more profitable, but as they retire, many move out of the metropolis and, in all likelihood, return less often to central London to have their hair attended to. When asked if he could do one thing to change hairdressing, Mr Brooks pondered a moment and then replied that he wished people would stop aging as hairdressers and continue to be dynamic and well-informed. Too many, he thought, made themselves redundant.[53] Both Brooks and Brooks in London and Cienté in Berkhamsted have issued newsletters to advertise their services, including catwalk stylings done by their staff, new hair trends, and special offers such as bridal services. Increasingly subtle hair services will lead to greater specialisation and likely higher prices. Staff training is ongoing and ever more nuanced; traditional service is reinforced through outreach into the community through sponsorship of sports teams, participation in charity events, and an openness to serving the (normally unprofitable) children of regular clients. Service in some of the best salons has recently become a seven-days-a-week enterprise – catering for business people early in the morning, and late in the day for those readying themselves for a night on the town, and whole days – or more – for weddings and other celebratory events.

The repealing of the 1950 Shops Act made much of this possible but it was demanding clients that made it imperative. These and other progressive salons have all the concerns of small businesses. But the best of them are more than a business, for they embrace a passion for hair and the creativity that can be achieved through the social and empathetic dimensions of the profession.

✂ ✂ ✂ ✂

Hairdressing salons are now, in the second decade of the twenty-first century, virtually ubiquitous. In September 2010, when I travelled on foot in Ely, Cambridgeshire, from the marina to the cathedral – a short walk – I counted five beauty salons. On another stroll, this time through King's Lynn, Norfolk, I counted seven hairdressers in one block and another one around the corner – as well as two male stylist/barbers. The telephone directory for Swindon, Wiltshire, in 2007/2008 listed 175 hairdressers. Nowadays in Britain communities that lack (and often have recently lost) a grocery store commonly have at least one hairdressing shop. National statistics confirm these anecdotal impressions. A 1986 booklet titled *Becoming a Hairdresser* advised prospective entrants to the trade that 'in this country approximately 500 million pounds are spent in salons each year, and that there are over 40 thousand salons employing more than 120 thousand people … Because a large number leave the industry for various reasons, the craft needs renewing at an annual rate of 24 thousand, and that is why there are hardly any redundancies even during this time of high unemployment.'[54] Two decades later a careers website noted that 'hairdressing is a huge industry and one of the most widespread types of business in the UK'; it accounted for over 35,000 salons, a number that another source raised to 38,000 a year later.[55] Even these substantial numbers fail to take into account mobile hairdressers, whose numbers were thought to bring the total of hair and beauty professionals to 44,000 in 2011.[56] The year 2011 was a challenge for the British economy and many other Western economies. Consumers were cutting back on purchases that they considered non-essential and were often cautious in all their spending. Yet, significantly, Mintel's 2010 British Lifestyles report found that Britons spent more than £13 billion on hairdressing and cosmetics, an average of £216 per person and that spending in hair and beauty salons had *increased* by 50 percent over the previous decade.[57]

✂ ✂ ✂ ✂

However diligent hairdressers in salons might be in their efforts to anticipate and satisfy the needs of clients, they cannot please everyone. Having your hair done in a salon overlooking a busy high street, or in a shopping mall, may be a cheerful diversion to one woman but an agony of self-exposure to another. Some women have said they feel intimidated in a salon, either by the atmosphere – too posh, too slickly modern, gratingly unisex – or by the uncertainty of the outcome. Visits to the hairdresser are wrenching experiences for some women:

'You can come out disgusted when the perm, set, or whatever – such as highlights – are *not* what you asked for.'[58] Occasionally childhood recollections such as having been left alone in a cubicle, enduring an overheated dryer, or feeling nauseated by the smell of perming chemicals, or perhaps just the later memory of one humiliatingly horrid hairdo, have induced a woman to steer clear of salons. Hairdressers have often liked to compare themselves with medical professionals, but they might be distressed to know the professional they tend to get compared to is, in fact, the dentist.[59] A woman who simply does not like her appearance might say, 'I hate my hair. And I don't like going to the hairdresser's.'[60] Other women have disliked salons for practical reasons – distance, difficult transportation, the cost of hiring a babysitter, reluctance to leave a dependent relative.

One solution for those averse to salons has been mobile hairdressing. Women with young children and those working long hours or who for some other reason find it difficult to get to a salon can employ a hairdresser who will work in the client's own home. The hairdresser arrives at a time convenient to the client and provides just the services and products she wants. A professional cut, an experienced dye job or perm, a blow-dry or set may be given by the hairdresser while the client supplies her own shampoo, hair dye, gel, spray, etc – what is known generically in the profession as 'product'. 'For some years when living in Norfolk', reported one Mass Observer, 'a local girl used to come to the house, she brought her dryer but I used my own towels'.[61] The woman whose hair is looked after in the comfort of her own home can keep an eye on children, monitor cooking or housework, or catch up with paperwork while waiting for a time-consuming hairdressing process to be completed. Not least, she does not run the risk that her new coiffure will be ruined. 'I have a hairdresser who comes to my home', noted a satisfied customer in Suffolk. 'So if it's a bad day weather wise it doesn't get ruined afterwards. She comes once a month to cut and blow-dry it and she is marvellous. If I have got a special occasion I also make extra appointments to have it done for that time. I have great confidence in her and she has done it for approximately 10 years. I have known her parents for years through our church and watched her grow up. So as well as being a hairdresser she is almost like a member of the family, because she is a just slightly older than my own daughter.'[62] A visiting hairdresser may sometimes care for several family members, cutting the children's hair and even their father's . 'I think visiting hairdressers do awfully well. They certainly do in Worthing', observed one woman in 2001, 'and I would never go to a shop again. It's all so much easier in one's own home and no need to turn out if it's pouring rain.'[63]

Having a hairdresser visit can save money as well be as a convenience. The *New York Times* reported that, in the wake of the 2008 recession, some New Yorkers had begun to hold 'cutting parties', hiring a hairdresser for the evening to cut friends' hair at a bargain rate while sharing glasses of wine and good company. Sometimes a party emerges when a client convinces her regular hairdresser that she will produce a guaranteed number of guests, a festive atmosphere and cash under the table for reduced rates.[64] Janna Levine, a New Yorker, reported that it had been two years since she had stepped in a salon. Not that her hair care is low maintenance: 'Her blowout, her cuts, her highlights and even her frizz-reducing Brazilian-keratin treatments are all done in the privacy of her Manhattan apartment' by a stylist who makes house-calls before 11 am or after 8 pm (slotted around his day job at a salon).[65] This segment of the hairdressing market has become so lucrative that some hairdressers forego salon service entirely. Tara Colavecchio is one of them. No longer associated with a salon, but able to charge big-city prices, she cuts hair for $125 US a head in New York, where she is prepared to do her work in a woman's garage with pets, children, and spouses underfoot.[66] Another modern form of mobility is the salon on wheels, for a few hairdressers bring their business premises to the client's front door, or any other place a client might want services. Stylist Sarah-Jane Haffrey Davis of Heathfield, East Sussex, converted an old fire engine into a mobile salon kitted out with three hairdressing chairs, a basin and other facilities.

Besides serving clients at home, she planned to make herself available for public events such as music festivals.[67]

Perhaps the fastest-growing part of the mobile hairdressing business in 2011 was the most elaborate and the one many women care about most – bridal hairdressing. In recent years weddings have become increasingly extravagant as couples marry later in life and have the means and the inclination to make their weddings a very special occasion for their friends and relatives as well as themselves. Brides, their attendants, and relatives are prepared to spend lavishly on hairdos that may be complex and/or bejewelled. Our increasingly multicultural society has absorbed something of the ritual splendour – including hair presentation – associated with extended families of South Asian origin. Elaborate styles imported with pride by Afro-Caribbean women from their African forebears have occasionally been adopted by their white fellow citizens for special events. At the same time hairstyling artistry, once available only to the elite, has become democratised. One young hairstylist working in Vancouver uses inspiration gained from her BA in Fine Arts to give a special character to the products of her mobile hairdressing business and provides bridal and other services to an ethnically diverse clientele.[68] (Hers is one of many internet sites promoting the services of mobile hairdressers.)

Hairdressing at home has advantages for hairdressers as well as their clients. A novice hairdresser can supplement small earnings at a salon by doing her friends' or neighbours' hair or visiting a long-term care home to attend to the needs of its residents. A young mother can keep up her skills while earning a little money. Hairdressers thinking of setting up on their own can test the waters and look for potential clients before investing in rent or equipment. A young Reading, Berkshire, software developer recalled that 'all the family's hair was cut by a lady named H who lived up the road. She was a trained hairdresser, but no longer worked as such since she'd had children. Instead she popped into friends' houses and did their hair, probably more cheaply than a salon would have offered, and probably without telling the taxman!'[69] Working in a mobile way is also appealing to hairdressers who want only part-time employment, such as those who are semi-retired. 'The freedom you have being a mobile hairdresser is unbelievable', gushed one internet site. 'Mobile hairdressing makes life easier for us all. Not just for the clients, but for the stylists. No more being told what to do by a boss, no more standing around for hours on end, no pressure to sell products, no more doing things you hate. Also, the main things are a lot more holidays, a lot more money and a lot more freedom. You get to choose what clients you like … you get to charge what you like and the money is yours … Can you imagine the measly £200 per week wage from a salon being made a day instead by working for yourself? Much better!'[70] Moreover, there are social advantages for those who value them – both client and hairdresser can enjoy shared cups of tea, glasses of wine at the end of the week, have 'a blether and catch up with the gossip', and, sometimes, develop a relationship close enough to rate invitations to each other's special occasions.

There are, of course, downsides to mobile hairdressing. Setting up an independent business initially requires long and irregular hours of work, many of which are likely to persist — weddings are usually on weekends, professionals often want home services before or after conventional hours of work, and photo or fashion shots can involve especially unpredictable hours and difficult personalities. As with other self-employed entrepreneurs, mobile hairdressers may need to buy their own supplies, maintain and keep track of equipment, pay for their own skill upgrading, and set prices, do bookkeeping and taxes, and arrange transport for themselves, any staff they employ, and needed equipment. A typical range of devices needed by a mobile hairdresser, ranging from scissors and combs to hairdryer and curling/straightening irons was estimated by one source in 2011 at close to £200 before VAT, not including transport costs, insurance, licensing or membership in trade associations.[71] A mobile hairdresser's costs are highly variable: some clients supply their own product while residential facilities like long-term care homes may provide hairdryers or even an in-facility salon. Overall responsibility and autonomy remain with the hairdresser, as do the problems. The difficult or demanding client, and any other personnel problems, must be handled personally by the mobile hairdresser.

Mobile hairdressing, on the whole, can be mutually beneficial. But it can get complicated too. The person who comes into your home every week or two gets to know you, your family, some of your habits, how orderly you are, and so forth, and may have become a bit of a friend in the process. How easy will it be if you wish to move to another hairdresser? Perhaps you want someone who is more up to date or who understands that you want a new image to match your new job or your new love interest. Consider too someone like Sally (not her real name), a thrifty and buoyant woman in her senior years, living in the North of England. Her hair is done by her hairdresser neighbour – in the following manner: Sally washes her hair at home and walks to the neighbour's home, where it is cut, sometimes permed, and set. Sally returns home and dries her hair using her 1950s hood dryer and then returns next door to have her hair combed out and styled. She pays her hairdresser whatever is thought to be fair – the hairdresser wants little because her neighbour has shown numerous kindnesses to her disabled child.[72] This is a relationship that would be difficult to end. Sally admits that her neighbour really does only one hairstyle (which does suit her) but implies that, for her, the social cost of trying out a new look with another hairdresser would be far too high.

A hairdressing salon is a business with a difference. Its mood and tone and purposes are not like those of any other business on the High Street. It is not, for the customer, a place to be quickly in and out. It is a personal, intimate space where clients go regularly to restore or renew their self-image, to enjoy a bit of chit-chat, to seek out a sympathetic and non-judgmental listener, to savour a bit of rare personal time – or just to try out something new at less cost than a full wardrobe; and, if the experiment does not work, it will be more readily reversible than cosmetic surgery. Some recent research suggests that the average woman between the ages of 13 and 65 changes her hairstyle twice a year and that the once sartorially conservative over-50s are now more attentive to their appearance and (unlike their grandmothers at similar ages) are commonly seen 'toned, tanned, and tinted', as one article put it.[73] The salon is often one of the first places a woman will visit to mark a change in the course of her life. A new hairstyle is commonly a marker of a woman's first steps towards a renewed sense of self after a divorce, a bereavement, a job change, or some other major development with deep personal meaning. It can also be a way to put a little zip into a life become bland, or over-domesticated, or it can be a simple assertion that 'I *am* worth it' – that it is good to do something for oneself alone. For so many women, hair is an important signifier of who they are, or wish to be, and hairdressers are tasked with helping them express – perhaps even uncover – these fervent desires.

References

1   'Developments at Douglas's', *Hairdressers' Weekly Journal*, 21 Sept 1901, 1149-50.

2   'Harrods' Ladies' Hair-dressing Court de Luxe', *The Fashions at Harrods*, c. 1907, p. 39 (Harrods Company Archive, Kensington, London). Gieben-Gamal, 'Gendered Spaces: Design and Display Strategies of British Hair Salons in the 1920s and 1930s', V&A/RCA MA, History of Design, 2nd Year Dissertation (unpublished) National Art Library, Victorian & Albert Museum, 1999.

3   'Women's Hairdressing Department', 9 June 1937, (Harrods Company Archive, RB11).

4   Johanna Lenander, 'Ladies Man', *Fashion*, April 2011, 126.

5   Personal communication, Pino Spadafora, *Rapunzel* salon, Toronto, early 2000s.

6   As quoted in *Fashion*, 128.

7   As quoted in Ibid, 128.

8   *Globe and Mail*. 12 February 2008. L, 8.

9   Wendy Baldwin, *Careerscope17: Careers in Hairdressing* (Creaton, Northampton: Hamilton House Publishing, 1983) p. 7.

10   Jamie Brooks, personal communication, 27 January 2012.

11   'Hair and Beauty', *Guardian,* 22 May 2010, M, 8.

12   *New York Times,* Thursday, 6 December, 2007, E, 3.

13   Jo Craven, 'Britain's love affair with hair', *The Times*, 13 June 2009, Archived Article, www.women.timesonline.co.uk/tol/life_stylewomen/.../article6455666.ece.

14   Lesley Hatton and Philip Hattton, *Foundation Hairdressing* (Oxford: BSP Professional Books, 1990), p. 330 and Chapter 11, 'Client Communication and Selling', pp. 322-333 passim.

15   Craven, Op cit.

16   Trisha Buller, Manager and Consultant Trichologist, Cienté, personal interview, 19 January 2012.

17   Jamie Brooks, co-manager, Brooks and Brooks, personal interview, 27 January 2012.

18   Craven, Op cit.

19   Ibid.

20   *New York Times,* 6 December, 2007, E, 3.

21   Ibid.

22   Amanda Stewart, personal communication, October 2010.

23   Janet Bailey, email communication, January 2010.

24   'Britain's love affair with hair, *The Times*, 13 June 2009, Archived Article, www.timesonline.co.uk.

25   University of Sussex, Mass Observation Archive, File Reports, Personal Appearance, July 1939, DC0281/1, 6.emma.

26   Geoffrey Browne, *Patterns of British Life* (London: Hulton Press, 1950), Table 60, p. 136.

27   Radford, *Art and Craft of Hairdressing*, p. ix.

28   As cited in Julie A Willett, *Permanent Waves: The Making of the American Beauty Shop* (New York: New York University Press, 2000), p. 135.

29   See for example, Eliza Potter, *A Hairdresser's Experience in High Life* (Cincinnati, published for the author), 1859.

30   "Britain's love affair with hair', *The Times*, 13 June 2009, Archived Article.

31   Ben Caplan, 'Such great lengths' *National Post*, Saturday, 1 August

2009, TO, 1&3.

32   L2281, Ex-teacher, 68, St. Albans.

33   P1796, Married PA, 54.

34   Nancy Sutherland, email, 2/12/2010.

35   T 1843, Married, 51, Cheshire civil servant.

36   Nella Last, manuscript diary, Friday 24 January 1941 (held at Mass Observation Archive, University of Sussex).

37   P1637, Widow, 71, retired Secretary/PA, Berkshire.

38   C2844, Married, 41, full-time mother, ex-University administrator, Perth, Australia.

39   D 1685.

40   C2053, Married, 47, librarian ,Norwich.

41   E 743, Married, 51, Part-time teacher and museum attendant, Warrington, Cheshire.

42   As quoted in Frederick H Radford, Ed., *The Art and Craft of Hairdressing including Beauty Culture and Therapy: A standard and complete guide to modern techniques and salon management* 5th Edition, Vol. I (London: Pitman & Sons, 1968), p. viii.

43   Radford, *Art and Craft of Hairdressing*, p. vii.

44   For more detail on hair salon design changes in the 1920s and 1930s see Gieben-Gamal, "Gendered Spaces", passim.

45   Frederick H Radford, Ed.,*The Art and Craft of Hairdressing including including Beauty Culture and Therapy: A standard and complete guide to modern techniques and salon management* 5th Editions, Vol. I (London: Pitman & Sons, 1968), p. viii.

46   As quoted in Alison Pressley, *Changing Times: being young in Britain in the '60s* (London: Michael O'Mara, 2000), p. 24.

47   *Time*, 15 April 1966, cover: 'London: The Swinging City'.

48   'The Mister Hairitorium opens in Lancaster', *Lancaster Guardian,* 18 October 1974, 18.

49   ' 'Medusa's Ankles', A S Byatt, *The Matisse Stories* (London: Chatto & Windus, 1993), pp. 3-27.

50   Gilbert A Foan, Ed., *The Art and Craft of Hairdressing* (London: New Era Publishing, 1931), passim.

51   Foan, Ed, *The Art and Craft of Hairdressing* (London: New Era Publishing, Fourth Edn, 1958, reprinted 1963), p. 589.

52   John Steinberg with Alexandra Innes *Follicles: 50 Stories of Life and the art of hairdressing* (2008, ISBN 978-0-9809401-0-7 online and print on demand publication), as quoted pp. 12-13, also 7.

53   Jamie Brooks, Personal communication, 27 January 2012.

54   Pauline M Wheatley, *Becoming a Hairdresser* (London: Batsford, 1986), p. 11.

55   Cobweb Information, *Hairdresser*, No 32 March 2009 (Amended June 2010), 1; Mini BOP, *Children's Hairdresser*, MBP433/October 2010, n.p. Both online sources held at the British Library.

56   Cobweb Information, *Mobile Hairdresser*, No 303, March 2011, 1. It is difficult if not impossible to directly compare these numbers. They are meant only to suggest relative scale.

57   *Mobile Hairdresser*, pp. 1, 2.

58   MOA, Spring Directive 2001, W 563, housewife, former MO worker.

59   For instance. MOA, Spring Directive 2001, Y2498, widow, West London.

60   MOA, Spring Directive 2001, W 632, widow, retired business analyst.

61   MOA, Spring Directive, 2001, H266, widow, Horncastle.

62   MOA Spring Directive 2001, housewife, 60, Ipswich, Suffolk.

63   MOA, Spring Directive, S521.

64   Lauren Lipton, 'Get bobbed, but don't get clipped', *New York Times*, Thursday, 10 December 2008, E, 1.

65   'Undercover Beauty', *Globe and Mail*, Saturday 3 April 2010, L, 10.

66   'Get bobbed', E, 10.

67   'Fire engine salon for the hottest hair cuts', *Metro*, 20 May 2010, 43. More unusual were the 'Cosmic Barbers', a pair of Australian hairdressers who parked their van at public places and sold or bartered their services to finance their travels in North America, CBC Daybreak, CBC Radio (Kelowna, BC) 11 August 2010. The following month I saw their van parked alongside the Saturday farmer's market in Nelson, BC. Among the advertising painted on the van were 'Cut your locks for a pair of socks' and 'Cut the lot for what you got'.

68   Hairstylist@victoriakuzma.com. Kuzma graduated with a Bachelor of Fine Art from Queen's University, Kingston, Canada in 2004. In February 2011 her mobile bridal service was already booked for spring and summer weekends a year ahead. A web search reveals large numbers of other mobile hairdressers.

69 MOA, Spring Directive, 2001, W2782, single, 24, software developer.

70 http: www.hairfinder.com/tips/mobilehairdressing.htm.

71 Cobweb Information, *Mobile Hairdresser*, No 303, March 2011, 2.

72 Personal communication, May 2009, anonymity requested.

73 *Mobile Hairdresser*, 2; www.saga.co.uk/media-centre/press-release/2010/over-50s-toned-tanned-and-tinted.asp.

EPILOGUE

In the late summer of 1941, Olivia Cockett, a woman in her late twenties who lived in London, wrote in her diary of a nasty experience: 'I had my hair "set" on Thursday morning for the party. First time ever. And it looked very nice and I didn't really begrudge the 6s 6d until Sunday, when it all fell straight and I realised the girl had cut out all the "perm". Got more and more miserable about it till in the early evening I wept! Never considered myself vain before, but it really was pure miserable injured vanity. Man [her lover] cleverly realised it and suggested going on the Monday for a new perm. Otherwise I'd be so sick for the three days precious leave [from work] beginning that day. He was even angelic enough to come to Town with me! Had a successful perm and went to Flemings for lunch.'[1]

This was a wartime version of a bad hair day, as endured by an intelligent, free-thinking, independent woman. Virtually no man would have written in this way about his hair. Men have bad days, but they don't have bad hair days. Hair may not be entirely a woman's concern, but, with the important exception of baldness, it is mostly so. The hundreds of books published in the last thirty years, in English alone, on hair care – what style to choose and what styles to avoid, whether to colour or not colour, how to deal with problem hair – are testimony to the fact that hair is a major issue for tens of millions of women. One recent book is aptly titled *The Hair Bible*; its subtitle is *The Ultimate Guide to Healthy, Beautiful Hair Forever* (2003, by Susan Craig Scott). Such extravagant language is commonplace in writing about hair. The book's title reflects the strength of women's feelings about how their hair appears – to others and to themselves. Few women feel they can afford to be careless about their hair.

I am certainly one of these women. I am also an historian whose main interest is in everyday life. So in this book I have tried to connect my feelings about hair with my pleasure in writing history. I have wanted to understand more fully the ways in which past generations of women have dealt with a feature of themselves that could not be erased (except if they became nuns or, more recently, if they underwent chemotherapy), and thus has always required decisions to be made about it. Even when hair has been concealed, as by a hijab, or eliminated and replaced by a wig, as in some Jewish traditions, it remains a significant matter for the presentation of self. Hair is a major aspect of a woman's self-consciousness, and rarely a matter of indifference. And because so many women are hair-conscious, caring for hair has become big business. It has also become a major part of the world of small business, as beauty salons have proliferated. Hairdressing is an important sector of employment, especially for women – though most of the high-profile hairdressers are still men – and numerous writers and careers advisors since the 1950s have encouraged teenagers to enter the trade.

While in certain respects it might be said that hair has been taken for granted, certainly by most historians, hairdressing is clearly not in the category of brushing your teeth or carrying an umbrella, for hair almost always makes a statement, and sometimes a fairly strong one. Some of these statements have been rooted in religion, including the fear that lush hair, exuberantly displayed, conveys dangerously erotic messages. Others have been rooted in wealth and/or social standing, since until recent decades most fashionable hairstyles were unaffordable for most women. Auburn hair, curls, and blondeness have had different significance at different times – but thin, lank, mousy, or unruly hair has rarely been in fashion. As a young woman in the 1940s, the New Zealand novelist Janet Frame received 'continued advice about my frizzy hair' and recalled being 'baffled' by her hair and 'the attention it drew, and the urgency with which people advised that I have it "straightened", as if it posed a threat'.[2] Those women with access to adept hairdressers – Janet Frame marked an important passage in her life by having 'my hair "washed and set", with the hairdresser assuring me that my hair would never be attractive unless it was professionally straightened'[3] – and perhaps a willingness to experiment with hairpieces, hair ornaments, and other hair treatments have generally been the best equipped to deflect or cushion criticism of their hair. Then there are the various life circumstances, some of them inescapable, which can determine a woman's hairstyle – age, illness, marital status, motherhood, ambition, a change in career.

Hairstyles are socially and psychologically embedded; they are entangled in a society's attitudes and anxieties and derive most of their significance from what has been going on in that society and, very much today, in individuals' lives. Indeed, the pronounced individualism of modern life underlies the virtual anarchy of hairstyles in contemporary Britain and North America, most obviously among the young, and especially for dress-up occasions. Most of us, across the age spectrum, are encouraged to reinvent ourselves, and hair affords a way of doing this that can be fun and perhaps reassuring and that makes no permanent commitment.

References

1   Robert Malcolmson, ed., *Love & War in London: The Mass Observation Diary of Olivia Cockett* (Stroud, Gloucestershire: The History Press, 2008), p. 197.

2   Janet Frame, *The Complete Autobiography* (London: The Women's Press, 1990), pp. 246 and 203.

3   Ibid p.240

.

APPENDIX

One Woman's Reflections on her Hair, 2001

The writer, who responded to Mass Observation's Spring Directive in 2001 (she is no. B2760), was 66 years old, had grown children and grandchildren, and lived north of London.

I actually like my hair, which I think is quite unusual. It is light brown with very little loss of colour so I am very lucky. It is straight but has a slight wave at times. I have a good cut about every eight weeks. I would like it to be thicker but am now used to it! It was a problem in the past when I tried to have perms because it all broke off for ages after; now I am happy to keep it straight as this is fashionable. When or if it eventually goes grey or white then I will probably have it coloured back to its natural light brown, but as a family we keep our hair colouring well into old age.

I used to wear wigs years ago when I worked as a store detective as it was fun and a good way of altering my appearance.

I think regular care is important as it is good to look well groomed, for work, comfort and self esteem. I notice other people's hair styles and always tell people if their hair looks exceptionally nice.

When I was a child I was taken regularly to the hairdresser's. It was cut in a pudding basin style and much shorter than I wanted it because I was cared for by an Aunt who 'Didn't like hair' – she had an Eton crop, which is very short. When I see old photos now I can see that my hair style actually looked very nice. The way I have it cut now is actually very similar and it still suits me. I dried it by rubbing with a towel and going into the garden in the summer or leaning over the fire in the winter. I can remember being very cold after hair washing. It was washed once a week. My Grandma never washed her hair. She used to sprinkle talc on it and then brush the talc out to remove the grease. My Granddad never washed his hair either. He washed himself once a week in a bowl of water – he washed down to his neck and up to his knees. The rest of him never got washed at all. My Grandma had an all-over strip wash from a bowl once a week. We actually lived in a house with a bathroom and the rest of us had weekly baths.

As I got older I had my hair permed to be in fashion and in the sixties it was all back brushed, making it look as though I had lots of hair, which I never had. I still only washed it once a week. I went through a stage of changing the colour regularly – home dyes as I couldn't afford the hairdresser. The perms were horrific, all connected to the electricity. We sat in individual compartments so you never saw the other customers and the hairdresser would never have more than two customers in the shop at a time. No one washed their hair more than once a week and I remember the advert saying 'Friday night is Amami night'.

My husband now does notice my hair and when it is different will always say whether he likes it or not.

In my childhood we had a rain water butt and used the water from that to give the final rinse – problem being that it was always so cold. I also bought a bottle of beer to put some in the final rinse as it was said to give body and there were no products on the market to do this. I would use the same bottle for several weeks and it would smell terrible after a while.

I last went to the hairdresser two days ago for a trim and blow dry. He knows exactly how I like it and if I want a change he will do whatever I want. I have to book up three weeks in advance as he is very good. I regard him as a friend. There is no music there. He doesn't talk a lot unless I initiate it. I hate being talked to when having my hair done. It is a small studio, very clean and tidy, with displays of hair products but no pictures. There are flowers – lilies. Also a few magazines, Tatler, Country Life. I paid £20 and gave a £1 tip to the girl who washed my hair. I don't tip Brian as he owns the hair salon and I pay more to go to him anyway. There is one girl working there and she charges a lot less, so I've been told. There is also a beautician there who works in a different room. Sometimes I get her to do my nails.

I hope I am not influenced by adverts. I try not to be. I am aware of the L'Oreal advert that says 'Because I'm worth it'. At home I use Andrew Colling products because I went through a stage of trying out different makes and decided these really did suit my hair and give it body. Before that I used 'Thicken Hair' for many years and then it suddenly disappeared.

INSTEAD OF A GLOSSARY

A social history of hair – over more than 100 years and in various economic circumstances – inevitably involves a range of terminology, so a brief note of explanation is in order. First, and most obviously, some common contemporary hairdressing practices are described in different ways in different places. What the British call plaits, North Americans usually call braids, while hair cut across the forehead are bangs on one side of the Atlantic and a fringe on the other. The most durable modern hairstyle, the bob, has generally kept its name over the decades while a very short boyish cut might be called a shingle or an Eton crop in the 1920s but an Italian boy or gamin style in the 1950s. Hairdressers and beauty journalists have given coiffures a great variety of labels to distinguish their product, or create a sometimes a specious sense of novelty, or generate a frisson of fashion excitement. In addition a young woman's 'bedhead' look might be thought fashionable by her, derided as messy by her mother, and make her grandmother remark that she looks like she's been dragged through a hedge backwards. In this book I have tried to explain a hairstyle or treatment in its historic context, identifying an era's iconic styles but generally avoiding reference to arcane variants.

It is in the area of false hair (whether human or artificial) that today's reader may notice the most unfamiliar terminology. Most of us are familiar with wigs and extensions but may not be aware of the vast array of supplemental hair products that were available to Victorian and Edwardian women or what they were sometimes called. Wigs, both full and partial, were frequently given the more elegant name transformation or postiche – the latter just a suitably high-end word that means fake (from the Italian *posticcio* for counterfeit or feigned). Since hairpieces were enormously profitable, purchasers were usually wealthy, and fickle fashion demanded constant change, there was lots of incentive to create ever more kinds of artificial hair work to market to the client. The fact that ladies' maids and sometimes the wearer herself, had the arduous daily task of constructing elaborate hairdressing added a further demand for pre-dressed hairpieces that could more readily be added to madam's coiffure. So a false fringe might be fashioned as temple curls, a waved Regency front, a pompadour fringe, or a sleek wavelet while switches or tails of hair (extensions) could be purchased already styled as clusters of puffs, ringlets, knots, chignons, elaborate plaits and cable twists. For small embellishments , there were little pincurls, waved tendrils and the like. Finally, this was the big hair era *par excellence* so there was a need to support all that hair and, by Edwardian times, the enormous hats that perched upon it. Thus there were pads of false hair, widely called rats, as well as a huge variety of nets, pads or frisettes, and frames through or around which natural or supplemental hair could be wound or pulled over. A whole wardrobe of hairpieces might grace a boudoir in Grosvenor Square. The following list of sources can provide guidance for readers who wish to know more.

SOURCES

A key source is Richard Corson's *Fashions in Hair: The First Five Thousand Years* (London: Peter Owen, 9th edition, 2001). It was originally meant in part to give guidance to theatrical designers and includes extensive sketches of hairstyles over the centuries. The most recent edition includes a new section by Caroline Cox updating the survey with a chapter on hairstyles to the end of the twentieth century. *An Illustrated Dictionary of Hairdressing and Wigmaking* by J Stevens Cox (London: Hairdressers' Technical Council, 1966) contains a myriad of technical terms and over 600 historic photographs. But perhaps the best overview of a large range of topics and perspectives relating to hair is Victoria Sherrow's *Encyclopedia of Hair: A Cultural History* (Westport, Connecticut: Greenwood Press, 2006). This reference book contains a wealth of information, dozens of excellent short essays, and an extensive bibliography. It is an indispensable text. Three useful books that are full of illustrations are *The History of Hair: Fashion and Fantasy Down the Ages* by Robin Bryer (London: Philip Wilson Publishers, 2003), which is mainly British; Marian I Doyle's *An Illustrated History of Hairstyles 1830-1930* (Atgen, PA: Schiffer Publishing, 2003), which is mainly American; and *Hairstyles: Ancient to Present* edited by Charlotte Fiell (London: Fiell Books, 2012).

Surprisingly little has been written on the history of hair and the hairdressing industry since the nineteenth century. Perhaps the two most useful books for my work have been Grant McCracken's *Big Hair: A Journey into the Transformation of Self* (Toronto: Viking, 1995) and Caroline Cox's *Good Hair Days: A History of British Hairstyling* (London: Quartet Books, 1999). Other modern books that I have learned from include *Hair: Styling, Culture and Fashion* edited by Geraldine Biddle-Perry and Sarah Cheang (Oxford: Berg, 2008); *Hair and Fashion* by Caroline Cox and Lee Widdows (London: V&A Publications, 2005); Diane Simon's *Hair: Public, Political, Extremely Personal* (New York: St.

Martin's Press, 2000); Rose Weitz's *Rapunzel's Daughters: What Women's Hair Tells Us about Women's Lives* (New York: Farrer, Strauss & Giroux, 2004); Julie A Willett's *Permanent Waves: The Making of the American Beauty Shop* (New York: NYU Press, 2000); and *Hairstyles and Fashion: A Hairdresser's History of Paris, 1910-1920* edited by Steven Zdatney (Oxford: Berg, 1999).

It is important to get a sense of hairdressing as a trade and profession by examining a few of the many guides and training manuals that have been published, for they often include, as well as instructions and revelations of the conventional wisdom of the time, some history of the trade and copious illustrations. Aside from Gilbert Foan's classic, *The Art and Craft of Hairdressing* (1931), which was revised and enlarged by N E B Wolters (1950) and Frederick H Radford (1968), useful information may be found in S G Flitman's *The Craft of Ladies Hairdressing* (London: Odhams, 1956) and *Foundation Hairdressing* by Lesley and Philip Hatton (Oxford: BSP Professional Books, 1990). For another perspective, a reader may want to look at a sample of the many books produced by or on behalf of celebrity hairdressers, such as Joshua and Daniel Galvin, Charles Worthington or Vidal Sassoon. These titles are readily found and I have not included examples here since they are usually some combination of self-advertisement, memoir, and proprietary product or salon advancement. They reveal less about their clients' attitudes towards hair than do the books written about the social and cultural meaning of – for example – hair colour, notably Natalia Ilyin's *Blonde Like Me: The Roots of the Blonde Myth in our Culture* (New York: Touchstone, 2000); Joanna Pitman's *On Blondes* (London: Bloomsbury, 2003); Marion Roach's *The Roots of Desire: The Myth, Meaning, and Sexual Power of Red Hair* (New York: Bloomsbury, 2005); and Anne Kreamer's *Going Gray: What I Learned about Beauty, Sex, Work, Motherhood, Authenticity, and Everything Else that Really Matters* (New York: Little, Brown, 2007).

As the notes to each chapter reveal, my understanding of hair and society is dependent on readings from a wide rage of primary sources – newspapers and magazines; trade directories;

diaries, memoirs, and other literary material; some government documents – along with interviews of knowledgeable people and searches of online sources. Perhaps the single most important body of relevant testimony is found in the Mass Observation Archive at the University of Sussex, particularly the Directive sent to Mass Observers in the spring of 2001 and some of the diaries it holds (mainly from the 1940s). Finally, I have benefitted from extensive reading of several trade periodicals, of which the most important are *Hairdresser and Beauty Trade* (1932-1950), which became *Hair and Beauty* (1951-1990); *Hairdressers' Weekly Journal* (1882-1948), which became *Hairdressers' Journal* (1949-1976); and *Hairdressers Journal International* (since 1976). I have also been educated by walking the streets of London and Toronto and many smaller cities on both sides of the Atlantic for almost fifty years and making my own observations. And almost everywhere, and occasionally in the strangest circumstances, women have been eager to talk about 'me and my hair'.

INDEX